Thomas S. Coleman
Close Mountain Advisors LLC
Adjunct Faculty, Fordham University and
Rensselaer Polytechnic Institute

A Practical Guide to Risk Management

Statement of Purpose

The Research Foundation of CFA Institute is a
not-for-profit organization established to promote
the development and dissemination of relevant
research for investment practitioners worldwide.

The Research Foundation of CFA Institute and the Research Foundation logo are
trademarks owned by The Research Foundation of CFA Institute. CFA®, Chartered
Financial Analyst®, AIMR-PPS®, and GIPS® are just a few of the trademarks owned by
CFA Institute. To view a list of CFA Institute trademarks and the Guide for the Use of
CFA Institute Marks, please visit our website at www.cfainstitute.org.

©2011 The Research Foundation of CFA Institute

This publication is designed to provide accurate and authoritative information in regard to
the subject matter covered. It is sold with the understanding that the publisher is not engaged
in rendering legal, accounting, or other professional service. If legal advice or other expert
assistance is required, the services of a competent professional should be sought.

ISBN 978-1-934667-41-5

8 July 2011

Editorial Staff

Maryann Dupes
Book Editor

Mary-Kate Brissett
Assistant Editor

Christina Hampton
Publishing Technology Specialist

Lois Carrier
Production Specialist

Cindy Maisannes
Publishing Technology Specialist

Biography

Thomas S. Coleman has worked in the finance industry for more than 20 years and has considerable experience in trading, risk management, and quantitative modeling. Mr. Coleman currently manages a risk advisory consulting firm. His previous positions have been head of Quantitative Analysis and Risk Control at Moore Capital Management, LLC (a large multi-asset hedge fund manager), and a director and founding member of Aequilibrium Investments Ltd., a London-based hedge fund manager. Mr. Coleman worked on the sell side for a number of years, with roles in fixed-income derivatives research and trading at TMG Financial Products, Lehman Brothers, and S.G. Warburg in London.

Before entering the financial industry, Mr. Coleman was an academic, teaching graduate and undergraduate economics and finance at the State University of New York at Stony Brook, and more recently he has taught as an adjunct faculty member at Fordham University Graduate School of Business Administration and Rensselaer Polytechnic Institute. Mr. Coleman earned his PhD in economics from the University of Chicago and his BA in physics from Harvard. He is the author, together with Roger Ibbotson and Larry Fisher, of *Historical U.S. Treasury Yield Curves* and continues to publish in various journals.

Risk management is the art of using lessons from the past in order to mitigate misfortune and exploit future opportunities—in other words, the art of avoiding the stupid mistakes of yesterday while recognizing that nature can always create new ways for things to go wrong.

****

"You haven't told me yet," said Lady Nuttal, "what it is your fiancé does for a living."

"He's a statistician," replied Lamia, with an annoying sense of being on the defensive.

Lady Nuttal was obviously taken aback. It had not occurred to her that statisticians entered into normal social relationships. The species, she would have surmised, was perpetuated in some collateral manner, like mules.

"But Aunt Sara, it's a very interesting profession," said Lamia warmly.

"I don't doubt it," said her aunt, who obviously doubted it very much. "To express anything important in mere figures is so plainly impossible that there must be endless scope for well-paid advice on how to do it. But don't you think that life with a statistician would be rather, shall we say, humdrum?"

Lamia was silent. She felt reluctant to discuss the surprising depth of emotional possibility which she had discovered below Edward's numerical veneer.

"It's not the figures themselves," she said finally, "it's what you do with them that matters."

—K.A.C. Manderville
The Undoing of Lamia Gurdleneck
quoted in Kendall and Stuart (1979, frontispiece)

Contents

Foreword

Having been the head of the risk management department at Goldman Sachs for four years and having collaborated on a book titled *The Practice of Risk Management*, I suppose it is not a surprise that I have a point of view about the topic of this book.

Thomas Coleman, who was, likewise, a risk manager and trader for several derivatives desks as well as a risk manager for a large hedge fund, also brings a point of view to the topic of risk management, and it turns out that, for better or for worse, we agree. A central theme of this book is that "in reality, risk management is as much the art of managing people, processes, and institutions as it is the science of measuring and quantifying risk." I think he is absolutely correct.

The title of this book also highlights an important distinction that is sometimes missed in large organizations. Risk measurement, per se, which is a task usually assigned to the "risk management" department, is in reality only one input to the risk management function. As Coleman elaborates, "Risk measurement tools . . . help one to understand current and past exposures, which is a valuable and necessary undertaking but clearly not sufficient for actually managing risk." However, "the art of risk management," which he notes is squarely the responsibility of senior management, "is not just in responding to anticipated events but in building a culture and organization that can respond to risk and withstand unanticipated events. In other words, risk management is about building flexible and robust processes and organizations."

The recognition that risk management is fundamentally about communicating risk up and managing risk from the top leads to the next level of insight. In most financial firms, different risks are managed by desks requiring very different metrics. Nonetheless, there must be a comprehensive and transparent aggregation of risks and an ability to disaggregate and drill down. And as Coleman points out, consistency and transparency in this process are key requirements. It is absolutely essential that all risk takers and risk managers speak the same language in describing and understanding their risks.

Finally, Coleman emphasizes throughout that the management of risk is not a function designed to *minimize* risk. Although risk usually refers to the downside of random outcomes, as Coleman puts it, risk management is about taking advantage of opportunities: "controlling the downside and exploiting the upside."

In discussing the measurement of risk, the key concept is, of course, the distribution of outcomes. But Coleman rightly emphasizes that this distribution is unknown and cannot be summarized by a single number, such as a measure of dispersion. Behavioral finance has provided many illustrations of the fact that, as Coleman notes, "human intuition is not very good at working with randomness and probabilities." To be successful at managing risk, he suggests, "We must give up any illusion that there is certainty in this world and embrace the future as fluid, changeable, and contingent."

One of my favorite aspects of the book is its clever instruction on working with and developing intuition about probabilities. Consider, for example, a classic problem—that of interpreting medical test results. Coleman considers the case of testing for breast cancer, a disease that afflicts fewer than 1 woman in 200 at any point in time. The standard mammogram tests actually report false positives about 5 percent of the time. In other words, a woman without cancer will get a negative result 95 percent of the time and a positive result 5 percent of the time. Conditional on receiving a positive test result, a natural reaction is to assume the probability of having cancer is very high, close to 95 percent. In fact, that assumption is not true. Consider that out of 1,000 women, approximately 5 will have cancer but approximately 55 will receive positive results. Thus, conditional on receiving a positive test result, the probability of having cancer is only about 9 percent, not 95 percent. Using this example as an introduction, the author then develops the ideas of Bayesian updating of probabilities.

Although this book appropriately spends considerable effort describing quantitative risk measurement techniques, that task is not its true focus. It takes seriously its mission as a practical guide. For example, in turning to the problem of managing risk, Coleman insightfully chooses managing people as his first topic, and the first issue addressed is the principal–agent problem. According to Coleman, "Designing compensation and incentive schemes has to be one of the most difficult and underappreciated, but also one of the most important, aspects of risk management." Although he does not come to a definitive conclusion about how to structure employment contracts, he concludes that "careful thinking about preferences, incentives, compensation, and principal–agent problems enlightens many of the most difficult issues in risk management—issues that I think we as a profession have only begun to address in a substantive manner."

Coleman brings to bear some of the recent insights from behavioral finance and, in particular, focuses on the problem of overconfidence, which is, in his words, "the most fundamental and difficult [issue] in all of risk management because confidence is necessary for success but overconfidence can lead to disaster." Later, he elaborates: "Risk management . . . is also about managing ourselves—managing our ego, our arrogance, our stubbornness, our mistakes. It is not about fancy quantitative techniques but about making good decisions in the face of uncertainty, scanty information, and competing demands." In this context, he highlights four characteristics of situations that can lead to risk management mistakes: familiarity, commitment, the herding instinct, and belief inertia.

When focusing on the understanding and communication of risk, Coleman delves deeply into a set of portfolio analysis tools that I helped to develop and used while managing risk at Goldman Sachs. These tools—for example, the marginal contribution to risk, risk triangles, best hedges, and the best replicating portfolio—were all designed to satisfy the practical needs of simplifying and highlighting the most important aspects of inherently complex combinations of exposures. As we used to repeat often, risk management is about communicating the right information to the right people at the right time.

After covering the theory, the tools, and the practical application, Coleman finally faces the unsatisfying reality that the future is never like the past, and this realization is particularly true with respect to extreme events. His solution is to recognize this limitation. "Overconfidence in numbers and quantitative techniques and in our ability to represent extreme events should be subject to severe criticism because it lulls us into a false sense of security." In the end, the firm relies not so much on risk measurement tools as on the good judgment and wisdom of the experienced risk manager.

Robert Litterman
Executive Editor
Financial Analysts Journal

Acknowledgments

I would like to thank those who helped make this book possible. First and foremost thanks to Larry Siegel for his valuable insights, suggestions, and diligent editing and shepherding of the manuscript through the process. The Research Foundation of CFA Institute made the whole project possible with its generous funding. Many others have contributed throughout the years to my education in managing risk, with special thanks owed to my former colleagues Gian Luca Ambrosio and Michael du Jeu—together we learned many of the world's practical lessons. I thank all those from whom I have learned; the errors, unfortunately, remain my own.

1. Risk Management vs. Risk Measurement

What Are Risk Management and Risk Measurement?

Managing risk is at the core of managing any financial organization. This statement may seem obvious, even trivial, but remember that the "risk management" department is usually separate from trading management or line management. Words matter, and using the term "risk management" for a group that does not actually manage anything leads to the notion that managing risk is somehow different from managing other affairs within the firm. Indeed, a director at a large financial group was quoted in the *Financial Times* as saying that "A board can't be a risk manager."[1] In reality, the board has the same responsibility to understand and monitor the firm's risk as it has to understand and monitor the firm's profit or financial position.

To repeat, managing risk is at the core of managing any financial organization; it is too important a responsibility for a firm's managers to delegate. Managing risk is about making the tactical and strategic decisions to control those risks that should be controlled and to exploit those opportunities that can be exploited. Although managing risk does involve those quantitative tools and activities generally covered in a "risk management" textbook, in reality, risk management is as much the art of managing people, processes, and institutions as it is the science of measuring and quantifying risk. In fact, one of the central arguments of this book is that risk management is not the same as risk measurement. In the financial industry probably more than any other, risk management must be a central responsibility for line managers from the board and CEO down through individual trading units and portfolio managers. Managers within a financial organization must be, before anything else, risk managers in the true sense of managing the risks that the firm faces.

Extending the focus from the passive measurement and monitoring of risk to the active management of risk also drives one toward tools to help identify the type and direction of risks and tools to help identify hedges and strategies that alter risk. It argues for a tighter connection between risk management (traditionally focused on monitoring risk) and portfolio management (in which one decides how much risk to take in the pursuit of profit).

---

[1]Guerrera and Larsen (2008).

Risk measurement is necessary to support the management of risk. Risk measurement is the specialized task of quantifying and communicating risk. In the financial industry, risk measurement has, justifiably, grown into a specialized quantitative discipline. In many institutions, those focused on risk measurement will be organized into an independent department with reporting lines separate from line managers.

Risk measurement has three goals:

- Uncovering "known" risks faced by the portfolio or the firm. By "known" risks, I mean risks that can be identified and understood with study and analysis because these or similar risks have been experienced in the past by this particular firm or others. Such risks often are not obvious or immediately apparent, possibly because of the size or diversity of a portfolio, but these risks can be uncovered with diligence.

- Making the known risks easy to see, understand, and compare—in other words, the effective, simple, and transparent display and reporting of risk. Value at risk, or VaR, is a popular tool in this arena, but there are other, complementary, techniques and tools.

- Trying to understand and uncover the "unknown" or unanticipated risks— those that may not be easy to understand or anticipate, for example, because the organization or industry has not experienced them before.

Risk management, as I just argued, is the responsibility of managers at all levels of an organization. To support the management of risk, risk measurement and reporting should be consistent throughout the firm, from the most disaggregate level (say, the individual trading desk) up to the top management level. Risk measured at the lowest level should aggregate in a consistent manner to firmwide risk. Although this risk aggregation is never easy to accomplish, a senior manager should be able to view firmwide risk but then, like the layers of an onion or a Russian nesting doll, peel back the layers and look at increasingly detailed and disaggregated risk. A uniform foundation for risk reporting across a firm provides immense benefits that are not available when firmwide and desk-level risk are treated on a different basis.

Contrasting "Risk Management" and "Risk Measurement." The distinction I draw between risk management and risk measurement argues for a subtle but important change in focus from the standard risk management approach: a focus on understanding and managing risk in addition to the independent measurement of risk. Unfortunately, the term "risk management" has been appropriated to describe what should be termed "risk measurement": the measuring and quantifying of risk. Risk measurement requires specialized expertise and should generally be organized into a department separate from the main risk-taking units within the organization. Managing risk, in contrast, must be treated as a core competence of a financial firm and of those charged with managing the firm. Appropriating the term "risk management" in this way can mislead one to think that the risk takers' responsibility to manage risk is somehow lessened, diluting their responsibility to make the decisions necessary to effectively manage risk. Managers cannot delegate their responsibilities to manage risk, and there should no more be a separate *risk management* department than there should be a separate *profit management* department.

The standard view posits *risk management* as a separate discipline and an independent department. I argue that *risk measurement* indeed requires technical skills and should often form a separate department. The risk measurement department should support line managers by measuring and assessing risk—in a manner analogous to the accounting department supporting line managers by measuring returns and profit and loss. It still remains line managers' responsibility to manage the risk of the firm. Neither risk measurement experts nor line managers (who have the responsibility for managing risk) should confuse the measurement of risk with the management of risk.

Re-Definition and Re-Focus for "Risk Management." The focus on managing risk argues for a modesty of tools and a boldness of goals. Risk measurement tools can only go so far. They help one to understand current and past exposures, which is a valuable and necessary undertaking but clearly not sufficient for actually managing risk. In contrast, the goal of risk management should be to use the understanding provided by risk measurement to manage future risks. The goal of managing risk with incomplete information is daunting precisely because quantitative risk measurement tools often fail to capture unanticipated events that pose the greatest risk. Making decisions with incomplete information is part of almost any human endeavor. The art of risk management is not just in responding to anticipated events but in building a culture and organization that can respond to risk and withstand unanticipated events. In other words, risk management is about building flexible and robust processes and organizations with the flexibility to identify and respond to risks that were not important or recognized in the past, the robustness to withstand unforeseen circumstances, and the ability to capitalize on new opportunities.

Possibly the best description of my view of risk management comes from a book not even concerned with financial risk management, the delightful *Luck* by the philosopher Nicholas Rescher (2001):

> The bottom line is that while we cannot *control* luck [risk] through superstitious interventions, we can indeed *influence* luck through the less dramatic but infinitely more efficacious principles of prudence. In particular, three resources come to the fore here:

Risk management: managing the direction of and the extent of exposure to risk, and adjusting our risk-taking behavior in a sensible way over the overcautious-to-heedless spectrum.

Damage control: protecting ourselves against the ravages of bad luck by prudential measures, such as insurance, "hedging one's bets," and the like.

Opportunity capitalization: avoiding excessive caution by positioning oneself to take advantage of opportunities so as to enlarge the prospect of converting promising possibilities into actual benefits. (p. 187)

Quantitative Measurement and a Consistent Framework

The measurement of risk, the language of risk, seemingly even the definition of risk itself—all these can vary dramatically across assets and across levels of a firm. Traders might talk about DV01 or adjusted duration for a bond, beta for an equity security, the notional amount of foreign currency for a foreign exchange (FX) position, or the Pandora's box of delta, gamma, theta, and vega for an option. A risk manager assessing the overall risk of a firm might discuss the VaR, or expected shortfall, or lower semivariance.

This plethora of terms is often confusing and seems to suggest substantially different views of risk. (I do not expect that the nonspecialist reader will know what all these terms mean at this point. They will be defined as needed.) Nonetheless, these terms all tackle the same question in one way or another: What is the variability of profits and losses (P&L)? Viewing everything through the lens of P&L variability provides a unifying framework across asset classes and across levels of the firm, from an individual equity trader up through the board.

The underlying foundations can and should be consistent. Measuring and reporting risk in a consistent manner throughout the firm provides substantial benefits. Although reporting needs to be tailored appropriately, it is important that the foundations—the way risk is calculated—be consistent from the granular level up to the aggregate level.

Consistency provides two benefits. First, senior managers can have the confidence that when they manage the firmwide risk, they are actually managing the aggregation of individual units' risks. Senior managers can drill down to the sources of risk when necessary. Second, managers at the individual desk level can know that when there is a question regarding their risk from a senior manager, it is relevant to the risk they are actually managing. The risks may be expressed using different terminology, but when risk is calculated and reported on a consistent basis, the various risks can be translated into a common language.

An example will help demonstrate how the underlying foundations can be consistent even when the language of risk is quite different across levels of a firm. Consider the market risk for a very simple portfolio:

- $20 million nominal of a 10-year U.S. Treasury (UST) bond, and
- €7 million nominal of CAC 40 Index (French equity index) futures.

We can take this as a very simple example of a trading firm, with the bond representing the positions held by a fixed-income trading desk or investment portfolio and the futures representing the positions held by an equity trading desk or investment portfolio. In a real firm, the fixed-income portfolio would have many positions, with a fixed-income trader or portfolio manager involved in the minute-to-minute management of the positions, and a similar situation would exist for the equity portfolio. Senior managers would be responsible for the overall or combined risk but would not have involvement in the day-to-day decisions.

Desk-level traders require a very granular view of their risk. They require, primarily, information on the exposure or sensitivity of a portfolio to market risk factors. The fixed-income trader may measure exposure using duration, DV01 (also called BPV or dollar duration), or 5- or 10-year bond equivalents.[2] The equity trader might measure the beta-equivalent notional of the position.

In both cases, the trader is measuring only the exposure or sensitivity—that is, how much the position makes or loses when the market moves a specified amount. A simple report for the fixed-income and equity portfolios might look like **Table 1.1**, which shows the DV01 for the bond and the beta-equivalent holding for the equity. The DV01 of the bond is $18,288, which means that if the yield falls by 1 bp, the profit will be $18,288.[3] The beta-equivalent position of the equity holding is €7 million or $9.1 million in the CAC index.

Market P&L and the distribution of P&L are always the result of two elements interacting: the exposure or sensitivity of positions to market risk factors and the distribution of the risk factors. The sample reports in Table 1.1 show only the first, the exposure to market risk factors. Desk-level traders will

---

[2]Fixed-income exposure measures such as these are discussed in many texts, including Coleman (1998).

[3]Instead of the DV01 of $18,288, the exposure or sensitivity could be expressed as an adjusted or modified duration of 8.2 or five-year bond equivalent of $39 million. In all cases, it comes to the same thing: measuring how much the portfolio moves for a given move in market yields. The DV01 is the dollar sensitivity to a 1 bp move in yields, and the modified duration is the percentage sensitivity to a 100 bp move in yields. Modified duration can be converted to DV01 by multiplying the modified duration times the dollar holding (and dividing by 10,000 because the duration is percent change per 100 bps and the DV01 is dollars per 1 bp). In this case, $20 million notional of the bond is worth $22.256 million, and 8.2 × 22,256,000/10,000 = $18,288 (within rounding).

Table 1.1. Sample Exposure Report

Yield Curve (per 1 bp down)		Equity (beta-equivalent notional)	
10-year par yield	$18,288	CAC	$9,100,000

usually have knowledge of and experience with the markets, intuitively knowing how likely large moves are versus small moves, and so already have an understanding of the distribution of market risk factors. They generally do not require a formal report to tell them how the market might move but can form their own estimates of the distribution of P&L. In the end, however, it is the distribution of P&L that they use to manage their portfolios.

A more senior manager, removed somewhat from day-to-day trading and with responsibility for a wide range of portfolios, may not have the same intimate and up-to-date knowledge as the desk-level trader for judging the likelihood of large versus small moves. The manager may require additional information on the distribution of market moves.

Table 1.2 shows such additional information, the daily volatility or standard deviation of market moves for yields and the CAC index. We see that the standard deviation of 10-year yields is 7.1 bps and of the CAC index is 2.5 percent. This means that 10-year yields will rise or fall by 7.1 bps (or more) and that the CAC index will move by 2.5 percent (or more) roughly one day out of three. In other words, 7.1 bps provides a rough scale for bond market variability and 2.5 percent a rough scale for equity market volatility.

Table 1.2. Volatility or Standard Deviation of Individual Market Yield Moves

Yield Curve (bps per day)		Equity (% per day)	
10-year par yield	7.15	CAC	2.54

The market and exposure measures from Tables 1.1 and 1.2 can be combined to provide an estimate of the P&L volatility for the bond and equity positions, shown in **Table 1.3**:[4]

- Bond P&L volatility ≈ $18,288 × 7.15 ≈ $130,750;
- Equity P&L volatility ≈ $9,100,000 × 0.0254 ≈ $230,825.

---

[4]Assuming linearity as we do here is simple but not necessary. There are alternate methodologies for obtaining the P&L distribution from the underlying position exposures and market risk factors; the linear approach is used here for illustration.

Table 1.3. Portfolio Sensitivity to One Standard Deviation Moves in Specific Market Risk Factors

Yield Curve (yield down)		Equity (index up)	
10-year par yield	$130,750	CAC	$230,825

These values give a formal measure of the P&L variability or P&L distribution: the standard deviation of the P&L distributions. The $130,750 for the fixed-income portfolio means that the portfolio will make or lose about $130,750 (or more) roughly one day out of three; $130,750 provides a rough scale for the P&L variability. Table 1.3 combines the information in Tables 1.1 and Table 1.2 to provide information on the P&L distribution in a logical, comprehensible manner.

A report such as Table 1.3 provides valuable information. Nonetheless, a senior manager will be most concerned with the variability of the overall P&L, taking all the positions and all possible market movements into account. Doing so requires measuring and accounting for how 10-year yields move in relation to equities—that is, taking into consideration the positions in Table 1.1 and possible movements and co-movements, not just the volatilities of yields considered on their own as in Table 1.2.

For this simple two-asset portfolio, an estimate of the variability of the overall P&L can be produced relatively easily. The standard deviation of the combined P&L will be[5]

$$\text{Portfolio volatility} \approx \sqrt{\text{Bond vol}^2 + 2 \times \rho \times \text{Bond vol} \times \text{Eq vol} + \text{Eq vol}^2}$$
$$= \sqrt{130,750^2 + 2 \times 0.24 \times 130,750 \times 230,825 + 230,825^2} \qquad (1.1)$$
$$\approx \$291,300.$$

Diagrammatically, the situation might be represented by **Figure 1.1**. The separate portfolios and individual traders with their detailed exposure reports are represented on the bottom row. (In this example we only have two, but in a realistic portfolio there would be many more.) Individual traders focus on exposures, using their knowledge of potential market moves to form an assessment of the distribution of P&L.

Managers who are more removed from the day-to-day trading may require the combination of exposure and market move information to form an estimate of the P&L distributions. This is done in Table 1.3 and shown diagrammatically

---

[5]How volatilities combine is discussed more in Chapter 5. The correlation between bonds and the CAC equity is 0.24.

Figure 1.1. Representation of Risk Reporting at Various Levels

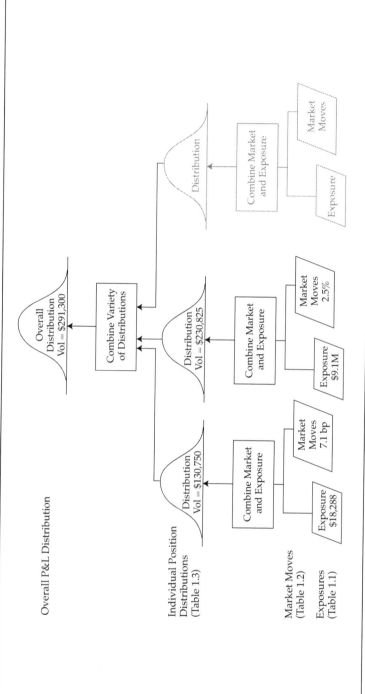

Note: M = million.

in the third row of Figure 1.1. Assessing the overall P&L requires combining the distribution of individual portfolios and assets into an overall distribution—performed in Equation 1.1 and shown diagrammatically in the top row of Figure 1.1.[6]

The important point is that the goal is the same for all assets and at all levels of the firm: measure, understand, and manage the P&L. This is as true for the individual trader who studies bond DV01s all day as it is for the CEO who examines the firmwide VaR.

The portfolio we have been considering is particularly simple and has only two assets. The exposure report, Table 1.1, is simple and easy to comprehend. A more realistic portfolio, however, would have many assets with exposures to many market risk factors. For example, the fixed-income portfolio, instead of having a single DV01 of $18,288 included in a simple report like Table 1.1, might show exposure to 10 or 15 yield curve points for each of 5 or 8 currencies. A granular report used by a trader could easily have 30 or 50 or 70 entries—providing the detail necessary for the trader to manage the portfolio moment by moment but proving to be confusing for anyone aiming at an overview of the complete portfolio.

The problem mushrooms when we consider multiple portfolios (say, a government trading desk, a swap trading desk, a credit desk, an equity desk, and an FX trading desk). A senior manager with overall responsibility for multiple portfolios requires tools for aggregating the risk, from simple exposures to individual portfolio distributions up to an overall distribution. The process of aggregation shown in Figure 1.1 becomes absolutely necessary when the number and type of positions and subportfolios increase.

Building the risk and P&L distributions from the bottom up as shown in Figure 1.1 is easy in concept, even though it is invariably difficult in practice. Equally or even more important, however, is going in the opposite direction: drilling down from the overall P&L to uncover and understand the sources of risk. This aspect of risk measurement is not always covered in great depth, but it is critically important. Managing the overall risk means making decisions about what risks to take on or dispose of, and making those decisions requires understanding the sources of the risk.

Consistency in calculating risk measures, building from the disaggregate up to the aggregate level and then drilling back down, is critically important. It is only by using a consistent framework that the full benefits of managing risk throughout the firm can be realized.

---

[6]For more complicated portfolios and for risk measures other than volatility (e.g., VaR or expected shortfall), the problem of combining multiple asset distributions into an overall distribution may be difficult but the idea is the same: Combine the individual positions to estimate the variability or dispersion of the overall P&L.

Systemic vs. Idiosyncratic Risk

There is an important distinction, when thinking about risk, between what we might call "idiosyncratic risk" and "systemic risk." This distinction is different from, although conceptually related to, the distinction between idiosyncratic and systemic (beta or marketwide) risk in the capital asset pricing model. Idiosyncratic risk is the risk that is specific to a particular firm, and systemic risk is widespread across the financial system. The distinction between the two is sometimes hazy but very important. Barings Bank's 1995 failure was specific to Barings (although its 1890 failure was related to a more general crisis involving Argentine bonds). In contrast, the failure of Lehman Brothers and AIG in 2008 was related to a systemic crisis in the housing market and wider credit markets.

The distinction between idiosyncratic and systemic risk is important for two reasons. First, the sources of idiosyncratic and systemic risk are different. Idiosyncratic risk arises from within a firm and is generally under the control of the firm and its managers. Systemic risk is shared across firms and is often the result of misplaced government intervention, inappropriate economic policies, or exogenous events, such as natural disasters. As a consequence, the response to the two sources of risk will be quite different. Managers within a firm can usually control and manage idiosyncratic risk, but they often cannot control systemic risk. More importantly, firms generally take the macroeconomic environment as given and adapt to it rather than work to alter the systemic risk environment.

The second reason the distinction is important is that the consequences are quite different. A firm-specific risk disaster is serious for the firm and individuals involved, but the repercussions are generally limited to the firm's owners, debtors, and customers. A systemic risk management disaster, however, often has serious implications for the macroeconomy and larger society. Consider the Great Depression of the 1930s, the developing countries' debt crisis of the late 1970s and 1980s, the U.S. savings and loan crisis of the 1980s, the Japanese crisis post-1990, the Russian default of 1998, the various Asian crises of the late 1990s, and the worldwide crisis of 2008, to mention only a few. These events all involved systemic risk and risk management failures, and all had huge costs in terms of direct (bailout) and indirect (lost output) costs.

It is important to remember the distinction between idiosyncratic and systemic risk because in the aftermath of a systemic crisis, the two often become conflated in discussions of the crisis. Better idiosyncratic (individual firm) risk management cannot substitute for adequate systemic (macroeconomic and policy) risk management. Failures of "risk management" are often held up as the primary driver of systemic failure. Although it is correct that better idiosyncratic risk management can mitigate the impact of systemic risk, it cannot substitute for appropriate macroeconomic policy. Politicians—indeed, all of us participating in the political process—must take responsibility for setting the policies that determine the incentives, rewards, and costs that shape systemic risk.

This book is about idiosyncratic risk and risk management—the risks that an individual firm can control. The topic of systemic risk is vitally important, but it is the subject for a different book—see, for example, the classic *Manias, Panics, and Crashes: A History of Financial Crises* by Kindleberger (1989) or the recent *This Time Is Different: Eight Centuries of Financial Folly* by Reinhart and Rogoff (2009).

2. Risk, Uncertainty, Probability, and Luck

What Is Risk?

Before asking, "What is risk management?" we need to ask, "What is risk?" This question is not trivial; risk is a very slippery concept. To define risk, we need to consider both the uncertainty of future outcomes and the utility or benefit of those outcomes. When someone ventures onto a frozen lake, that person is taking a risk not just because the ice may break but because if it does break, the result will be bad. In contrast, for a lake where no one is trying to cross it on foot, we would talk of the "chance" of ice breaking; we would only use the term "risk" if the breaking ice had an impact on someone or something. Or, to paraphrase the philosopher George Berkeley, if a tree might fall in the forest but there is nobody to be hit, is it risky?

The term "risk" is usually associated with downside or bad outcomes, but when trying to understand financial risk, limiting the analysis to just the downside would be a mistake. Managing financial risk is as much about exploiting opportunities for gain as it is about avoiding downside. It is true that, everything else held equal, more randomness is bad and less randomness is good. It is certainly appropriate to focus, as most risk measurement texts do, on downside measures (e.g., lower quantiles and VaR). But upside risk cannot be ignored. In financial markets, everything else is never equal and more uncertainty is almost invariably associated with more opportunity for gain. Upside risk might be better termed "opportunity," but downside risk and upside opportunity are mirror images, and higher risk is compensated by higher expected returns. Successful financial firms are those that effectively manage all risks: controlling the downside and exploiting the upside.[7]

Risk combines both the uncertainty of outcomes and the utility or benefit of outcomes. For financial firms, the "future outcomes" are profits—P&L measured in monetary units (i.e., in dollars or as rates of return). The assumption that only profits matter is pretty close to the truth because the primary objective of financial firms is to maximize profits. Other things—status, firm ranking, jobs for life, and so on—may matter, but these are secondary and are ignored here.

Future outcomes are summarized by P&L, and the uncertainty in profits is described by the distribution or density function. The distribution and density

---

[7]Gigerenzer (2002, p. 26) emphasizes the importance of thinking of "risk" as both positive and negative.

©2011 The Research Foundation of CFA Institute

functions map the many possible realizations for the P&L, with profits sometimes high and sometimes low. **Figure 2.1** shows the possible P&L from a $10 coin toss bet (only two possible outcomes) and from a hypothetical yield curve strategy (many possible outcomes). The vertical axis measures the probability of a particular outcome, and the horizontal axis measures the level of profit or loss. For the coin toss, each outcome has a probability of one-half. For the yield curve strategy, there is a range of possible outcomes, each with some probability. In the end, however, what matters is the distribution of P&L—how much one can make or lose.

Figure 2.1. P&L from Coin Toss Bet and Hypothetical Yield Curve Strategy

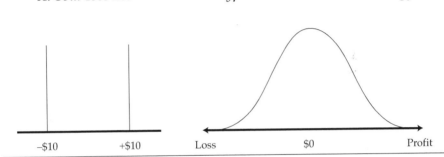

The distribution function contains all the "objective" information about the random outcomes, but the *benefit* (positive or negative) provided by any given level of profit or loss depends on an investor's preferences or utility function—how much an investor values each positive outcome and how much he or she is averse to each negative one. Whether one distribution is ranked higher than another (one set of outcomes is preferred to another) will depend on an investor's preferences.

Generally, there will be no unique ranking of distributions, in the sense that distribution *F* is preferred to distribution *G* by all investors. In certain cases, we can say that distribution *F* is unambiguously less "risky" than *G*, but these cases are of limited usefulness. As an example, consider the two distributions in Panel A of **Figure 2.2**. They have the same mean, but distribution *F* has lower dispersion and a density function that is "inside" *G*. Distribution *G* will be considered worse and thus more "risky" by all risk-averse investors.[8]

---

[8]Technically, the distribution *F* is said to dominate *G* according to second-order stochastic dominance. For a discussion of stochastic dominance, see the essay by Haim Levy in Eatwell, Milgate, and Newman (1987, *The New Palgrave*, vol. 4, pp. 500–501) or on the internet (New School, undated). In practice, distributions *F* and *G* rarely exist simultaneously in nature because the price system ensures that they do not. Because virtually anyone would consider *G* "worse" than *F*, the asset with distribution *G* would have to go down in price—thus ensuring that the expected return (mean) would be higher.

Figure 2.2.   Distributions with and without Unique "Risk" Ranking

A. With Unique Risk Ranking

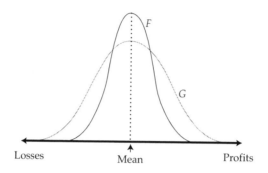

B. Without Unique Risk Ranking

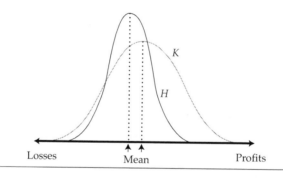

More often there will be no unique ranking, and some investors will prefer one distribution while others will prefer another. Panel B of Figure 2.2 shows two distributions: *H* with less dispersion but lower mean and *K* with more dispersion but higher mean. A particular investor could determine which distribution is worse given his or her own preferences, and some investors may prefer *H* while others prefer *K*, but there is no unique ranking of which is "riskier."

The bottom line is that the "riskiness" of a distribution will depend on the particular investor's preferences. There is no unique "risk" ranking for all distributions and all investors. To rank distributions and properly define risk, preferences must be introduced.

Markowitz (1959) implicitly provided a model of preferences when he introduced the mean–variance portfolio allocation framework that is now part of our financial and economic heritage. He considered a hypothetical investor who places positive value on the mean or expected return and negative value on the variance (or standard deviation) of return. For this investor, the trade-off between sets of outcomes depends only on the mean and variance. "Risk" is usually equated to variance in this framework because variance uniquely measures the disutility resulting from greater dispersion in outcomes.

In the mean–variance Markowitz framework, the problem is reduced to deciding on the trade-off between mean and variance (expected reward and risk). The exact trade-off will vary among investors depending on their relative valuation of the benefit of mean return and the cost of variance. Even here the variance uniquely ranks distributions on a preference scale only when the means are equal. In Figure 2.2, Panel B, distribution K might be preferred to H by some investors, even though K has a higher variance (K also has a higher mean). Even when limiting ourselves to quadratic utility, we must consider the precise trade-off between mean and variance.

Markowitz's framework provides immense insight into the investment process and portfolio allocation process, but it is an idealized model. Risk can be uniquely identified with standard deviation or volatility of returns only when returns are normally distributed (so that the distribution is fully characterized by the mean and standard deviation) or when investors' utility is quadratic (so they only care about mean and standard deviation, even if distributions differ in other ways ["moments"]).

Although "risk" properly depends on both the distribution and investor preferences, for the rest of this book I will focus on the distribution and largely ignore preferences. Preferences are difficult to measure and vary from one investor to another. Importantly, however, I do assume that preferences depend only on P&L: If we know the whole P&L distribution, we can apply it to any particular investor's preferences. Thus, as a working definition of risk for this book, I will use the following: *Risk is the possibility of P&L being different from what is expected or anticipated; risk is uncertainty or randomness measured by the distribution of future P&L.* This statement is relatively general and, effectively, evades the problem of having to consider preferences or the utility of future outcomes, but it achieves the simplification necessary for a fruitful discussion of risk measurement and risk management to proceed.[9]

---

[9]If we know the whole distribution, we can apply that to any particular investor's preferences to find the utility of the set of P&L outcomes. Thus, focusing on the full distribution means we can evade the issue of preferences.

Risk Measures

One important consequence of viewing "risk" as the distribution of future P&L is that risk is multifaceted and cannot be defined as a single number; we need to consider the full distribution of possible outcomes. In practice, however, we will rarely know or use the full P&L distribution. Usually, we will use summary measures that tell us things about the distribution because the full distribution is too difficult to measure or too complicated to easily grasp or because we simply want a convenient way to summarize the distribution.

These summary measures can be called "risk measures": numbers that summarize important characteristics of the distribution (risk). The first or most important characteristic to summarize is the dispersion or spread of the distribution. The standard deviation is the best-known summary measure for the spread of a distribution, and it is an incredibly valuable risk measure. (Although it sometimes does not get the recognition it deserves from theorists, it is widely used in practice.) But plenty of other measures tell us about the spread, the shape, or other specific characteristics of the distribution.

Summary measures for distribution and density functions are common in statistics. For any distribution, the first two features that are of interest are location, on the one hand, and scale (or dispersion), on the other. Location quantifies the central tendency of some typical value, and scale or dispersion quantifies the spread of possible values around the central value. Summary measures are useful but somewhat arbitrary because the properties they are trying to measure are somewhat vague.[10] For risk measurement, scale is generally more important than location, primarily because the dispersion of P&L is large relative to the typical value.[11]

Figure 2.3 shows the P&L distribution (more correctly the density function) for a hypothetical bond portfolio. The distribution is fairly well behaved, being symmetrical and close to normal or Gaussian. In this case, the mean of the distribution is a good indication of the central tendency of the distribution and serves as a good measure of location. The standard deviation gives a good indication of the spread or dispersion of the distribution and is thus a good measure of scale or dispersion.

---

[10]See, for example, Cramer (1974), sections 15.5 and 15.6. The following comments are appropriate: "All measures of location and dispersion, and of similar properties, are to a large extent arbitrary. This is quite natural, since the properties to be described by such parameters are too vaguely defined to admit of unique measurement by means of a single number. Each measure has advantages and disadvantages of its own, and a measure which renders excellent service in one case may be more or less useless in another" (pp. 181–182).

[11]For the S&P 500 Index, the daily standard deviation is roughly 1.2 percent and the average daily return is only 0.03 percent (calculated from Ibbotson Associates data for 1926–2007, which show the annualized mean and standard deviation for monthly capital appreciation returns are 7.41 percent and 19.15 percent).

Figure 2.3. P&L Distribution for Hypothetical Bond Portfolio

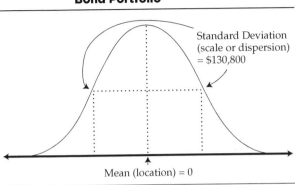

Standard Deviation
(scale or dispersion)
= $130,800

Mean (location) = 0

Particular measures work well in particular cases, but in general, one single number does not always work well for characterizing either location or scale. It is totally misleading to think there is a single number that is the "risk," that risk can be summarized by a single number that works in all cases for all assets and for all investors. Risk is multifaceted. There are better and worse numbers, some better or worse in particular circumstances, but it will almost never be the case (except for textbook examples such as normality or quadratic utility) that a single number will suffice. Indeed, the all-too-common tendency to reduce risk to a single number is part of the "illusion of certainty" (to use a phrase from Gigerenzer 2002) and epitomizes the difficulty of thinking about uncertainty, to which I turn next.

Randomness and the "Illusion of Certainty"

Thinking about uncertainty and randomness is hard, if only because it is more difficult to think about what we do not know than about what we do. Life would be easier if "risk" could be reduced to a single number, but it cannot be. There is a human tendency and a strong temptation to distill future uncertainty and contingency down to a single, definitive number, providing the "illusion of certainty." But many mistakes and misunderstandings ensue when one ignores future contingency and relies on a fixed number to represent the changeable future. The search for a single risk number is an example of the human characteristic of trying to reduce a complex, multifaceted world to a single factor.

To understand, appreciate, and work with risk, we have to move away from rigid, fixed thinking and expand to consider alternatives. We must give up any illusion that there is certainty in this world and embrace the future as fluid, changeable, and contingent. In the words of Gigerenzer (2002), "Giving up the illusion of certainty enables us to enjoy and explore the complexity of the world in which we live" (p. 231).

Difficulties with Human Intuition. Randomness pervades our world, but human intuition is not very good at working with randomness and probabilities. Experience and training do not always groom us to understand or live comfortably with uncertainty. In fact, a whole industry and literature are based on studying how people make mistakes when thinking about and judging probability. In the 1930s, "researchers noted that people could neither make up a sequence of [random] numbers . . . nor recognize reliably whether a given string was randomly generated" (Mlodinow 2008, p. ix). The best-known academic research in this area is by the psychologists Daniel Kahneman and Amos Tversky.[12]

Kahneman and Tversky did much to develop the idea that people use heuristics (rules of thumb or shortcuts for solving complex problems) when faced with problems of uncertainty and randomness. They found that heuristics lead to predictable and consistent mistakes (cognitive biases). They worked together for many years, publishing important early work in the 1970s. Kahneman received the 2002 Nobel Prize in Economic Sciences "for having integrated insights from psychological research into economic science, especially concerning human judgment and decision-making under uncertainty."[13] (Tversky died in 1996, and the Nobel Prize is not awarded posthumously.)

One oft-cited experiment shows the difficulty in thinking about randomness and probability. Subjects were asked to assess the probability of statements about someone's occupation and interests given information about the person's background and character.[14] In the experiment, Tversky and Kahneman presented participants with a description of Linda—31 years old, single, outspoken, and very bright. In college, Linda majored in philosophy, was deeply concerned with discrimination and social justice, and participated in antinuclear demonstrations. The experiment participants were then asked to rank the probability of three possible descriptions of Linda's current occupation and interests (i.e., extrapolating forward from Linda's college background to her current status):

(A)   Linda is a bank teller.

(B)   Linda is active in the feminist movement.

(C)   Linda is a bank teller and is active in the feminist movement.

Eighty-seven percent of the subjects ranked the probability of bank teller and feminist together higher than bank teller alone (in other words, they ranked C, which is both A and B together, above A alone). But this is mathematically

---

[12]See, for example, Kahneman and Tversky (1973) and Tversky and Kahneman (1974).

[13]http://nobelprize.org/nobel_prizes/economics/laureates/2002/.

[14]See Kahneman, Slovic, and Tversky (1982, pp. 90–98) for the original reference. The present description is a somewhat abbreviated version of that in Mlodinow (2008).

impossible. Whatever Linda's current employment and interests are, the probability that Linda is both a bank teller *and also* an active feminist (C—that is, A and B together) cannot be higher than the probability of her being just a bank teller. No matter what the particulars, the probability of A and B together is never higher than the probability of A alone. Another way to see this problem is to note that the total universe of bank tellers is much larger than the subset of bank tellers who are also active feminists, so it has to be more likely that someone is a bank teller than that she is a bank teller who is also an active feminist.

Further Thoughts about Linda the Bank Teller

The bank teller/feminist combination may be less likely, yet psychologically it is more satisfying. Possibly the explanation lies in our everyday experience and in the tasks we practice regularly. The essence of Kahneman and Tversky's experiment is to take Linda's college life and make probability statements about her future occupation. We do not commonly do this. More frequently we do the reverse: meet new acquaintances about whom we have limited information and then try to infer more about their character and background. In other words, it would be common to meet Linda at age 31, find out her current status, and make probability inferences about her college life. The likelihood that Linda had the college background ascribed to her would be much higher if she were currently a bank teller and active feminist than if she were a bank teller alone. In other words, P[college life|bank teller & feminist] > P[college life|bank teller], and P[bank teller & feminist|college life] < P[bank teller|college life]. It may be that we are good at solving the more common problem, whether through practice or innate psychological predisposition, and fail to account for the unusual nature of the problem presented in the experiment; we think we are solving the familiar problem, not the unfamiliar one. This explanation would be consistent with another Kahneman and Tversky experiment (Tversky and Kahneman 1983; Mlodinow 2008, p. 25) in which doctors are essentially asked to predict symptoms based on an underlying condition. Doctors are usually trained to do the reverse: diagnose underlying conditions based on symptoms.

Alternatively, the explanation may be in how the problem is posed. Possibly when we read C ("bank teller and feminist"), we unconsciously impose symmetry on the problem and reinterpret A as "bank teller and nonfeminist." Given the information we have about Linda, it would be reasonable to assign a higher probability to C than the reinterpreted A. Perhaps the experimental results would change if we chose a better formulation of the problem—for example, by stating A as "Linda is a bank teller, but you do not know if she is active in the feminist movement or not" because this restatement would make it very explicit that C is, in a sense, a subset of A.

The argument about heuristics (how we think about problems) and how a problem is posed is related to Gigerenzer (2002) and discussed more later.

Such mistakes are not uncommon. Kahneman and Tversky developed the concepts of representativeness, availability of instances or scenarios, and adjustment from an anchor as three heuristics that people use to solve probability problems and deal with uncertainty.[15] These heuristics often lead to mistakes or biases, as seen in the Linda example. The fields of behavioral economics and behavioral finance are in large part based on their work, and their work is not limited to the academic arena. Many books have popularized the idea that human intuition is not well suited to dealing with randomness. Taleb (2004, 2007) is well known, but Gigerenzer (2002) and Mlodinow (2008) are particularly informative.

Probability Is Not Intuitive. Thinking carefully about uncertainty and randomness is difficult but genuinely productive. The fact is that dealing with probability and randomness is hard and sometimes just plain weird. Mlodinow (2008), from which the description of the Linda experiment is taken, has further examples. But one particularly nice example of how probability problems are often nonintuitive is the classic birthday problem. It also exhibits the usefulness of probability theory in setting our intuition straight.

The birthday problem is discussed in many texts, with the stimulating book by Aczel (2004) being a particularly good presentation. The problem is simple to state: What is the probability that if you enter a room with 20 people, 2 of those 20 will share the same birthday (same day of the year, not the same year)? Most people would say the probability is small because there are, after all, 365 days to choose from. In fact, the probability is just over 44 percent, a number that I always find surprisingly high. And it only takes 56 people to raise the probability to more than 99 percent. As Aczel put it:

> when fifty-six people are present in a room, there is a ninety-nine percent probability that at least two of them share a birthday! How can we get so close to certainty when there are only fifty-six people and a total of three hundred and sixty-five possible days of the year? Chance does seem to work in mysterious ways. If you have three hundred and sixty-five open boxes onto which fifty-six balls are randomly dropped, there is a ninety-nine percent chance that there will be at least two balls in at least one of the boxes. Why does this happen? No one really has an intuition for such things. The natural inclination is to think that because there are over three hundred empty boxes left over after fifty-six balls are dropped, no two balls can share the same spot.

---

[15] See Tversky and Kahneman (1974).

20

The mathematics tells us otherwise, and reality follows the mathematics. In nature, we find much more aggregation—due to pure randomness—than we might otherwise suspect. (pp. 71–72)[16]

Another example of how intuition can mislead and where probability is not intuitive is in assessing streaks or runs. Random sequences will exhibit clustering or bunching (e.g., runs of multiple heads in a sequence of coin flips), and such clustering often appears to our intuition to be nonrandom. The "random" shuffle on an iPod has actually been adjusted so it appears to us as "more random." When the iPod was originally introduced, the random order of songs would periodically produce repetition and users hearing the same song or artist played back-to-back believed the shuffling was not random. Apple altered the algorithm to be "less random to make it feel more random," according to Steve Jobs.[17] The clustering of random sequences is also why sub-random or quasi-random sequences are used for Monte Carlo simulation and Monte Carlo numerical integration; these sequences fill the space to be integrated more uniformly.[18]

To appreciate how runs can mislead, consider observing 10 heads in a row when flipping a coin. Having 10 in a row is unlikely, with a probability of 1 in 1,024 or 0.098 percent. Yet, if we flip a coin 200 times, there is a 17 percent chance we will observe a run of either 10 heads or 10 tails.[19]

Runs or streaks occur in real life, and we need to be very careful in interpreting such streaks. As the example of 10 heads shows, unlikely events do occur in a long-repeated process. A very practical example, highly relevant to anyone interested in risk management, is that of Bill Miller, portfolio manager of Legg Mason Value Trust Fund. Through the end of 2005, Bill Miller had a streak of 15 years of beating the S&P 500,[20] which is an extraordinary accomplishment, but is it caused by skill or simply luck? We will see that it could easily be entirely because of luck.

The likelihood of a single fund beating the S&P 500 for 15 years in a row is low. Say we choose one particular fund, and let us assume that the fund has only a 50/50 chance of beating the index in a given year (so that no exceptional skill is involved, only luck). The probability of that fund beating the index for the next 15 years is only 1 in 32,768 or 0.003 percent—very low.

---

[16]Feller (1968, p. 33) also discusses the problem and gives approximations to the probability that two or more people in a group of size r have the same birthday. For a small r (say, around 10), P[2 or more with same birthday] $\approx r(r-1)/730$. For a larger r (say, 15 or more), P[2 or more with same birthday] $\approx 1 - \exp[-r(r-1)/730]$. These work quite well. For $r = 23$ people, the true probability is 0.507 and the approximation is 0.500, and for $r = 56$, the true is 0.988 and the approximation is 0.985.

[17]See Mlodinow (2008, p. 175) and Maslin (2006).

[18]For discussion of sub-random sequences, see, for example, Press, Teukolsky, Vetterling, and Flannery (2007, section 7.8).

[19]I use simulation to arrive at this answer; I do not know of any simple formula for calculating the probability of such a run.

[20]The discussion of results through 2005 follows Mlodinow (2008).

But 0.003 percent is not really the relevant probability. We did not select the Value Trust Fund before the streak and follow just that one fund; we are looking back and picking the one fund out of many that had a streak. The streak may have been caused by exceptional skill, but it may also have been caused by our looking backward and considering the one lucky fund that did exceptionally well. Among many funds, one will always be particularly lucky, even if we could not say beforehand which fund that would be.

When we look at many funds, how exceptional would it be to observe a streak of 15 years? Say that only 1,000 funds exist (clearly an underestimate), that each fund operates independently, and that each fund has a 50/50 chance of beating the index in a particular year. What would be the chance that, over 15 years, we would see at least 1 of those 1,000 funds with a 15-year streak? It turns out to be much higher than 1 in 32,768—roughly 1 in 30 or 3 percent.[21] Therefore, observing a 15-year streak among a pool of funds is not quite so exceptional.

But we are not done yet. Commentators reported in 2003 (earlier in the streak) that "no other fund has ever outperformed the market for a dozen consecutive years over the last 40 years."[22] We really should consider the probability that some fund had a 15-year streak during, say, the last 40 years. What would be the chance of finding 1 fund out of a starting pool of 1,000 that had a 15-year streak sometime in a 40-year period? This scenario gives extra freedom because the streak could be at the beginning, middle, or end of the 40-year period. It turns out that the probability is now much higher, around 33 percent. In other words, the probability of observing such a streak, purely caused by chance, is high.[23]

---

[21]If each fund has probability p of outperforming in a year (in our case, $p = 0.5$), then the probability that one fund has a streak of 15 years is $p^{15} = 0.000031$ because performance across years is assumed to be independent and we multiply the probability of independent events to get the joint probability (one of the laws of probability—see Aczel 2004, ch. 4, or Hacking 2001, ch. 6). Thus, the probability the fund does not have a streak is $1 - p^{15} = 0.999969$. Each fund is independent, so for 1,000 funds, the probability that no fund has a streak is $(1 - p^{15})^{1,000} = 0.9699$ (again, we multiply independent events), which means the probability that at least 1 fund has a streak is $1 - 0.9699 = 0.0301$.

[22]Mauboussin and Bartholdson (2003, quoted in Mlodinow 2008, p. 180).

[23]I arrive at 33 percent by simulating the probability that a single fund would have a 15-year (or longer) run in 40 years ($p = 0.000397$) and then calculating the probability that none of 1,000 identical and independent funds would have a 15-year streak $[(1 - p^{15})^{1,000} = 0.672]$. Thus, the probability that at least one fund has a streak is $(1 - 0.672 = 0.328)$. Mlodinow (2008, p. 181) arrives at a probability of roughly 75 percent. Mlodinow may have assumed a more realistic pool of funds—say, 3,500, which would give a probability of 75 percent for at least one streak. Whether the probability is 33 percent or 75 percent, however, does not matter for the point of the argument because either way the probability is high.

The point of this exercise is not to prove that Bill Miller has only average skill. Possibly he has extraordinary skill, possibly not. The point is that a 15-year streak, exceptional as it sounds, does not prove that he has extraordinary skill. We must critically evaluate the world and not be misled by runs, streaks, or other quirks of nature. A streak like Bill Miller's sounds extraordinary. But before we get carried away and ascribe extraordinary skill to Bill Miller, we need to critically evaluate how likely such a streak is due to pure chance. We have seen that it is rather likely. Bill Miller may have exceptional skill, but the 15-year streak does not, on its own, prove the point.[24]

****

Probability Paradoxes and Puzzles: A Long Digression[25]

There are many probability paradoxes and puzzles. In this long digression, I will explore random walks and the "Monty Hall problem."

Random walks

One interesting and instructive case of a probability paradox is that of random walks—specifically, the number of changes of sign and the time in either positive or negative territory.

The simplest random walk is a process where, each period, a counter moves up or down by one unit with a probability of ½ for each. (This example is sometimes colloquially referred to as the drunkard's walk, after a drunkard taking stumbling steps from a lamppost—sometimes going forward and sometimes back but each step completely at random.) A random walk is clearly related to the binomial process and Bernoulli trials because each period is up or down—in other words, an independent Bernoulli trial with probability $p = $ ½.

Random walks provide an excellent starting point for describing many real-life situations, from gambling to the stock market. If we repeatedly toss a fair coin and count the number of heads minus the number of tails, this sequence is a simple random walk. The count (number of heads minus number of tails) could represent a simple game of chance: If we won $1 for every heads and lost $1 for every tails, the count would be our total winnings. With some elaborations (such as a p of not quite one-half and very short time periods), a random walk can provide a rudimentary description of stock market movements.

---

[24]As a side note, since 2005 the performance for the Legg Mason Value Trust has been not merely average but abysmal. For the four years 2006–2009, the Value Trust underperformed the S&P 500 three years out of four, and overall from year-end 2005 through year-end 2009, it was *down* 37.5 percent while the S&P 500 was down roughly 2.7 percent.

[25]Note that this section is a digression that can be read independently of the rest of the chapter.

Let us consider more carefully a simple random walk representing a game of chance in which we win $1 for every heads and lose $1 for every tails. This is a fair game. My intuition about the "law of averages" would lead me to think that because heads and tails each have equal chance, we should be up about half the time and we should go from being ahead to being behind fairly often. This assumption may be true in the long run, but the long run is very deceptive. In fact, "intuition leads to an erroneous picture of the probable effects of chance fluctuations."[26]

Let us say we played 10,000 times. **Figure 2.4** shows a particularly well-known example from Feller (1968). In this example, we are ahead (positive winnings) for roughly the first 120 tosses, and we are substantially ahead for a very long period, from about toss 3,000 to about 6,000. There are only 78 changes of sign (going from win to lose or vice versa), which seems to be a small number but is actually more than we should usually expect to see. If we repeated this game (playing 10,000 tosses) many times, then roughly 88 percent of the time we would see fewer than 78 changes of sign in the cumulative winnings. To me this is extraordinary.

Even more extraordinary would be if we ran this particular example of the game in reverse, starting at the end and playing backwards. The reverse is also a random walk, but for this particular example, we would see only eight changes of sign and would be on the negative side for 9,930 out of 10,000 steps—on the winning side only 70 steps. And yet, this outcome is actually fairly likely. The probability is better than 10 percent that in 10,000 tosses of a fair coin, we are almost always on one side or the other—either winning or losing for more than 9,930 out of the 10,000 trials. This result sounds extraordinary, but it is simply another example of how our intuition can mislead. As Feller says, if these results seem startling, "this is due to our faulty intuition and to our having been exposed to too many vague references to a mysterious 'law of averages'" (p. 88).

As a practical matter, we must be careful to examine real-world examples and compare them with probability theory. In a game of chance or other events subject to randomness (such as stock markets), a long winning period might lead us to believe we have skill or that the probability of winning is better than even. Comparison with probability theory forces us to critically evaluate such assumptions.

---

[26]Feller (1968, p. 78). This discussion is taken from the classic text on probability, Feller (1968, sections III.4–6).

Figure 2.4. Sample of 10,000 Tosses of an Ideal Coin

A. First 550 Trials

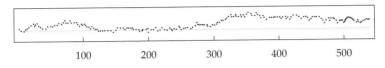

B. Trial 1–6,000 Compressed

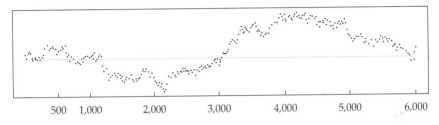

C. Trial 6,000–10,000 Compressed

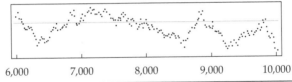

Note: The compressed scale is 10 times smaller.
Source: Based on Feller (1968, Figure 4).

The Monty Hall problem

One of the best-known probability puzzles goes under the name of the Monty Hall problem, after the host of the old TV game show *Let's Make a Deal.* One segment of the original show involved Monty Hall presenting a contestant with three doors. Behind one door was a valuable prize (often a car), and behind the other two were less valuable or worthless prizes (invariably referred to in current presentations as "goats"). The contestant chose one door, but before the chosen door was opened, Monty Hall would step in and open one of the doors and then give the contestant the opportunity to either stay with his or her original choice or switch. The probability puzzle is this: Is it better to stay with your original door or switch?

The answer we will eventually come to is that it is better to switch: The chance of winning is one-third if you stay with the original door and two-thirds if you switch.

Before delving into the problem more deeply, however, two particulars are needed. First, the problem as I have written it is actually not well posed and really cannot be answered properly. The heart of the problem, as we will see, is exactly what rules Monty Hall uses to open the doors: Does he always open a door, no matter which door the contestant chooses? Does he always open a door with a goat? The outline of the problem just given is too sloppy in laying out the rules.

Second, this problem has created more controversy and more interest both inside and outside the mathematical community than any comparable brainteaser. The history of the problem is itself interesting, but the controversy also serves to highlight some important truths:

- Thinking carefully about probability is hard but does have value. By doing so, we can get the right answer when intuition may mislead us.

- Assumptions and the framework of the problem are vitally important. We shall see that the answer for the Monty Hall problem depends crucially on the details of how the game show is set up.

- When we get an answer that does not make sense, we usually need to go back and refine our thinking about and assumptions behind the problem. Often we find that we did not fully understand how to apply the solution or the implications of some assumption. Ultimately, we end up with deeper insight into the problem and a better understanding of how to apply the solution in the real world. (This is somewhat along the lines of Lakatos's [1976] *Proofs and Refutations*.)

- Related to the preceding point, probability problems and models are just representations of the world and it is important to understand how well (or how poorly) they reflect the part of the world we are trying to understand. The Monty Hall problem demonstrates this point well. In the actual TV show, Monty Hall did not always act as specified in this idealized problem. Our solution does, however, point us toward what is important—in this case, understanding Monty Hall's rules for opening the doors.

The Monty Hall problem has been around for a considerable time, and its more recent popularity has generated a considerable literature. A recent book by Jason Rosenhouse (2009), on which many points in this exposition are based, is devoted entirely to Monty Hall.[27] The first statement of the problem, under a different name but equivalent mathematically, was apparently made by Martin Gardner (1959) in a *Scientific American* column. That version of the problem, although it generated interest in the mathematical community, did not become famous.

---

[27]The Monty Hall problem is discussed widely—Mlodinow (2008); Gigerenzer (2002); and Aczel (2004), although under a different formulation. Vos Savant (1996) covers the topic in some depth.

The first appearance of the problem under the rubric of Monty Hall and *Let's Make a Deal* appears to have been in 1975, in two letters published in the *American Statistician* by Steve Selvin (1975a, 1975b). Once again, this presentation of the problem generated interest but only within a limited community.

The Monty Hall problem took off with the answer to a question in *Parade* magazine in September 1990 from reader Craig Whitaker to the columnist Marilyn vos Savant, author of the magazine's "Ask Marilyn" column. Vos Savant was famous for being listed in the *Guinness Book of World Records* (and inducted into the Guinness Hall of Fame) as the person with the world's highest recorded IQ (228) but is now better known for her (correct) response to the Monty Hall problem.

The question that started the furor was as follows:

> Suppose you are on a game show, and you are given the choice of three doors. Behind one door is a car, behind the others, goats. You pick a door, say Number 1, and the host, who knows what is behind the doors, opens another door, say Number 3, which has a goat. He says to you, "Do you want to pick door Number 2?" Is it to your advantage to switch your choice of doors? (vos Savant, 1990a, p. 15)

The reply was:

> Yes, you should switch. The first door has 1/3 chance of winning, but the second door has a 2/3 chance. Here's a good way to visualize what happened. Suppose there are a *million* doors, and you pick door Number 1. Then the host, who knows what is behind the doors and will always avoid the one with the prize, opens them all except door number 777,777. You would switch to that door pretty fast, wouldn't you? (vos Savant, 1990b, p. 25)

This simple exchange led to a flood of responses—thousands of letters from the general public and the halls of academe. Vos Savant was obliged to follow up with at least two further columns. The responses, many from professional mathematicians and statisticians, were often as rude as they were incorrect (from vos Savant 1996, quoted in Rosenhouse 2009, pp. 24–25):

> Since you seem to enjoy coming straight to the point, I will do the same. In the following question and answer, you blew it!

> You blew it, and you blew it big!

> May I suggest that you obtain and refer to a standard textbook on probability before you try to answer a question of this type again?

> You made a mistake, but look at the positive side. If all those PhD's were wrong, the country would be in some very serious trouble.

Unfortunately for these correspondents, vos Savant was absolutely correct, although possibly less careful than an academic mathematician might have been in stating the assumptions of the problem. All those PhDs *were* wrong.

Let me state the problem in a reasonably precise way:

- There are three doors, with a car randomly placed behind one door and goats behind the other two.
- Monty Hall, the game show host, knows the placement of the car and the goats; the contestant does not.
- The contestant chooses one door, but that door is not opened.
- Monty Hall then opens a door. He follows these rules in doing so:
  - Never open the door the contestant has chosen.
  - If the car is behind the contestant's door (so that the two nonchosen doors have goats), randomly choose which goat door to open.
  - If the car is behind one of the two nonchosen doors (so only one nonchosen door has a goat), open that goat door.
- As a result of these rules, Monty Hall will always open a nonchosen door and that door will always show a goat.
- Most importantly, the rules ensure that a goat door is opened deliberately and systematically, in a decidedly nonrandom way so that a goat door is always opened and a car door is never opened.
- The contestant is now given the choice of staying with his or her original door or switching to the remaining closed door.

The natural inclination is to assume that there are now two choices (the door originally chosen and the remaining unopened door), and with two choices, there is no benefit to switching; it is 50–50 either way. This natural inclination, however, is mistaken. The chance of winning the car by remaining with the original door is 1/3, the chance of winning by switching is 2/3.

As pointed out earlier, there is a vast literature discussing this problem and its solution. I will outline two explanations for why the 1/3 versus 2/3 answer is correct, but take my word that, given the rules just outlined, it is correct.[28]

The first way to see that switching provides a 2/3 chance of winning is to note that the originally chosen door started with a 1/3 chance of having the car and the other two doors, together, had a 2/3 chance of winning. (Remember that the car was randomly assigned to a door, so any door a contestant might choose has a 1/3 chance of being the door with the car.) The way that Monty Hall chooses to open a door ensures that he always opens one of the other two doors and always chooses a door with a goat. The manner of his choosing does not alter the 1/3 probability that the contestant chose the car door originally, nor does it alter the 2/3 probability that the car is behind one of the other two. By switching, the contestant can move from 1/3 to 2/3 probability of winning.

---

[28]These arguments are intended to show why the solution is correct, not as a formal proof of the solution. See Rosenhouse (2009) for a proof of the classical problem, together with a large choice of variations.

(Essentially, in 2/3 of the cases where the car is behind one of the other two doors, Monty Hall reveals which door it is not behind. Monty Hall's door opening provides valuable information.)

An alternative approach, and the only one that seems to have convinced some very astute mathematicians, is to simulate playing the game.[29] Take the role of the contestant, always pick Door 1, and try the strategy of sticking with Door 1. (Because the car is randomly assigned to a door, always picking Door 1 ends up the same as randomly picking a door.) Use a random number generator to generate a uniform random variable between 0 and 1 (for example, the RAND() function in Microsoft Excel). If the random number is less than 1/3 or 0.3333, then the car is behind Door 1 and you win. Which other door is opened does not matter. Try a few repeats, and you will see that you win roughly 1/3 of the time.

Now change strategies and switch doors. If the random number is less than 1/3 or 0.3333, then the car is behind Door 1 and you lose by switching doors. Which other door is opened really does not matter because both doors have goats and by switching you lose. If the random number is between 0.3333 and 0.66667, then the car is behind Door 2; Door 3 must be opened, and you switch to Door 2 and win. If the random number is between 0.66667 and 1.0, then the car is behind Door 3; Door 2 must be opened, and you switch to Door 3 and win. Try several repeats. You will soon see that you win 2/3 of the time and lose 1/3.

In the end, the strategy of switching wins 2/3 of the time and the strategy of staying wins only 1/3. Although nonintuitive, this strategy is correct. In the literature, there are many discussions of the solution, many that go into detail and present solutions from a variety of perspectives.[30]

In this problem, the rules for choosing the doors are the critical component. Consider an alternate rule. Say that Monty Hall does not know the car location and randomly chooses an unopened door, meaning that he sometimes opens a door with the car and the game ends. In this case, the solution is that if a door with a goat is opened, staying and switching each have a 50–50 chance of winning and there is no benefit to switching.

In the original game, Monty Hall's opening a goat door tells you nothing about your original door; the rules are designed so that Monty Hall always opens a goat door, no matter what your original choice. Heuristically, the probability of the originally chosen door being a winner does not change; it remains at 1/3. (This can be formalized using Bayes' rule.)

---

[29]Hoffman (1998) relates how Paul Erdös, one of the most prolific 20th century mathematicians, was only convinced of the solution through a Monte Carlo simulation. This is also the method by which I came to understand that switching is the correct strategy.

[30]Rosenhouse (2009) discusses the problem and solutions in detail. It is also covered in Mlodinow (2008) and Gigerenzer (2002).

In the alternate game, opening a door does tell you something about your original choice. When Monty Hall opens a door with a car (roughly 1/3 of the time), you know for sure that your door is a loser. When Monty Hall opens a goat door (2/3 of the time), you know that now only two choices are left, with your originally chosen door one of those possibilities.

The actual TV show apparently did not abide by either of these sets of rules but, rather, by a set of rules we might call somewhat malevolent.[31] If the contestant chose a "goat," Monty Hall would usually open the contestant's door to reveal the goat and end the game. When the contestant chose the car, Monty Hall would open one of the other doors to reveal a goat and then try to convince the contestant to switch. Under these rules, Monty Hall's opening one of the other doors would be a sure sign that the originally chosen door was a winner. In this case, the best strategy would be to stick with the original door whenever Monty Hall opened another door.

For the actual TV game, the standard problem does not apply and the probability arguments are not relevant. Nonetheless, the analysis of the problem would have been truly valuable to any contestant. The analysis highlights the importance of the rules Monty Hall uses for choosing which door to open. For the actual game, contestants familiar with the probability problem could examine past games, determine the scheme used by Monty Hall to open doors, and substantially improve their chance of winning.

****

Past/Future Asymmetry. One aspect of uncertainty and randomness that is particularly important is what might be called "past/future asymmetry." It is often easy to explain the past but very difficult to predict the future, and events that look preordained when viewed in hindsight were often uncertain at the time. Mlodinow (2008) discusses this topic at some length. One nice example he gives in chapter 10 is chess:

> Unlike card games, chess involves no explicit random element. And yet there is uncertainty because neither player knows for sure what his or her opponent will do next. If the players are expert, at most points in the game it may be possible to see a few moves into the future; if you look out any further, the uncertainty will compound, and no one will be able to say with any confidence exactly how the game will turn out. On the other hand, looking back, it is usually easy to say why each player made the moves he or she made. This again is a probabilistic process whose future is difficult to predict but whose past is easy to understand. (pp. 197–198)

---

[31] See Rosenhouse (2009, p. 20).

In chapter 1, Mlodinow gives examples of manuscripts rejected by publishers: John Grisham's manuscript for *A Time to Kill* by 26 publishers, J.K. Rowling's first *Harry Potter* manuscript by 9, and Dr. Seuss's first children's book by 27. Looking back, it is hard to believe that such hugely popular books could ever have been rejected by even one publisher, but it is always easier to look back and explain what happened than it is to look forward and predict what will happen.

Because we always look back at history and so often it is easy to explain the past, we can fall into the trap of thinking that the future should be equally easy to explain and understand. It is not, and the chess example is a good reminder of how uncertain the future can be even for a game with well-defined rules and limited possible moves. We must continually remember that the future is uncertain and all our measurements only give us an imperfect view of what might happen and will never eliminate the inherent uncertainty of the future.

Do Not Worry Too Much about Human Intuition. It is true that thinking about uncertainty is difficult and human intuition is often poor at solving probability problems. Even so, we should not go too far worrying about intuition. So what if human intuition is ill suited to situations involving uncertainty? Human intuition is ill suited to situations involving quantum mechanics, or special relativity, or even plain old classical mechanics. That does not stop us from developing DVD players and MRI scanners (which depend on quantum mechanics) and GPS devices (requiring both special and general relativistic timing corrections) or from calculating projectile trajectories (using classical mechanics). None of these are "intuitive"; they require science and mathematics to arrive at correct answers, and nobody is particularly surprised that quantitative analysis is required to inform, guide, and correct intuition.

If we were to conduct experiments asking people about relativistic physics, nobody would get the right answers. The paradoxes in relativity are legion and, in fact, are widely taught in undergraduate courses in special relativity. And quantum mechanics is worse: Einstein never could accept quantum entanglement and what he called "spooky action at a distance," but it is reality nonetheless. Lack of intuition does not stop the development of relativistic physics or quantum mechanics or their practical application.

In the realm of probability, why should anybody be surprised that quantitative analysis is necessary for understanding and dealing with uncertainty? We should be asking how good are the quantitative tools and how useful is the quantitative analysis, not fret that intuition fails. "The key to understanding randomness and all of mathematics is not being able to intuit the answer to every problem immediately but merely having the tools to figure out the answer" (Mlodinow 2008, p. 108).

This discussion is not meant to belittle intuition. Intuition can be valuable, and not all problems can be solved mathematically. The best-seller *Blink* by Gladwell (2005) extols the virtues of intuition[32] and is itself based in part on research performed by Gigerenzer (2007). My point is that the failure of intuition in certain circumstances does not invalidate the usefulness or importance of formal probabilistic analysis.

Steps toward Probabilistic Numeracy. I am not saying that understanding and working with probability is easy. Nor am I saying that risk management is a science comparable to physics; in many ways, it is harder because it deals with the vagaries of human behavior. But neither should we, as some commentators seem to advocate, just walk away and ignore the analytical and mathematical tools that can help us to understand randomness and manage risk. Risk management and risk measurement are hard, and there are and will continue to be mistakes and missteps and problems that cannot be solved exactly, or even approximately. But without the mathematics to systematize and organize the problems, the task would be plain impossible.

Gigerenzer (2002), who takes a critical approach to the work of Kahneman and Tversky, has a refreshing approach to the problem of living with uncertainty. (Indeed, Gigerenzer [2002] was published outside the United States under the title *Reckoning with Risk: Learning to Live with Uncertainty*.) Gigerenzer argues that sound statistical (and probabilistic) thinking can be enhanced, both through training and through appropriate tools and techniques:

> Many have argued that sound statistical thinking is not easily turned into a "habit of mind." . . . I disagree with this habit-of-mind story. The central lesson of this book is that people's difficulties in thinking about numbers need not be accepted, because they can be overcome. The difficulties are not simply the mind's fault. Often, the solution can be found in the mind's environment, that is, in the way numerical information is presented. With the aid of intuitively understandable representations, statistical thinking can become a habit of mind. (p. 245)

Gigerenzer (2002, p. 38) aims to overcome statistical innumeracy through three steps:

- Defeat the illusion of certainty (the human tendency to believe in the certainty of outcomes or the absence of uncertainty).

---

[32]Gladwell's book spawned a counterargument (Adler 2009) in which the author makes the case that first impressions are usually wrong and that one ought to do the hard work of analyzing a situation before making a decision.

- Learn about actual risks of relevant events and actions.

- Communicate risks in an understandable way.

These three steps apply equally to risk management. Most work in risk management focuses on the second—learning about risks—but the first and third are equally important. Thinking about uncertainty is hard, but it is important to recognize that things happen and the future is uncertain. And communicating risk is especially important. The risks a firm faces are often complex and yet need to be shared with a wide audience in an efficient, concise manner. Effectively communicating these risks is a difficult task that deserves far more attention than it is usually given.

Probability and Statistics

Probability is the science of studying uncertainty and systematizing randomness. Given uncertainty of some form, what should happen, what should we see? A good example is the analysis of streaks, the chance of a team winning a series of games. This kind of problem is discussed in any basic probability text, and Mlodinow (2008) discusses this type of problem.

Consider two teams that play a series of three games, with the first team to win two games being the winner of the series. There are four ways a team can win the series and four ways to lose the series, as laid out in the following table. If the teams are perfectly matched, each has a 50 percent chance of winning a single game, each individual possibility has a probability of one-eighth ($0.125 = 0.5 \times 0.5 \times 0.5$), and each team has a 50 percent chance of winning the series:

Win	Probability	Lose	Probability
WWL	0.125	LLW	0.125
WLW	0.125	LWL	0.125
LWW	0.125	WLL	0.125
WWW	0.125	LLL	0.125
	0.500		0.500

The analysis seems fairly obvious.[33] But consider if the teams are not evenly matched and one team has a 40 percent chance of winning and a 60 percent chance of losing. What is the probability the inferior team still wins the series?

[33]It might seem odd to include the possibilities WWL and WWW separately because in both cases the final game would not be played. They need to be included, however, because the series sometimes goes to three games (as in WLW). And because the series sometimes goes to three games, we must keep track of all the possible ways it could go to three games and count WWL and WWW as separate possibilities.

We can write down all the possibilities as before, but now the probabilities for outcomes will be different—for example, a WWL for the inferior team will have probability 0.096 (0.4 × 0.4 × 0.6):

Win	Probability	Lose	Probability
WWL	0.096	LLW	0.144
WLW	0.096	LWL	0.144
LWW	0.096	WLL	0.144
WWW	0.064	LLL	0.216
	0.352		0.648

It turns out the probability of the inferior team winning the series is 35 percent, not a lot less than the chance of winning an individual game.

The problem becomes more interesting when considering longer series. The winner of the World Series in baseball is the winner of four out of seven games. In baseball, the best team in a league wins roughly 60 percent of its games during a season and the worst team wins roughly 40 percent, so pitting a 60 percent team against a 40 percent team would be roughly equivalent to pitting the top team against the bottom team. What would be the chance that the inferior team would still win the series? We need only write down all the possible ways as we just did (but now there are 128 possible outcomes rather than 8), calculate the probability of each, and sum them up. The result is 29 percent.

To me, a 29 percent chance of such an inferior team winning the series is surprisingly high. It is also a good example of how probability theory can help guide our intuition. I would have thought, before solving the problem, that the probability would be lower, much lower. The analysis, however, forces me to realize that either my intuition is wrong or that my assumptions are wrong.[34] Probability theory and analysis help us to critically evaluate our intuition and assumptions and to adjust both so that they more closely align with experience and reality.

The analysis of win/lose situations turns out to be quite valuable and applicable to many problems. It is the same as coin tossing: heads versus tails (although not necessarily with a balanced 50/50 coin). It applies to the streak of the Legg Mason Value Trust Fund. The name given to such a process with two

---

[34]It may be that the worst team in the league has a probability lower than 40 percent of winning a single game. Nonetheless, the World Series pits the best teams from the American and National Leagues, and these teams will be more closely matched than 60 percent/40 percent. Yet, the analysis shows that there is a reasonable chance (better than 30 percent) that the better team will lose the World Series.

outcomes, one outcome usually (for convenience) labeled "success" and the other "failure," is a Bernoulli trial. When a Bernoulli trial is repeated a number of times, the number of successes that occurs is said to have a binomial distribution.

Bernoulli

Bernoulli trials are named after Jakob Bernoulli (1654–1705, also known as Jacob, James, and Jacques). The Bernoulli family was so prolific that it is difficult to keep all the Bernoullis straight. Over the period 1650–1800, the family produced eight noted mathematicians with three (Jakob, brother Johann, and nephew Daniel) among the world's greatest mathematicians.

The weak law of large numbers originated with Jakob and also goes by the name of Bernoulli's theorem. It was published as the "Golden Theorem" in *Ars Conjectandi* in 1713 after Jakob's death. The probabilistic Bernoulli's theorem should not be confused with the fluid dynamics Bernoulli's theorem or principle, which originated with nephew Daniel (1700–1782).

Bernoulli trials and the binomial distribution have immediate application to finance and risk management. We often know (or are told) that there is only a 1 percent chance of losses worse than some amount Y (say, $100,000) in one day. This is the essence of VaR, as I will show in Chapter 5. We can now treat losses for a given day as a Bernoulli trial: 99 percent chance of "success," and 1 percent chance of "failure" (losses worse than $100,000). Over 100 days, this is a sequence of 100 Bernoulli trials, and the number of successes or failures will have a binomial distribution.

We can use probability theory to assess the chance of seeing one or more days of large losses. Doing so provides an example of how we must move toward embracing randomness and away from thinking there is any certainty in our world. The number of days worse than $100,000 will have a binomial distribution. Generally, we will not see exactly 1 day out of 100 with large losses, even though with a probability of 1 out of 100 we *expect* to see 1 day out of 100. Over 100 days, there is only a 37 percent chance of seeing a single day with large losses. There is a 37 percent chance of seeing no losses worse than $100,000, a 19 percent chance of two days, and even an 8 percent chance of three or more days of large losses.[35]

---

[35] According to the binomial distribution with p = probability of "success" and $q = 1 - p$ = probability of "failure," the probability of k failures out of n trials is $\binom{n}{k} q^k (1-q)^{n-k}$, where $\binom{n}{k} = \dfrac{n!}{k!(n-k)!}$ is the binomial coefficient. For $q = 0.01$, $n = 100$, $P(k=0) = 0.366$, $P(k=1) = 0.370$, $P(k=2) = 0.185$, $P(k \geq 3) = 0.079$.

The intent of this section is not to cover probability theory in depth but, rather, to explain what it is and show how it can be used. Books such as Mlodinow (2008), Gigerenzer (2002), Hacking (2001), Kaplan and Kaplan (2006), and in particular Aczel (2004) are very useful. Probability systematizes how we think about uncertainty and randomness. It tells us what we should expect to observe given a certain model or form of randomness in the world—for example, how likely a team is to win a series or how likely it is to see multiple bad trading days in a set of 100 days. Building probabilistic intuition is valuable, I would even say necessary, for any success in managing risk.

Statistics. Although probability theory starts with a model of randomness and from there develops statements about what we are likely to observe, statistics, roughly speaking, works in the opposite direction. We use what we observe in nature to develop statements about the underlying probability model. For example, probability theory might start with knowing that there is a 1 percent chance of a day with losses worse than $100,000 and then tell us the chance that, in a string of 100 days, we will observe exactly 1 or exactly 2 or exactly 3 such days. Statistics starts with the actual losses that we observe over a string of 100 days and attempts to estimate the underlying process: Is the probability of a loss worse than $100,000 equal to 1 percent or 2 percent? Statistics also provides us with estimates of confidence about the probabilities so that we can know, for example, whether we should strongly believe that it is a 1 percent probability or (alternately) whether we should only feel confident that it is somewhere between 0.5 percent and 1.5 percent.

For the technical side of risk measurement, statistics is equally or more important than probability. For the application of risk management, for actually managing risk, however, probability is more important. A firm understanding of how randomness may affect future outcomes is critical, even if the estimation of the underlying model has to be left to others. Without an appreciation of how randomness governs our world, understanding risk is impossible.

Theories of Probability: Frequency vs. Belief (Objective vs. Subjective). There are deep philosophical questions concerning the foundations of probability, with two theories that are somewhat at odds. These theories often go under the name of "objective probability" versus "subjective probability" or by the terms "risk" versus "uncertainty," although better names (used by Hacking 2001) are "frequency-type" versus "belief-type" probability. Fortunately, we can safely sidestep much of the debate over the alternate approaches and, for most practical purposes, use the two interchangeably. Nonetheless, the distinction is relevant, and I will discuss the issues here before turning back to more strictly risk management issues.

The objective or frequency-type theory of probability is the easiest to understand and is tied to the origins of probability theory in the 17th century. Probability theory started with games of chance and gambling, and the idea of frequency-type probability is best demonstrated in this context. Consider an ideal coin, with a 50 percent chance of heads versus tails. Each flip of the coin is a Bernoulli trial, and we "know" that the probability of a heads is 50 percent. How do we know? It is an objective fact—one that we can measure by inspecting the coin or even better by counting the frequency of heads versus tails over a large number of trials. (The terms "objective" and "frequency" are applied to this probability approach exactly because this probability approach measures objective facts and can be observed by the frequency of repeated trials.)

Repeated throws of a coin form the archetypal frequency-type probability system. Each throw of the coin is the same as any other, each is independent of all the others, and the throw can be repeated as often and as long as we wish.[36] Frequency-type probability reflects *how the world is* (to use Hacking's phrase). It makes statements that are either true or false: A fair coin either has a one-half probability of landing heads on each throw or it does not; it is a statement about how the world actually is.

For frequency-type probability, laws of large numbers and central limit theorems are fundamental tools. Laws of large numbers tell us that as we repeat trials (flips of the coin), the relative frequency of heads will settle down to the objective probability set by the probabilistic system we are using, one-half for a fair coin. Not only that, but laws of large numbers and central limit theorems tell us how fast and with what range of uncertainty the frequency settles down to its "correct" value. These tools are incredibly powerful. For example, we can use the usual central limit theorem to say that in a coin-tossing experiment with 100 flips, we have a high probability that we will observe between 40 and 60 heads (and a low probability that we will observe outside that band).[37]

Frequency-type probability is ideally suited to games of chance, in which the game is repeated always under the same rules. Much of the world of finance fits reasonably well into such a paradigm. Trading in IBM stock is likely to look tomorrow like it does today—not in terms of the stock going up by the exact amount it did yesterday but, rather, in the likelihood that it will go up or down

---

[36] A die would be another simple and common example of a system to which frequency-type probability would naturally apply. An ideal die would have a one-sixth chance of landing with any face up. For an actual die, we could examine the die itself and verify its symmetry, and we could also perform repeated throws to actually measure the frequency for each of the six faces.

[37] The number of heads will be approximately normally distributed, $N(\mu = 50, \sigma^2 = 25)$, so that there will be a 95 percent probability the actual number of heads will be within $\mu \pm 2\sigma$ or 50 ± 10.

and by how much. New information might come out about IBM, but news about IBM often comes out, which is part of the repeated world of trading stocks. Whether IBM goes up or down is, in effect, as random as the flip of a coin (although possibly a biased coin because stocks generally grow over time). For many practical purposes, the coin that is flipped today can be considered the same as the coin flipped yesterday: We do not know whether IBM will go up or down tomorrow, but we usually do not have any particular reason to think it more likely to go up tomorrow than it has, on average, in the past.

For many problems, however, a frequency-type approach to probability just does not work. Consider the weather tomorrow. What does it mean to say the probability of precipitation tomorrow is 30 percent? This is not a true or false statement about how the world is. Viewed from today, tomorrow is a one-time event. Saying the probability is 30 percent is a statement about our confidence in the outcome or about the credibility of the evidence we use to predict that it will rain tomorrow. We cannot consider frequencies because we cannot repeat tomorrow. What about the probability that an asteroid impact led to the extinction of the dinosaurs? Or the probability that temperatures will rise over the next century (climate change)? None of these are repeatable events to which we can apply frequency concepts or the law of large numbers. Yet we need to apply, commonly do apply, and indeed can sensibly apply probabilistic thinking to these areas.

For these kinds of one-off or unique or nonfrequency situations, we rely on belief-type probabilities, what are often termed "subjective probabilities."[38] Belief-type probabilities must follow the same rules as frequency-type probabilities but arise from a very different source.

The probability of one-off events, or more precisely our assessment or beliefs about the probabilities, can be uncovered using a neat trick developed by Bruno de Finetti (1906–1985), an Italian mathematician and co-developer of mean–variance optimization.[39] The de Finetti game is a thought experiment, a hypothetical lottery or gamble in which an event is compared with drawing balls from a bag.

---

[38]The term "subjective" is unfortunate. It suggests that this type of probability is somehow inferior to the frequency-type or "objective" probability. Furthermore, belief-type probability statements can be based on logical relations and evidence that can reasonably be labeled "objective"; an example is a forecast of rain tomorrow based on the observations that a storm system lies to the west and that weather in the middle northern latitudes usually moves from west to east. Like Hacking (2001), I will generally not use the terms "objective" and "subjective" probability but rather "frequency-type" and "belief-type" probability.

[39]See Markowitz (2006). See also Bernstein (2007, p. 108).

Say the event we are considering is receiving a perfect score on an exam; a friend took an exam and claims she is absolutely, 100 percent sure she got a perfect score on the exam (and she will receive the score tomorrow).[40] We might be suspicious because, as Ben Franklin so famously said, "nothing can be said to be certain, except death and taxes," and exam grades in particular are notoriously hard to predict.

We could ask our friend to choose between two no-lose gambles: The first is to receive $10 tomorrow if our friend's test is a perfect score, and the second is to receive $10 if our friend picks a red ball from a bag filled with 100 balls. The bag is filled with 99 red balls and only one black ball so that there is a 99 percent chance our friend would pick a red ball from the bag. Most people would presumably draw from the bag rather than wait for the exam score. It is almost a sure thing to win the $10 by drawing from the bag, and our friend, being reasonable, probably does not assign a higher than 99 percent chance of receiving a perfect score.

Assuming our friend chooses to draw a ball from the bag with 99 red balls, we can then pose another choice between no-lose gambles: $10 if the test score is perfect versus $10 if a red ball is drawn from a bag—this one filled with 80 red and 20 black balls. If our friend chooses the test score, we know the subjective probability is between 99 percent and 80 percent. We can further refine the bounds by posing the choice between $10 for a perfect test score versus $10 for a red ball from a bag with 90 red and 10 black. Depending on the answer, the probability is between 99 percent and 90 percent or 90 percent and 80 percent.

Such a scheme can be used to uncover our own subjective probabilities. Even using the scheme purely as a thought experiment can be extremely instructive. Aczel (2004, p. 23) points out that people often restate their probabilities when playing this game; it forces us to think more carefully about our subjective probabilities and to make them consistent with assessments of other events. Aczel also points out that, interestingly, weather forecasters do not tend to change their assessments very much; presumably their profession forces them to think carefully about belief-type or subjective probabilities.

Note that the theory of belief-type probability includes more than just personal degrees of belief. Logical probability (i.e., statements about the probability of events conditional on evidence or logical relations) is another form of belief-type probability. An example of a logical probability statement would be the following (taken from Hacking 2001, p. 142): "Relative to recent evidence about a layer of iridium deposits . . . the probability is 90 percent that the reign of the dinosaurs was brought to an end when a giant asteroid hit the Earth."

---

[40]This example is modified from the nice explanation in Aczel (2004, pp. 21–24).

This is a statement about the probability of some event conditional on evidence. It is intended to express a logical relationship between some hypothesis (here the extinction of dinosaurs) and relevant evidence (here the presence of iridium in asteroids and the distribution of iridium in geological deposits around the globe). In the theory of logical probability, any probability statement is always relative to evidence.

The good news in all this is that the laws of probability that we apply to frequency-type (objective) probability carry over to these belief-type (subjective) probability situations. Laws concerning independence of events, unions of events, conditional probability, and so on, all apply equally to frequency-type and belief-type probability. In fact, for most practical purposes, in our daily lives and in risk management applications, we do not need to make any definite distinction between the two; we can think of probability and leave it at that.

The History of Theories of Probability

The history of the philosophical debate on the foundations of probability is long. The distinction between objective and subjective probability is often ascribed to Knight (1921), but LeRoy and Singell (1987) argue that it more properly belongs to Keynes (1921). (LeRoy and Singell argue that Knight is open to various interpretations but that he drew a distinction between insurable risks and uninsurable uncertainty where markets collapse because of moral hazard or adverse selection, rather than between objective risks and subjective uncertainties or the applicability or nonapplicability of the probability calculus. They state that "Keynes [1921] explicitly set out exactly the distinction commonly attributed to Knight" [p. 395].)

Frequency-Type Probability. John Venn (1834–1923), the inventor of Venn diagrams, developed one of the first clear statements of limiting frequency theories about probability. Richard von Mises (1883–1953), an Austrian-born applied mathematician, philosopher, and Harvard professor, systematically developed frequency ideas, and A.N. Kolmogorov (1903–1987) published definitive axioms of probability in 1933 and developed fundamental ideas of computational complexity. Karl Popper (1902–1994), an Austrian-born philosopher and professor at the London School of Economics, developed the propensity approach to frequency-type probability.

Belief-Type Probability. John Maynard Keynes (1883–1946), in *A Treatise on Probability* (1921), provided the first systematic presentation of logical probability. Frank Plumpton Ramsey (1903–1930) and Bruno de Finetti (1906–1985) independently invented the theory of personal probability, but its success is primarily attributed to Leonard J. Savage (1917–1971), who made clear the importance of the concept, as well as the importance of Bayes' rule. De Finetti (and Savage) thought that only personal belief-type probability made sense, whereas Ramsey saw room for a frequency-type concept, especially in quantum mechanics.

There has been, and continues to be, considerable debate over the various theories of probability. To gain an inkling of the potential ferocity of the debate, keep in mind the comment of John Venn, an early developer of the frequency theory, regarding the fact that in the logical theory of probability, a probability is always *relative* to evidence: "The probability of an event is no more relative to something else than the area of a field is relative to something else" (quoted in Hacking 2001, p. 143).

A valuable and straightforward exposition of the foundations of modern probability theory is given by the philosopher Ian Hacking (2001). And Hacking (1990, 2006) provides a nice history of probability.

Bayes' Theorem and Belief-Type Probability. One important divergence between the frequency-type and belief-type probability approaches is in the central role played by the law of large numbers versus Bayes' rule. The law of large numbers tells us about how relative frequencies and other observed characteristics stabilize with repeated trials. It is central to understanding and using frequency-type probability.

Bayes' rule (or theorem), in contrast, is central to belief-type probability—so central, in fact, that belief-type probability or statistics is sometimes termed "Bayesian" probability or statistics. Bayes' rule is very simple in concept; it tells us how to update our probabilities given some new piece of information. Bayes' rule, however, is a rich source of mistaken probabilistic thinking and confusion. The problems that Bayes' rule applies to seem to be some of the most counterintuitive.

A classic example of the application of Bayes' rule is the case of testing for a disease or condition, such as HIV or breast cancer, with a good but not perfect test.[41] Consider breast cancer, which is relatively rare in the general population (say, 5 in 1,000). Thus, the prior probability that a woman has breast cancer, given no symptoms and no family history, is only about 0.5 percent. Now consider the woman undergoing a mammogram, which is roughly 95 percent accurate (in the sense that the test falsely reports a positive result about 5 percent of the time). What is the chance that if a patient has a positive mammogram result, she actually has breast cancer? The temptation is to say 95 percent because the test is 95 percent accurate, but that answer ignores the fact that the prior probability is so low, only 0.5 percent. Bayes' rule tells us how to appropriately combine the prior 0.5 percent probability with the 95 percent accuracy of the test.

---

[41] Discussed in Aczel (2004, ch. 16), Gigerenzer (2002, ch. 4), and Mlodinow (2008, ch. 104). See also Hacking (2001, ch. 7).

Before turning to the formalism of Bayes' rule, let us reason out the answer, using what Gigerenzer (2002) calls "natural frequencies." Consider that out of a pool of 1,000 test-takers, roughly 5 (5 in 1,000) will actually have cancer and roughly 50 will receive false positives (5 percent false-positive rate, 5 in 100, or 50 in 1,000). That is, there will be roughly 55 positive test results, but only 5 will be true positives. This means the probability of truly having cancer given a positive test result is roughly 5 in 55 or 9 percent, not 95 in 100 or 95 percent. This result always surprises me, although when explained in this way, it becomes obvious.[42]

The formalism of Bayes' rule shows how the conditional probability of one event (in this case, the conditional probability of cancer given a positive test) can be found from its inverse (in this case, the conditional probability of a positive test given no cancer, or the false-positive rate).

Say we have two hypotheses—*HY*: cancer yes and *HN*: cancer no. We have a prior (unconditional) probability of each hypothesis:

$$P(HY) = 0.005$$

and

$$P(HN) = 0.995.$$

We also have a new piece of evidence or information—*EY*: evidence or test result yes (positive) or *EN*: evidence or test result no (negative). The test is not perfect, so there is a 95 percent chance the test will be negative with no cancer and a 5 percent chance it will be positive with no cancer:

$$P(EY \mid HN) = 0.05$$

and

$$P(EN \mid HN) = 0.95.$$

---

[42]Gigerenzer (2002) stresses the usefulness of formulating applications of Bayes' rule and conditional probability problems in such a manner. He argues that just as our color constancy system can be fooled by artificial lighting (so that his yellow-green Renault appears blue under artificial sodium lights), our probabilistic intuition can be fooled when presented with problems in a form that our intuition has not been adapted or trained to handle. Gigerenzer's solution is to reformulate problems in "natural frequencies" rather than bemoan the inadequacy of human intuition. This is an example of how proper presentation and communication of a risk problem can clarify rather than obfuscate the issues.

For simplicity, let us assume that the test is perfect if there is cancer (there are no false negatives):

$$P(EY \mid HY) = 1.00$$

and

$$P(EN \mid HY) = 0.00.$$

Now, what is the probability that there is actually cancer given a positive test (hypothesis yes given evidence yes)—that is, what is

$$P(HY \mid EY)?$$

Bayes' rule says that

$$P(HY \mid EY) = \frac{P(EY \mid HY) \times P(HY)}{P(EY \mid HY) \times P(HY) + P(EY \mid HN) \times P(HN)}. \tag{2.1}$$

This can be easily derived from the rules of conditional probability (see Hacking 2001, ch. 7), but we will simply take it as a rule for incorporating new evidence (the fact of a positive test result) to update our prior probabilities for the hypothesis of having cancer—that is, a rule on how to use EY to go from $P(HY)$ to $P(HY|EY)$. Plugging in the probabilities just given, we get

$$P(HY \mid EY) = \frac{1.00 \times 0.005}{1.00 \times 0.005 + 0.05 \times 0.995}$$
$$= 0.0913$$
$$= 9.13\%.$$

Bayes' rule has application throughout our everyday lives as well as in risk management. The breast cancer example shows how important it is to use the updated probability—$P(HY|EY)$ = 9 percent—rather than what our intuition initially gravitates toward—the test accuracy, $1 - P(EY|HN)$ = 95 percent. Failure to apply Bayes' rule is common and leads to harrowing encounters with doctors and severe miscarriages of justice. Mlodinow (2008) relates his personal experience of being told he was infected with HIV with 999 in 1,000 or 99.9 percent certainty; in reality, an appropriate application of Bayes' theorem to his positive test results in a probability of about 1 in 11 or 9.1 percent. (He did not have HIV.)[43] In legal circles, the mistake of using $1 - P(EY|HN)$ when $P(HY|EY)$ should be used is called the "prosecutor's fallacy." Mlodinow (2008) discusses the cases of Sally Clark and O.J. Simpson. Gigerenzer has carried out research in this arena, and Gigerenzer (2002) devotes considerable attention to the issue: chapter 8 to the O.J. Simpson trial and chapter 9 to a celebrated California case, *People v. Collins*, among others.

Bayes' rule is central to belief-type probability because it tells us how to consistently use new evidence to update our prior probabilities. Sometimes Bayesian probability theory is misunderstood, or caricatured, as a vacuous approach that can be used to arrive at whatever result the speaker desires. If the prior probability is silly (say, a prior probability of 1.0 that the equity risk premium is negative), then the resulting posterior will also be silly. Bayes' rule provides a standard set of procedures and formulas for using new evidence in a logical and consistent manner and as such is incredibly useful and powerful. Bayes' rule, however, does not excuse us from the hard task of thinking carefully and deeply about the original (prior) probabilities.

Thomas Bayes (1702–1761)

Thomas Bayes was a Presbyterian minister at Mount Sion, Tunbridge Wells, England. Bayes' considerable contribution to the theory of probability rests entirely on a single paper, which he never published. Bayes left the paper to fellow minister Richard Price (a mathematician in his own right and credited with founding the field of actuarial science), who presented it to the Royal Society on 23 December 1763. The paper apparently aroused little interest at the time, and full appreciation was left to Pierre-Simon Laplace (1749–1827). Yet, it has had a fundamental, lasting, and continuing influence on the development of probability and statistics, although it has often been considered controversial. "It is hard to think of a single paper that contains such important, original ideas as does Bayes'. His theorem must stand with Einstein's $E = mc^2$ as one of the great, simple truths" (D.V. Lindley 1987. In Eatwell, Milgate, and Newman 1987, *The New Palgrave*, vol. 1, p. 208).

---

[43]To apply Bayes' rule using Gigerenzer's idea of natural frequencies, we need to know that the prior probability of someone like Mlodinow having HIV is about 1 in 10,000 and that the test's false-positive rate is about 1 in 1,000 (or, its accuracy is 99.9 percent). So for a population of 10,000 test-takers, there would be 1 true positive and roughly 10 false positives, for a total of 11 positive tests. In other words, the probability of having HIV given a positive test would be about 1 in 11 or 9.1 percent. Using the formalism of Bayes' rule, we have $P(HY) = 0.0001$, $P(EY|HN) = 0.001$, and let us assume $P(EY|HY) = 1.00$. Then, $P(HY|EY) = (1.00 \times 0.0001)/(1.00 \times 0.0001 + 0.001 \times 0.9999) = 0.091 = 9.1$ percent. For the record, Mlodinow's test was a false positive and he was not infected. Also, note that the application of Bayes' rule is very dependent on the assumption that Mlodinow is at low risk of HIV infection. For an individual at high risk (say, with a prior probability of 1 percent rather than 0.01 percent), we would get: $P(HY|EY) = (1.00 \times 0.01)/(1.00 \times 0.01 + 0.001 \times 0.99) = 0.910 = 91$ percent. Bayes' rule tells us how to update the prior probabilities in the presence of new evidence; it does not tell us what the prior probabilities are.

Using Frequency-Type and Belief-Type Probabilities. I have spent time explaining the distinction between frequency-type and belief-type probability for one important reason. Financial risk often combines both frequency-type and belief-type probabilities. For one thing, in the real world the future will never be the same as the past; it may be different not just in the particulars but in the distribution of outcomes itself. There will always be totally new and unexpected events; a new product may be introduced, new competitors may enter our business, new regulations may change the landscape.

There is another important reason why we need to consider both frequency-type and belief-type probabilities: Single events always involve belief-type probability. What is the chance that losses *tomorrow* will be less than $50,000? That is a question about a *single event* and as such is a question about belief-type and not frequency-type probability. Probability statements about single events are, inherently, belief type. We may base the belief-type probability on frequency-type probability.

Hacking (2001, p. 137) discusses the *frequency principle*, a rule of thumb that governs when and how we switch between frequency-type and belief-type probability. He discusses the following example: A fair coin is tossed, but before we can see the result, the coin is covered. What is the probability that *this particular coin toss* is heads? This is a single event. We cannot repeat this particular experiment. And yet, it is clear that we should, rationally and objectively, say that the probability is one-half. We know the frequency-type probability for a fair coin turning up heads is one-half, and because we know nothing else about this single trial, we should use this frequency-type probability. The frequency principle is just this: When we know the frequency-type probability and nothing else about the outcome of a single trial, we should use the frequency-type probability.

Something like the frequency principle holds generally. The world is not a repeated game of chance to which fixed rules apply, and so we must always apply some component of subjective or belief-type probability to our management of risk. Aczel (2004) summarizes the situation nicely (emphasis in the original):

> *When an objective* [frequency-type] *probability can be determined, it should be used.* (No one would want to use a subjective probability to guess what side a die will land on, for example.) *In other situations, we do our best to assess our subjective* [belief-type] *probability of the outcome of an event.* (p. 24)

Bayes' Theorem, Streaks, and Fund Performance

We can use Bayes' theorem to help improve our understanding of fund performance and streaks, such as the streak experienced by the Legg Mason Value Trust Fund discussed earlier. Remember that through 2005, the Value Trust Fund had outperformed the S&P 500 for 15 years straight. And remember that for a single fund having no exceptional skill (i.e., with a 50/50 chance of beating the index in any year), the probability of such a streak is very small: $(1/2)^{15}$ or 0.000031 or 0.0031 percent. For a collection of 1,000 funds, however, the probability that 1 or more funds would have such a streak is 3 percent. The probability of having 1 or more such funds during a 40-year period out of a pool of 1,000 is about 32.8 percent.

Now let us turn the question around and consider what such a streak, when it occurs, tells us about funds in general and the Value Trust Fund in particular. Roughly speaking, our earlier application was probabilistic, using probability theory to say something about what we should observe. Our current application is more statistical, using data to make inferences about our underlying model.

Let us start with a simplistic hypothesis or model of the world, a model in which some managers have exceptional skill. Specifically, let us take the hypothesis HY to be that out of every 20 funds, 1 fund beats the index 60 percent of the time. In other words, there is a small proportion (5 percent) of "60 percent skilled" funds with the other 19 out of 20 (95 percent of funds) being "49.47 percent skilled." On average, funds have a 50 percent chance of beating the index. Of course, there is no certainty in the world, and it would be foolish to assume that exceptional skill exists with probability 1.00—that is, to assume $P(HY) = 1.00$. We must consider the alternative hypothesis, HN, that there is no special skill and each and every fund has a 50/50 chance of beating the market in any one year.

In this case, the evidence is observing a streak for some fund among all funds (say, for argument, the pool is 1,000 funds), with EY the evidence of *yes* observing a 15-year streak in 40 years and EN the evidence of *not* observing a 15-year streak. Now we can ask, what does this evidence, observing a streak, tell us about the probability of HY (the world has exceptional managers) versus HN (no managers have exceptional skill)?

We start by calculating the probability of observing a streak in a world with exceptional skill versus no exceptional skill:[i]

---

[i]By simulation, the probability that a single 60 percent skilled fund has a 15-year streak in 40 years is 0.005143, versus 0.000348 for a 49.47 percent skilled fund. Thus, P(15-yr run in 40 yrs$|HY$) = 0.05 × P(15-yr run$|$0.6 manager] + 0.95 × P(15-yr run$|$0.4947 manager) = 0.05 × 0.005143 + 0.95 × 0.000348 = 0.000588.

$$P(EY|HY) = P\left(\begin{array}{l}\text{Yes streak for some fund} \mid 5\% \text{ of funds are } 60\% \text{ skilled,}\\ 95\% \text{ are } 49.47\% \text{ skilled}\end{array}\right)$$

$$= 1 - (1 - 0.000588)^{1,000}$$

$$= 0.4447$$

$$\Rightarrow P(EN|HY) = 1 - 0.4447$$

$$= 0.5553.$$

$$P(EY|HN) = P(\text{Yes streak for some fund} \mid \text{All funds } 50\% \text{ skilled})$$

$$= 1 - (1 - 0.000397)^{1,000}$$

$$= 0.3277$$

$$\Rightarrow P(EN|HN) = 1 - 0.3277$$

$$= 0.6723.$$

Now we can ask, what is $P(HY|EY)$? That is, what is the probability of the world having skilled managers, given that we observe at least one fund with a streak of 15 years? Bayes' rule (Equation 2.1) says that

$$P(HY|EY) = \frac{P(EY|HY) \times P(HY)}{P(EY|HY) \times P(HY) + P(EY|HN) \times P(HN)}$$

$$= \frac{0.4447 \times P(HY)}{0.4447 \times P(HY) + 0.3277 \times P(HN)}.$$

There are two important lessons to take from this equation. First, Bayes' rule itself tells us nothing about what the prior probabilities should be (although Bayes' original paper tried to address this issue). We may start being highly confident that exceptional skill exists [say $P(HY) = 0.90$] or very skeptical [$P(HY) = 0.10$]. We are taking the probability $P(HY)$ as pure belief-type probability: We must use experience or judgment to arrive at it, but it is not based on hard, frequency-type evidence. The second lesson is that Bayes' rule tells us how to apply evidence to our belief-type probabilities to consistently update those probabilities in concert with evidence. In fact, when we apply enough and strong-enough evidence, we will find that divergent prior belief-type probabilities [$P(HY)$ and $P(HN)$] will converge to the same posterior probabilities [$P(HY|EY)$ and $P(HN|EY)$].

We can examine exactly how much the probabilities will change with the evidence of a streak. Let us say that I am skeptical that the world has managers with superior skill; my prior belief-type probability for HY, the hypothesis that there are funds with superior skill (60 percent skilled funds), is

$$P\left(\begin{array}{l}HY = 5\% \text{ of managers have superior skill and can}\\ \text{beat the index better than } 50/50\end{array}\right) = 0.10.$$

Then, applying Bayes' rule (Equation 2.1) gives

$$P(HY|EY) = P\left(\begin{array}{c}\text{5\% of managers have skill given there}\\\text{is at least one 15-year streak}\end{array}\right) = 0.13.$$

In other words, the evidence of a streak alters my initial (low) probability but not by very much.

Now consider the other extreme, where I strongly believe there are managers with superior skill so that my prior is $P(HY) = 0.90$. Then applying Bayes' rule gives $P(HY|EY) = 0.92$, and again my initial assessment is not altered very much. In sum, the evidence of a 15-year streak is not strong evidence in favor of superior manager skill. The streak does not prove (but neither does it disprove) the hypothesis that superior skill exists.

Let us now ask a subtly different question: Say we knew or were convinced for some reason that the world contained some managers with superior skill (we take as a given the hypothesis that 5 percent of the managers are 60 percent skilled funds). Now, what does a 15-year streak *for a particular fund* tell us about that fund? How does that change our assessment of whether that fund is a 60 percent skilled fund versus a 49.47 percent skilled fund?

In this case, the hypothesis HY is that a *particular* fund is 60 percent skilled and the evidence is a 15-year streak out of 40 years:

$$P(EY|HY) = P(\text{Yes streak for one fund}|\text{This fund is 60\% skilled}) = 0.005143$$
$$\Rightarrow (EN|HY) = 1 - 0.005143$$
$$= 0.99486.$$

$$P(EY|HN) = P(\text{Yes streak for one fund}|\text{This fund is 49.47\% skilled}) = 0.00035$$
$$\Rightarrow (EN|HY) = 1 - 0.00035$$
$$= 0.99965.$$

Now we can ask, what is $P(HY|EY)$? That is, what is the probability that this manager is 60 percent skilled given that this fund has a streak of at least 15 years? Bayes' rule says that

$$P(HY|EY) = \frac{P(EY|HY) \times P(HY)}{P(EY|HY) \times P(HY) + P(EY|HN) \times P(HN)}$$
$$= \frac{0.005143 \times 0.05}{0.005143 \times 0.05 + 0.00035 \times 0.95}$$
$$= 0.436.$$

In other words, the evidence that this fund has a 15-year streak changes our probability that this *particular* fund is a skilled fund from $P(HY) = 0.05$ to $P(HY|EY)$ = 0.436. (This result is conditional on the world containing a 5 percent smattering of skilled funds among the large pool of all funds.) We could view this either as a big change (from 5 percent probability to 43.6 percent probability) or as further indication that a 15-year streak is weak evidence of skill because we still have less than a 50/50 chance that this particular manager is skilled.

The Legg Mason Value Trust Fund outperformed for the 15 years up to 2005, but performance during the following years definitively broke the streak; the fund underperformed the S&P 500 for 3 out of the 4 years subsequent to 2005.[ii] We can use Bayes' theorem to examine how much this evidence would change our probability that the fund is 60 percent skilled. The hypothesis *HY* is still that the fund is 60 percent skilled, but now $P(HY) = 0.436$ and

$$P(EY|HY) = P\left(\begin{array}{l}\text{Fund underperforms 3 out of 4 years} \\ |\text{This fund is 60\% skilled}\end{array}\right)$$

$$= P\left(\begin{array}{l}\text{Binomial variable fails 3 out of 4 trials} \\ |\text{Prob of success} = 0.6\end{array}\right)$$

$$= 0.1536$$

$$P(EY|HN) = P\left(\begin{array}{l}\text{Fund underperforms 3 out of 4 years} \\ |\text{This fund is 49.47\% skilled}\end{array}\right)$$

$$= P\left(\begin{array}{l}\text{Binomial variable fails 3 out of 4 trials} \\ |\text{Prob of success} = 0.4974\end{array}\right)$$

$$= 0.2553.$$

Bayes' theorem gives

$$P(HY|EY) = \frac{P(EY|HY) \times P(HY)}{P(EY|HY) \times P(HY) + P(EY|HN) \times P(HN)}$$

$$= \frac{0.1536 \times 0.436}{0.1536 \times 0.436 + 0.2553 \times 0.564}$$

$$= 0.317.$$

This evidence drops the probability that the Value Trust Fund is skilled, but not as much as I would have thought.

[ii] As noted in an earlier footnote, for the four years 2006–2009, the Value Trust underperformed the S&P 500 for 2006, 2007, and 2008.

In conclusion, this example shows how we can use probability theory and Bayes' theorem to organize our belief-type probabilities and combine them with evidence and experience. It also shows how important it is to systematize and organize our probabilitistic thinking. A 15-year streak sounds quite impressive, but upon closer examination, we see that it is not as unusual as we might have thought.[iii]

[iii]I am not arguing here against the existence of special skill as much as I am arguing in favor of a critical approach to the data. Focusing only on Legg Mason Value Trust ignores the fact that there were many other winning funds with track records that were not quite as good. Their existence would (I think, greatly) raise the likelihood that funds with superior skill, not pure luck, exist. This assertion does not change the general observation, however, that "beating the market" is hard.

"Risk" vs. "Uncertainty" or "Ambiguity." The good news is that the rules of probability that apply to frequency-type probability apply equally to belief-type probability. We can use the two interchangeably in calculations and for many purposes can ignore any distinction between them.

Although I argue that we can often ignore any distinction between frequency-type (objective) and belief-type (subjective) probability, many writers argue otherwise. This distinction is usually phrased by contrasting "risk" (roughly corresponding to frequency-type probability) to "uncertainty" or "ambiguity" (where numerical probabilities cannot be assigned, usually corresponding to some form of belief-type or subjective probability). One expression of this view is Lowenstein (2000):

> Unlike dice, markets are subject not merely to risk, an arithmetic concept, but also to the broader uncertainty that shadows the future generally. Unfortunately, uncertainty, as opposed to risk, is an indefinite condition, one that does not conform to numerical straitjackets. (p. 235)

Lowenstein is a popular author and not a probabilist or statistician, but the same view is held by many who think carefully and deeply about such issues. For example, Gigerenzer (2002) states it as follows:

> In this book, I call an uncertainty a *risk* when it can be expressed as a number such as a probability or frequency on the basis of empirical data. . . . In situations in which a lack of empirical evidence makes it impossible or undesirable to assign numbers to the possible alternative outcomes, I use the term "uncertainty" instead of "risk." (p. 26)

The distinction between "risk" and "uncertainty" is usually attributed to Knight (1921) and often called "Knightian uncertainty." It is often argued that "uncertainty" or "ambiguity" is inherently distinct from "risk" in the sense that people behave differently in the face of "ambiguity" than they do when confronted with computable or known probabilities ("risk"). It is argued that there is "ambiguity aversion" separate from "risk aversion."

Various paradoxes are said to provide evidence in favor of ambiguity and ambiguity aversion, with probably the best known being the Ellsberg paradox (Ellsberg 1961). I am not convinced by these paradoxes, and I maintain that frequency-type (objective) and belief-type (subjective) probabilities can and should be used interchangeably.

My conclusion that frequency-type and belief-type probabilities can, and indeed should, be used interchangeably is not taken lightly, but on balance, I think we have no other choice, in risk management and in our daily lives. The future is uncertain, subject to randomness that is not simply replication of a repeated game. But we have to make decisions, and probability theory is such a useful set of tools that we have to use it. The utility of treating frequency-type and belief-type probabilities as often interchangeable outweighs any problems involved in doing so.

When using belief-type probabilities, however, we must be especially careful. We cannot rely on them in the same way as we can rely on frequency-type probabilities in a game of chance. We must be honest with ourselves that we do not, indeed cannot, always know the probabilities. The de Finetti game and Bayes' rule help keep us honest, in the sense of being both realistic in uncovering our prior (belief-type) probabilities and consistent in updating probabilities in the face of new evidence. The formalism imposed by careful thinking about belief-type probability may appear awkward to begin with, but careful thinking about probability pays immense rewards.

Ellsberg Paradox

Daniel Ellsberg (b. 1931) has the distinction of being far better known for political activities than for his contribution to probability and decision theory. Ellsberg obtained his PhD in economics from Harvard in 1962. In 1961, he published a discussion of a paradox that challenges the foundations of belief-type probability and expected utility theory. In the late 1960s, Ellsberg worked at the RAND Corporation, contributing to a top secret study of documents regarding affairs associated with the Vietnam War. These documents later came to be known as the Pentagon Papers. Ellsberg photocopied them, and in 1971, they were leaked and first published by the *New York Times*. At least partially in response to the leaked papers, the Nixon administration created the "White House Plumbers," whose apparent first project was breaking into Ellsberg's psychiatrist's office to try to obtain incriminating information on Ellsberg. The plumbers' best-known project, however, was the Watergate burglaries.

Ellsberg's 1961 paper discusses a series of thought experiments in which you are asked to bet on draws from various urns. (Although popularized by Ellsberg and commonly known by his name, a version of this paradox was apparently noted by Keynes 1921, paragraph 315, footnote 2.)

The experiment I discuss here concerns two urns, each having 100 balls. For Urn 1, you are told (and allowed to verify if you wish) that there are 100 balls, 50 of which are red and 50 black. For Urn 2, in contrast, you are told only that there are 100 balls, with some mix of red and black (and only red or black); you are not told the exact proportions. For the first part of the experiment, you will draw a single ball from Urn 1 and a single ball from Urn 2 and be paid $10 depending on the selection of red versus black. Before you draw, you must decide which payoff you prefer:

RED = $10 if Red, $0 if Black

BLACK = $0 if Red, $10 if Black

When asked to choose between the two payoffs, most people will be indifferent between red versus black for both the first and the second urn. For Urn 1, we have evidence on the 50/50 split, so we can assign a frequency-type probability of 50 percent to both red and black. For Urn 2, we do not have any frequency-type information, but we also do not have any information that red or black is more likely, and most people seem to set their subjective or belief-type probability at 50/50 (red and black equally likely).

In the second part of the experiment, you will draw a single ball and get paid $10 if red, but you get to choose whether the draw is from Urn 1 or Urn 2. It seems that most people have a preference for Urn 1, the urn with the known 50/50 split. (Remember that this is a thought experiment, so when I say "most people" I mean Ellsberg and colleagues he spoke with, and also myself and colleagues I have spoken with. Nonetheless, the conclusion seems pretty firm. And because this is a thought experiment, you can try this on yourself and friends and colleagues.) The preference for red from Urn 1 seems to establish that people assess red from Urn 1 as more likely than red from Urn 2.

Now we get to the crux of the paradox: The preference for Urn 1 is the same if the payoff is $10 on black, which seems to establish black from Urn 1 as more likely than black from Urn 2. In other words, we seem to have the following:

Red 1 preferred to Red 2 ⇒ Red 1 more likely than Red 2.

Black 1 preferred to Black 2 ⇒ Black 1 more likely than Black 2.

But this is an inconsistency. Red 2 and Black 2 cannot both be less likely because that would imply that the total probability for Urn 2 is less than 1.00. (Try it. For any probabilities for Red 1 and Black 1, the relations just given imply that the total probability for Urn 2 is less than 1.00.)

Ellsberg claimed that this inconsistency argues for "uncertainties that are not risk" and "ambiguity" and that belief-type or subjective probabilities (as for Urn 2) are different in a fundamental way from frequency-type probabilities. Subsequent authors have worked to develop theories of probability and expected utility to explain this "paradox" (see Epstein 1999; Schmeidler 1989).

There are a few obvious critiques of the paradox. Maybe we simply prefer the easier-to-understand Urn 1, not wanting to waste brain cells on thinking through all implications of the problem. Maybe we are "deceit averse," wanting to shy away from Urn 2 in case the experimenter somehow manipulates the red and black balls to our disadvantage. But I think the paradox goes deeper. When I think long and hard about the problem (I make sure I fully explain the problem to myself and reliably assure myself that I, as the experimenter, will not cheat), I still prefer the 50/50 Urn 1.

The resolution of the paradox lies in viewing the Ellsberg experiment in the context of a larger "meta-experiment":

- X percent probability of single draw (original Ellsberg experiment);
- $1 - X$ percent probability of repeated draws.

Real differences exist between Urn 1 and Urn 2, and Urn 1 is less risky (thus, preferable) in all cases *except* the Ellsberg single-draw experiment. It does not take much thinking to realize that repeated draws from Urn 2, where we do not know how many red or black, is more risky than repeated draws from Urn 1, where we know there are precisely 50 red and 50 black. With Urn 2, I might choose the red payoff but have the bad luck that there are no red and all black. For repeated draws, I am stuck with my initial choice. For a single draw it does not really matter—because I do not have any prior knowledge, and because I get to choose red or black up front, the urn really does behave like a 50/50 split. (Coleman 2011 discusses the problem in more detail and shows how a mixed distribution for Urn 2 will be more risky for repeated draws than the simple 50/50 distribution of Urn 1.)

So, we have a situation where for a single draw, Urn 1 and Urn 2 are probabilistically equivalent but for repeated or multiple draws, Urn 1 is preferable. For the meta-experiment, it is only in the special case where $X = 100$ percent that the two urns are equivalent; whenever $X < 100$ percent, Urn 1 is preferable. Even a small probability that there will be repeated draws leads to Urn 1 being preferred. So, what would be the rational response: Choose Urn 2, which is equivalent to 1 in the single-draw case but worse in any repeated-draw experiment, or for no extra cost, choose Urn 1? The choice is obvious: As long as there is some nonzero chance that the experiment could involve repeated draws (and psychologically it is hard to ignore such a possibility), we should choose Urn 1.

Stated this way, there is no paradox. From this perspective, preference for Urn 1 is rational and fully consistent with expected utility theory. In summary, I do not find the Ellsberg paradox to be evidence in favor of ambiguity or uncertainty. I do not see the need for "ambiguity aversion" as a supplement to the standard "risk aversion" of expected utility theory. Similarly, I do not believe that we need to amend the concept of subjective or belief-type probability.

The Curse of Overconfidence

Much of this chapter has been concerned with how our human intuition can be fooled by randomness and uncertainty. We have seen that it is easy to generate (random) runs and streaks that seem, intuitively, very nonrandom. Humans, however, crave control over their environment, and we will often impose an illusion of certainty and control over purely random events. It is all too easy, all too tempting, to mistake luck for skill, and the result can be overconfidence in our own abilities. There is a fundamental tension here because confidence in one's abilities is as necessary for successful performance in the financial arena as it is in any area of life, but overconfidence can also breed hubris, complacency, and an inability to recognize and adapt to new circumstances.

Gladwell (2009) is an interesting essay discussing the importance of psychology, in particular confidence and overconfidence, in the finance industry and in running an investment bank. He focuses specifically on Jimmy Cayne and the fall of Bear Stearns in 2008 (with interesting digressions to the debacle of Gallipoli). With hindsight, Cayne's words and actions can seem to be the purest hubris. But Gladwell argues, convincingly, that such confidence is a necessary component of running an investment bank. If those running the bank did not have such optimism and confidence, why would any customers or competitors have confidence in the bank? And yet such confidence can be maladaptive.

Both Gladwell and Mlodinow (2008) discuss the work of the psychologist Ellen Langer and our desire to control events. Langer showed that our need to feel in control clouds our perception of random events. In one experiment (Langer 1975), subjects bet against a rival. The rival was arranged to be either "dapper" or a "schnook." Against the schnook, subjects bet more aggressively, even though the game was pure chance and no other conditions were altered. Subjects presumably felt more in control and more confident betting against a nervous, awkward rival than against a confident one, although the probabilities were the same in both cases.

In another experiment (Langer and Roth 1975), Yale undergraduates were asked to predict the results of 30 random coin tosses. When queried afterwards, the students behaved as if predicting a random coin toss was a skill that could be improved with practice. Subjects for whom tosses were manipulated to exhibit early streaks (but also so that overall they guessed correctly half the time) rated themselves better at the guessing than other subjects, even though all subjects were correct half the time.

The problem of overconfidence may be the most fundamental and difficult in all of risk management because confidence is necessary for success but overconfidence can lead to disaster. This situation is made even worse by the natural human tendency to forget past bad events. Maybe that is just part of the human psyche; it would be hard to survive if past losses remained forever painful.

I know of no foolproof way to avoid overconfidence. Possibly the most insightful part of Gladwell (2009) is in the closing paragraphs, where he contrasts the bridge-playing expertise of Cayne and others at Bear Stearns with the "open world where one day a calamity can happen that no one had dreamed could happen" (p. 7). This discussion harks back to the distinction between frequency-type versus belief-type probability. Bridge is a game of chance, a repeated game with fixed and unchanging rules to which we can apply the law of large numbers. We may momentarily become overconfident as bridge players, but the repeated game will come back to remind us of the underlying probabilities. The real world, in contrast, is not a repeated game, and the truly unexpected sometimes happens. And most importantly, because the unexpected does not happen frequently, we may become overconfident for long periods before nature comes back to remind us that it does.

Luck

Luck is the irreducible chanciness of life. Luck cannot be "controlled," but it can be managed.

What do I mean by "luck" versus "risk"? Risk is the interaction of the uncertainty of future outcomes with the benefits and costs of those outcomes. Risk can be studied and modified. Luck is the irreducible chanciness of life—chanciness that remains even after learning all one can about possible future outcomes, understanding how current conditions and exposures are likely to alter future outcomes, and adjusting current conditions and behavior to optimally control costs and benefits. Some things are determined by luck, and it is a fool's errand to try to totally control luck.

The philosopher Rescher (2001) states it well:

> The rational domestication of luck is a desideratum that we can achieve to only a very limited extent. In this respect, the seventeenth-century philosophers of chance were distinctly overoptimistic. For while probability theory is a good guide in matters of gambling, with its predesignated formal structures, it is of limited usefulness as a guide among the greater fluidities of life. The analogy of life with games of chance has its limits, since we do not and cannot effectively play life by fixed rules, a fact that sharply restricts the extent to which we can render luck amenable to rational principles of measurement and calculation. (pp. 138–139)

Rescher's point is that luck is to be managed, not controlled. The question is not whether to take risks—that is inevitable and part of the human condition—but rather to appropriately manage luck and keep the odds on one's side.

The thrust of this chapter has been twofold: Randomness and luck are part of the world, and randomness is often hard to recognize and understand. The success or failure of portfolio managers, trading strategies, and firms is dependent on randomness and luck, and we need to recognize, live with, and manage that randomness and luck.

In the next chapter, I change gears, moving away from the theory of probability and focusing on the business side of managing risk. The insights and approach to uncertainty discussed in this chapter must be internalized to appropriately manage risk on a day-to-day basis.

3. Managing Risk

What Is Risk Management?

In the previous chapter, I discussed uncertainty, risk, and the theory of probability. Now, I change gears and move from hard science to soft business management because when all is said and done, risk management is about managing risk—about managing people, processes, data, and projects. It is not just elegant quantitative techniques; it is the everyday work of actually managing an organization and the risks it faces. Managing risk requires making the tactical and strategic decisions to control those risks that should be controlled and to exploit those opportunities that should be exploited. Managing profits cannot be separated from managing losses or the prospect of losses. Modern portfolio theory tells us that investment decisions are the result of trading off return versus risk; managing risk is just part of managing returns and profits.

Managing risk must be a core competence for any financial firm. The ability to effectively manage risk is the single most important characteristic separating financial firms that are successful and survive over the long run from firms that are not successful. At successful firms, managing risk always has been and continues to be the responsibility of line managers from the board through the CEO and down to individual trading units or portfolio managers. Managers have always known that this is their role, and good managers take their responsibilities seriously. The only thing that has changed in the past 10 or 20 years is the development of more sophisticated analytical tools to measure and quantify risk. One result has been that the technical skills and knowledge required of line managers have gone up. Good managers have embraced these techniques and exploited them to both manage risk more effectively and make the most of new opportunities. Not all firms and managers, however, have undertaken the human capital and institutional investments necessary to translate the new quantitative tools into effective management.

The value of quantitative tools, however, should not be overemphasized. If there is one paramount criticism of the new "risk management" paradigm, it is that the industry has focused too much on measurement, neglecting the old-fashioned business of *managing* the risk. Managing risk requires experience and intuition in addition to quantitative measures. The quantitative tools are invaluable aids that help to formalize and standardize a process that otherwise would be driven by hunches and rules of thumb, but they are no substitute for informed judgment. Risk management is as much about apprenticeship and learning by doing as it is about book learning. Risk management is as much about managing people, processes, and projects as it is about quantitative techniques.

Manage People

Managing people means thinking carefully about incentives and compensation. Although I do not pretend to have the answers for personnel or incentive structures, I do want to emphasize the importance of compensation and incentive schemes for managing risk and building a robust organization that can withstand the inevitable buffeting by the winds of fortune. Managing risk is always difficult for financial products and financial firms, but the principal–agent issues introduced by the separation of ownership and management substantially complicate the problems for most organizations.

As discussed in Chapter 2, risk involves both the uncertainty of outcomes and the utility of outcomes. The distribution of outcomes is "objective" in the sense that it can, conceptually at least, be observed and agreed upon by everyone. The utility of outcomes, in contrast, depends on individual preferences and is in essence subjective. The preferences that matter are the preferences of the ultimate owner or beneficiary. Consider an individual investor making his or her own risk decisions. The problem, although difficult, is conceptually straightforward because the individual is making his own decisions about his own preferences. Although preferences might be difficult to uncover, in this case at least it is only the preferences of the owner (who is also the manager of the risk) that matter.

Now consider instead a publicly traded firm—say, a bank or investment firm. The ultimate beneficiaries are now the shareholders. As a rule, the shareholders do not manage the firm, instead hiring professional managers and delegating the authority and responsibility for managing the risks. The preferences of the shareholders are still the relevant preferences for making decisions about risk, but now it is the managers who make most decisions. The shareholders must ensure that the decisions reflect their preferences, but two difficulties arise here. The first is that the managers may not know the owners' preferences, which is a real and potentially challenging problem but not the crux of the problem. Even if the owners' preferences are known, the second difficulty will intrude: The preferences of the managers will not be the same as those of the shareholders, and the interests of the managers and owners will not be aligned. The owners must design a contract or compensation scheme that rewards managers for acting in accordance with owners' preferences and punishes them for acting contrary to those preferences.

This issue goes by the name of the principal–agent problem in the economics literature.[44] The essence of the problem is in addressing the difficulties that arise when a principal hires an agent to perform some actions, the interests (preferences) of the two are not the same, and there is incomplete and asymmetric information so that the principal cannot perfectly monitor the agent's behavior. Employer–employee relations are a prime arena for principal–agent issues, and employment contracts are prime examples of contracts that must address principal–agent problems.

In virtually any employer–employee relationship, there will be some divergence of interests. The principal's interest will be to have some tasks or actions performed so as to maximize the principal's profit or some other objective relevant to the principal. Generally, the agent will have other interests. The agent will have to expend effort and act diligently, which is costly to the agent, to perform the actions. In a world of perfect information, no uncertainty, and costless monitoring, the principal–agent problem can be remedied. A contract can be written, for example, that specifies the required level of effort or diligence—rewarding the agent depending on the effort expended or on the observed outcome of the action. In such a world, the interests of the principal and agent can be perfectly aligned.

When there is uncertainty, asymmetric information, and costly monitoring, however, the principal–agent problem comes to the fore and designing a contract to align the interests of principal and agent can be very difficult. A compensation scheme generally cannot be based on the agent's effort because this effort can be observed only by the agent (asymmetric information) or is costly to monitor (costly monitoring). There will be difficulties in basing the compensation scheme on observed outcomes. First, it might be difficult or impossible to effectively measure the outcomes (costly monitoring and asymmetric information). Second, because of uncertainty, the outcome might not reflect the agent's effort; rewarding output may reward lazy but lucky agents while punishing diligent but unlucky agents to such a degree that it provides no incentive for agents to work hard. Furthermore, rewarding individuals based on individual measures of output may destroy incentives for joint effort and lead to free-riding problems.

Risk management usually focuses on the problem of measuring risk and the decisions that flow from that problem—combining the uncertainty of outcomes and the utility of outcomes to arrive at the decisions on how to manage

---

[44]See Stiglitz in Eatwell, Milgate, and Newman (1987, *The New Palgrave*, vol. 3, pp. 966–971 and references therein, including contributions by Ross 1973; Mirrlees 1974, 1976; and Stiglitz 1974, 1975). The problem is, of course, much older, with an entry in the original *Palgrave's Dictionary of Economics* (1894–1899) by J.E.C. Munro.

risk. In the real world, an additional layer of complexity exists—making sure that managers (agents) actually implement the appropriate measures, either by ensuring that they have the correct incentives or through constant monitoring and control.

Many types of compensation schemes are used in practice, including fixed versus variable compensation (salaries and bonuses or base and commission), deferred compensation, and granting of share ownership with various types and degrees of vesting. Designing compensation and incentive schemes has to be one of the most difficult and underappreciated, but also one of the most important, aspects of risk management. Substantial effort is devoted to measuring and monitoring risk, but unless those managers who have the information also have the incentives to act in concert with the owners' preferences, such risk measurement is useless.

Incentive and compensation schemes are difficult to design—for good times as well as bad times. During good times, it is easier to keep people happy—there is money and status to distribute—but difficult to design incentives that align the principal's and agent's interests. During bad times, it is harder to make people happy—money and status are often in short supply—and consequently it is difficult to retain good people. It is important to design compensation schemes for both good and bad times and to plan for times when the organization is under stress from both high profits (which breeds hubris and a tendency to ignore risk) and low profits (when everybody leaves).

As mentioned at the beginning of this section, I do not have answers for the puzzles of compensation and incentives. The topic is one, however, that rewards careful thinking. There is clearly no substitute for monitoring and measuring risk, but properly designed incentive schemes can go far toward managing and controlling risks. If the interests of managers throughout the organization can be properly aligned, these managers can move part of the way from being disasters in the waiting that require unrelenting monitoring and control to being allies of the principals in controlling and managing risk.

One final issue that I want to mention is the importance of embedded options and payout asymmetry in both compensation and capital structure. In compensation of traders and portfolio managers there is the well-known "trader's put," where a trader wins if things go well but loses little if things go badly. The trader receives a large bonus in a good year and is let go, with no claw-back of the bonus, in a bad year. Furthermore, traders can often find another trading position with large upside potential.

For hedge funds, the performance fee is often structured as a percentage of returns above a high-water mark (the high-water mark representing the highest net asset value previously achieved by the fund). A straight fee based on percentage of returns may encourage leverage and risk taking—behavior that can be discouraged by adjusting the fee for the risk taken, as discussed in Coleman and Siegel (1999). The high-water mark is designed (and probably originally intended) to make terms more favorable to the investor but, in fact, acts as a put option on returns. The manager receives fees in good times but after a period of losses will not earn performance fees. The payout becomes asymmetric, with performance fees if things go well but no fee penalty if they go badly (and if things go really badly, the manager may be able to close the fund and start again with a new and lower high-water mark). Thus, a high-water mark may hurt rather than help the investor.

The capital structure of publicly traded companies provides the final and possibly the most interesting example of embedded options. A classic article by Merton (1974) shows how shares of a publicly traded company whose capital structure includes both shares and bonds are equivalent to a call on the value of the company (and the risky bond includes a put option). The call option means that shareholders benefit from increased volatility in the value of the company assets (because the value of a call increases as volatility increases), to the detriment of bondholders. This effect becomes particularly important when the firm value is near the par value of the bonds and the company is thus near default. This way of thinking about share value raises the intriguing possibility that shareholders will have an incentive to take on more risk than desired by debtholders and possibly even more than company employees desire, particularly when a company is near default.

In the end, careful thinking about preferences, incentives, compensation, and principal–agent problems enlightens many of the most difficult issues in risk management—issues that I think we as a profession have only begun to address in a substantive manner.

Manage Process

Process and procedure, and the whole arena of operational process and controls, are critically important. These aspects of management are also vastly underappreciated. Many financial disasters—from large and world-renowned ones such as Barings Bank's collapse of 1995 to unpublicized misfortunes on individual trading desks—are the result of simple operational problems or oversights rather than complex risk management failures. To coin a phrase, processes and procedures are not rocket science; nonetheless, losses in this arena hurt as much as any others, possibly more so because they are so easy to prevent and so obvious after the fact. From Lleo (2009):

> Jorion (2007) drew the following key lesson from financial disasters: Although a single source of risk may create large losses, it is not generally enough to result in an actual disaster. For such an event to occur, several types of risks

usually need to interact. Most importantly, the lack of appropriate controls appears to be a determining contributor. Although inadequate controls do not trigger the actual financial loss, they allow the organization to take more risk than necessary and also provide enough time for extreme losses to accumulate. (p. 5)

Manage Technology, Infrastructure, and Data

Risk management and risk measurement projects are as much about boring data and information technology (IT) infrastructure as about fancy quantitative techniques; after all, if you do not know what you own, it is hard to do any sophisticated analysis. In building or implementing a risk management project, often 80 percent of the effort and investment is in data and IT infrastructure and only 20 percent in sophisticated quantitative techniques.

I cannot overemphasize the importance of data and the IT infrastructure required to store and manipulate the data for risk analytics. For market risk (but credit risk in particular), good records of positions and counterparties are critical, and these data must be in a form that can be used. An interest rate swap must be stored and recognized as a swap, not forced into a futures system. The cost and effort required to build, acquire, and maintain the data and IT infrastructure should not be underestimated, but neither should they stand as a significant impediment to implementing a risk management project. Building data and IT infrastructure is, again, not rocket science, and the available IT tools have improved vastly over the years.

Understand the Business

A cardinal rule of managing risk is that managers must understand risk. Managers must understand the risks embedded in the business, and they must understand the financial products that make up the risk. This is a simple and obvious rule but one that is often violated: Do the bank board members and CEO understand interest rate or credit default swaps? And yet these instruments make up a huge portion of the risk of many financial firms. And how often, when a firm runs afoul of some new product, has it turned out that senior managers failed to understand the risks?

Managers, both mid-level and senior, must have a basic understanding of and familiarity with the products that they are responsible for. In many cases, this means improving managers' financial literacy. Many financial products (derivatives in particular) are said to be so complex that they can be understood only by rocket scientists using complex models run on supercomputers. It may be true that the detailed pricing of many derivatives requires such models and computer power, but often the broad behavior of these same products can be surprisingly simple, analyzed using simple models and hand calculators. Many in research and trading benefit from the aura and status acquired as keepers of complex models, but a concerted effort must be made to reduce complex products to simple ideas. I do not wish to imply that "dumbing down" is advisable but rather that improved education for managers is required, together with simple and comprehensible explanations from the experts.

Simple explanations for thinking about and understanding risk are invaluable, even indispensable. In fact, when a simple explanation for the risk of a portfolio does not exist, it can be a sign of trouble—that somewhere along the line, somebody does not understand the product or the risk well enough to explain it simply and clearly. Even worse, it may be a sign that somebody does understand the risks but does not want others to understand.

****

Interest Rate Swaps and Credit Default Swaps: A Long Digression[45]

This book is not a text on financial products or derivatives, but in this long digression I will discuss two simple examples: interest rate swaps and credit default swaps. The goal is twofold. First, I want to show how the fundamental ideas can be easily presented even for products that are usually considered complex. Second, I want to show how these simple explanations have practical application in understanding what happens in financial markets.

Interest rate swaps and LTCM

Interest rate swaps (IRSs) are by now old and well-established financial instruments. Even so, they are often considered complex. In fact, they are very simple. For most purposes, particularly changes in interest rates, an IRS behaves like a bond. Its P&L has the same sensitivity as a bond to changes in interest rates but with no (or, more precisely, much reduced) credit risk.

I will assume that readers have a basic knowledge of how an interest rate swap is structured—that a swap is an agreement between two parties to exchange periodic fixed payments for floating interest rate payments for an agreed period.[46] Say that we are considering a four-year swap, receiving $5 annually and paying the floating rate annually.[47] The cash flows for the swap look like Panel A of **Figure 3.1**. One year from now, we receive $5 and pay the floating rate (which is set in the market today). In two years, we receive $5 and

---

[45] Note that this section is a digression that can be read independently of the rest of the chapter.

[46] See Coleman (1998) for a complete discussion.

[47] Standard swaps in U.S. dollars involve semiannual payments on the fixed side and quarterly on the floating side, but I will use annual payments here just to make the diagrams easier.

pay the appropriate floating rate (the rate that will be set at Year 1). On each payment date, we exchange only the net cash flow, so at Year 1 we would receive $1.50 if today's floating rate were 3.50 percent ($5.00 − $3.50).

Figure 3.1. Swap to Receive $5.00 Annual Fixed (Pay Floating) and Equivalence to Long Fixed Bond, Short Floating Bond

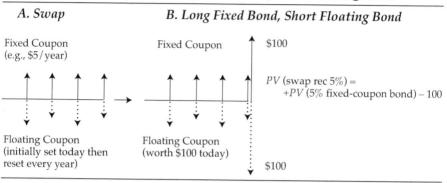

Understanding how to value the swap and what the risk is (that is, how it will move as underlying markets move) is not obvious from Panel A of Figure 3.1. We can use a simple trick, however, to make the valuation and risk clear. Because only net cash flows are exchanged on each payment date, it makes no difference to net overall value if we insert +$100 and −$100 at the end. It does, however, completely alter our view of the swap. Now we can view it as being long a fixed-coupon, four-year 5 percent bond and short a floating-rate bond, as shown in Panel B. Furthermore, a floating-rate bond is always worth $100 today, so we now know that the value of the swap is just the difference between the values of two bonds:

$$PV\left(\text{Swap to receive \$5 for 4 years}\right) = PV\left(\text{4-year 5\% bond}\right) - 100.$$

Not only do we know the value; we also know the interest rate risk: The risk of the swap will be exactly the same as the risk of the fixed-coupon bond (because a floating-coupon bond is always at par and has no interest rate risk).[48]

We thus have a very simple explanation of how any standard IRS will behave—like a bond of the same coupon, maturity, and notional amount. This approach may not be precise enough for trading swaps in today's competitive

---

[48]The exact equivalence between the swap and the net of the fixed coupon bond less the floating bond holds only for the instant before the first floating coupon is set and ignores any differences in day counts or other technical details. Furthermore, there will be some (although small) credit risk embedded in the swap because of counterparty exposure. I will ignore these issues for now because they do not matter for understanding the major component of the risk—the change in value with interest rates.

markets (we are ignoring details about day counts, etc.), but it is more than adequate for understanding the broad outlines of what a swap is and how a swap portfolio works.

We can, in fact, use this straightforward view of swaps to help understand what happened with the fund Long-Term Capital[49] in 1998. LTCM was a large hedge fund that spectacularly collapsed in September 1998 as a result of market disruptions following Russia's de facto debt default in August. At the beginning of 1998, LTCM's capital stood at $4.67 billion, but by the bailout at the end of September, roughly $4.5 billion of that had been lost; LTCM lost virtually all its capital.

The demise of LTCM is a fascinating story and has been extensively discussed, with the account of Lowenstein (2000) being particularly compelling (also see Jorion 2000 for an account). Many reasons can be given for the collapse, and I will not pretend that the complete explanation is simple, but much insight can be gained when one recognizes the size of the exposure to swaps. Lowenstein (2000, p. 187) recounts a visit by Federal Reserve and Treasury officials to LTCM's offices on 20 September, during which officials received a run-through of LTCM's risk reports. One figure that stood out was LTCM's exposure to U.S. dollar-denominated swaps: $240 million per 15 bp move in swap spreads (the presumed one standard deviation move).

As discussed earlier, receiving fixed on a swap is equivalent to being long a fixed-coupon bond, as regards sensitivity to moves in interest rates. The relevant interest rates are swap rates, not U.S. Treasury or corporate bond rates.[50] U.S. swap rates will usually be above U.S. Treasury rates and below low-rated corporate yields, although by exactly how much will vary over time.[51] The swap spread—the spread between swap rates and U.S. Treasury rates—will depend on the relative demand for U.S. Treasuries versus U.S. swaps. During a period of high risk aversion, such as during the 1998 Russia crisis, there will generally be an increase in demand for Treasuries as investors flock to a safe haven. This flight to safety will push the swap spread higher.

---

[49]Commonly referred to by the name of the management company, Long-Term Capital Management (LTCM).

[50]It may sound circular to say U.S. swaps depend on U.S. swap rates, but it is no more so than saying U.S. Treasuries depend on U.S. Treasury rates.

[51]Prior to 2008, I would have said that swap rates are always above Treasury rates, but since November 2008, 30-year swap rates have remained consistently below Treasury rates (with spreads as wide as −40 bps). This is generally thought to be the result of disruption in the repurchase agreement market and low risk appetite among dealers, combined with high demand from corporate customers to receive fixed payments. The combination has put downward pressure on swap rates relative to Treasury rates.

Whatever the determinants of the swap spread, it is common for traders to take positions with respect to the spread. Going short the spread (to benefit when the normally positive spread narrows or moves closer to zero) means going long swaps or receiving fixed—equivalent to going long a fixed-coupon bond and then going short U.S. Treasuries:

$$\text{Short swaps spreads} = \text{Receive fixed on swaps (Long swaps)}$$
$$\text{vs. Short U.S. Treasuries.}$$

There will be no net exposure to the level of rates because if both Treasury and swap rates go up, the swap position loses but the Treasury position benefits. There will be exposure to the swap spread because if swap rates go down and Treasury rates go up, there will be a profit as both the swap position (like a long bond position) benefits from falling rates and the short U.S. Treasury position benefits from rising Treasury rates.

LTCM's position was such that it benefited to the tune of $240 million for each 15 bp narrowing in U.S. swap spreads, or $16 million per 1 bp. We can easily calculate how large a notional position in bonds this exposure corresponds to. Ten-year swap rates in September 1998 were about 5.70 percent. Thus, a $1 million notional position in 10-year bonds (equivalent to the fixed side of a 10-year swap) would have had a sensitivity of about $750 per bp.[52] This analysis implies that the swap spread position was equivalent to a notional bond position of about $21.3 billion, which was a multiple of LTCM's total capital. Furthermore, the $21.3 billion represented only the *U.S. dollar* swap spread exposure. There was also exposure to U.K. swap spreads and to other market risk factors.

We can also easily calculate that a 45 bp move in swap spreads would have generated a profit or loss of $720 million. LTCM had estimated that a one-year move of one standard deviation was 15 bps. Three standard deviations would be very unlikely for normally distributed spreads (roughly 0.1 percent probability), but financial variables tend to have fat tails—thus, the possibility of a three standard deviation move should not be ignored. Indeed, from April through the end of August, 10-year U.S. swap spreads moved by almost 50 bps. This move is not so surprising when we consider that the default by Russia triggered a minor financial panic: "The morning's *New York Times* (27 August) intoned, 'The market turmoil is being compared to the most painful financial disasters in memory.' . . . Everyone wanted his money back. Burned by foolish speculation in

---

[52]See Coleman (1998) for a discussion of bond and swap sensitivity, or DV01.

Russia, investors were rejecting risk in any guise, even reasonable risk."[53] Everyone piled into the safe haven of U.S. Treasuries, pushing swap spreads higher.

A loss of $720 million would have been 15 percent of LTCM's beginning-year capital. We have to remember, however, that this analysis accounts only for the exposure to U.S. swap spreads. Including U.K. spreads would increase the number. Furthermore, the swap positions were so large (the U.S. position equivalent to $21.3 billion notional) that they could not be quickly liquidated, meaning that LTCM had no practical choice but to live with the losses. In the end, from January 1998 through the bailout, LTCM suffered losses of $1.6 billion because of swaps.[54]

This is by no means a full explanation of LTCM's collapse, but it is very instructive to realize that many of LTCM's problems resulted from large, concentrated, directional trades. The swap spread position was a directional bet on the swap spread—that the spread would narrow further from the levels earlier in the year. Instead of narrowing, swap spreads widened dramatically during August and September. LTCM simply lost out on a directional bet.

Swap spreads were one large directional bet, and long-term equity volatility was another.[55] Together, swap spreads and equity volatility accounted for $2.9 billion of losses out of a total of $4.5 billion. As Lowenstein says, "It was these two trades that broke the firm" (p. 234). There is much more to understanding LTCM's demise than this simple analysis, including the role of leverage and, importantly, the decisions and human personalities that led to taking such large positions. Lowenstein (2000) and Jorion (2000) cover these in detail, and Lowenstein's book in particular is a fascinating read. Nonetheless, this example shows how a simple, broad-stroke understanding of a portfolio and its risks is invaluable.

Credit default swaps and AIG

The market for credit default swaps (CDSs) has grown from nothing just 15 years ago to a huge market today. CDSs are often portrayed as complex, mysterious, even malevolent, but they are really no more complex or mysterious than a corporate bond. Indeed, a CDS behaves, in almost all respects, like a

---

[53] Lowenstein (2000, pp. 153–154).

[54] Lowenstein (2000, p. 234).

[55] According to Lowenstein (2000, p. 126), LTCM had positions equivalent to roughly $40 million per volatility point in both U.S. and European stock markets. (A volatility point is, say, a move from 20 to 21 in implied volatility. An example of an implied volatility index is the VIX index of U.S. stock market volatility.) Implied volatility for such options rose from roughly 20 percent to 35 percent (from early 1998 to September of that year), implying roughly $1.2 billion in losses. The actual losses from swaps were about $1.6 billion and from equity volatility, about $1.3 billion (Lowenstein 2000, p. 234).

leveraged or financed floating-rate corporate bond. The equivalence between a CDS and a floating-rate bond is very useful because it means that anyone acquainted with corporate bonds—anyone who understands how and why they behave in the market as they do, how they are valued, and what their risks are— understands the most important aspects of a CDS. In essence, a CDS is no harder (and no easier) to value or understand than the underlying corporate bond.

Once again I will assume that readers have a basic knowledge of credit default swaps.[56] A CDS is an agreement between two parties to exchange a periodic fixed payment in return for the promise to pay any principal shortfall upon default of a specified bond. **Figure 3.2** shows the CDS cash flows over time. The periodic premium payment is agreed up front, and (assuming I sell CDS protection) I receive premiums until the maturity of the CDS or default, whichever occurs first. If there is a default, I must cover the principal value of the bond: I must pay 100 less recovery (the recovery value of the bond). This payment of the principal amount is obviously risky, and because the premiums are paid to me only if there is no default, the premiums are also risky.

Figure 3.2. Timeline of CDS Payments, Sell Protection

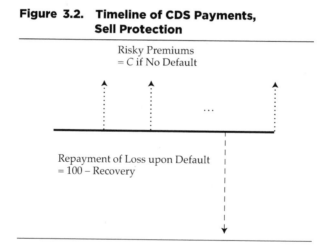

The details of CDSs are indeed more difficult to understand than those of many other securities, more difficult than bonds or interest rate swaps, but the equivalence between a CDS and a corporate bond mentioned earlier means that a broad view of how and why CDSs behave as they do is easy to grasp.

---

[56]See Coleman (2009) for a complete discussion.

To see why a CDS behaves like a floating-rate bond or note (FRN), consider a CDS where I receive the periodic fixed payments and promise to pay principal loss upon default of some bond or some company. That is, I *sell* CDS protection, which we will see shortly is the same as *buying* a financed FRN. Figure 3.2 shows the CDS cash flows: I receive premiums until the maturity or default, and I pay out the principal amount upon default.

Now we can use an elegant trick—in essence, the same as that used for the interest rate swap earlier. With any swap agreement, only net cash flows are exchanged. This means we can insert any arbitrary cash flows we wish so long as the same amount is paid and received at the same time and the net is zero. Let us add and subtract LIBOR[57] payments at each premium date and also 100 at CDS maturity but only when there is no default. These LIBOR payments are thus risky. But because they net to zero, they have absolutely no impact on the price or risk of the CDS. Panel A of **Figure 3.3** shows the original CDS plus these net zero cash flows. Panel B of Figure 3.3 rearranges these cash flows in a convenient manner:

- An FRN by combining

    - the CDS premium and +LIBOR into a risky floating coupon, paid only if there is no default;

    - +100 into a risky principal repayment, paid only if there is no default; and

    - conversion of the payment of −Recovery into receiving +Recovery, paid only if there is default (note that paying a minus amount is the same as receiving a positive amount).

- A LIBOR floater by combining

    - LIBOR into a risky floating coupon, paid until default or maturity, whichever occurs earlier;

    - 100 paid at maturity if there is no default; and

    - 100 paid at default if there is default.

In Panel B, the FRN behaves just like a standard floating-rate bond or note (FRN): If no default occurs, then I receive a coupon (LIBOR + Spread) and final principal at maturity, and if default occurs, then I receive the coupon up to default and then recovery. The LIBOR floater in Panel B looks awkward but is actually very simple: It is always worth 100 today. It is a LIBOR floating bond with maturity equal to the date of default or maturity of the CDS: Payments are LIBOR + 100 whether there is a default or not, with the date of the 100 payment being determined by date of default (or CDS maturity). The

---

[57]LIBOR is the London Interbank Offered Rate, a basic short-term interest rate.

Figure 3.3.   CDS Payments plus Offsetting Payments Equal FRN less LIBOR Floater

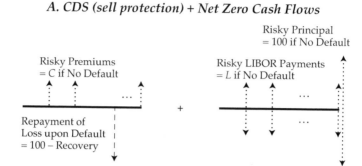

A. CDS (sell protection) + Net Zero Cash Flows

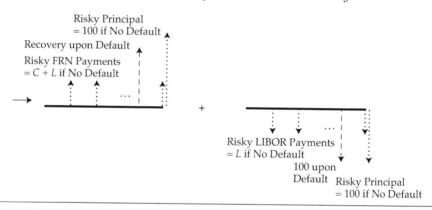

B. FRN + Floater of Indeterminate Maturity

timing of the payments may be uncertain, but that does not affect the price because any bond that pays LIBOR + 100, when discounted at LIBOR (as is done for CDSs), is worth 100 irrespective of maturity (i.e., irrespective of when the 100 is paid).

This transformation of cash flows is extraordinarily useful because it tells us virtually everything we want to know about the broad "how and why" of a CDS.[58] Selling CDS protection is the same as owning the bond (leveraged—that is, borrowing the initial purchase price of the bond). The CDS will respond to the credit spread of the underlying bond or underlying company in the same

---

[58]The equivalence is not exact when we consider FRNs that actually trade in the market. The technical issue revolves around payment of accrued interest upon default (see Coleman 2009). Although it may not be good enough for trading in the markets, the equivalence is more than satisfactory for our purposes.

way as the FRN would. This view of a CDS is quite different from the usual explanation of a CDS as an insurance product—that the seller of protection "insures" the bond upon default. Treating a CDS as an insurance contract is technically correct but profoundly uninformative from a risk management perspective, providing virtually no insight into how and why a CDS behaves as it does. In fact, a corporate bond can be treated as embedding an implicit insurance contract.[59] The insurance view of a corporate bond, like the insurance view of a CDS, is technically correct but generally uninformative from a portfolio risk management point of view, which is why corporate bonds are rarely treated as insurance products.

Having a simple and straightforward understanding of a CDS as an FRN can be very powerful for understanding the risk of portfolios and how they might behave. We can, in fact, use this approach to gain a better understanding of what brought AIG Financial Products (FP) to its knees in the subprime debacle of the late 2000s. According to press reports, in 2008 AIG FP had notional CDS exposure to highly rated CDSs of roughly $450 billion to $500 billion, with about $60 billion exposed to subprime mortgages and the balance concentrated in exposure to banks.[60] Viewing CDSs as leveraged FRNs has two immediate results. First, it reinforces how large a position $450 billion actually is. Outright purchase of $450 billion of bonds, with exposure concentrated in financial institutions and subprime mortgages, certainly would have attracted the attention of senior executives at AIG (apparently, the CDS positions did not). Even the mere recognition that the CDS position is, for all intents and purposes, $450 billion of bonds with all the attendant risks might have prompted a little more scrutiny.

The second result is that it allows us to easily calculate the risk of $450 billion of CDSs, in terms of how much the value might change as credit spreads change. I am not saying that we can calculate AIG FP's exact exposure, but we can get an order-of-magnitude view of what it probably was. We can do this quite easily using the equivalence between CDSs and FRNs. Most CDSs are five-year maturities, and rates were about 5.5 percent in 2008. A five-year par

---

[59]See Coleman (2009) for a discussion and also the mention by Stiglitz in Eatwell, Milgate, and Newman (1987, *The New Palgrave*, vol. 3, p. 967).

[60]The *Economist* ("AIG's Rescue: Size Matters" 2008) reported June 2008 notional exposure of $441 billion, of which $58 billion was exposed to subprime securities and $307 billion exposed to "instruments owned by banks in America and Europe and designed to guarantee the banks' asset quality." Bloomberg (Holm and Popper 2009) reported that AIG FP "provided guarantees on more than $500 billion of assets at the end of 2007, including $61.4 billion in securities tied to subprime mortgages." The *Financial Times* (Felsted and Guerrera 2008) reported that "based on mid-2007 figures, AIG had $465 billion in super-senior credit default swaps."

bond (FRN) with a rate of 5.5 percent has a sensitivity to credit spreads, or credit DV01, of about $435 per basis point for $1 million notional.[61] Thus, $450 billion of bonds would have sensitivity to credit spreads of very roughly $200 million per basis point. Once again, this analysis emphasizes how large the position was.

With a risk of $200 million per basis point, a widening of 10 bps in the spread would generate $2 billion of losses. A move of 50 bps would generate roughly $10 billion in losses. A 50 bp move in AAA spreads is large by pre-2008 historical standards, but not unheard of. Unfortunately, from mid-2007 through early 2008, spreads on five-year AAA financial issues rose from about 50 bps to about 150 bps. By the end of 2008, spreads had risen to roughly 400 bps; with a risk of $200 million per basis point, this change in spreads would mean losses of $70 billion.[62]

The exposure of $200 million is not precise, and the moves in aggregate spreads would not track exactly the spreads that AIG FP was exposed to. Nonetheless, given the size of the exposure and the moves in spreads, it is not hard to understand why AIG FP suffered large losses. AIG FP had a huge, concentrated, directional position in subprime, bank, and other bonds with exposure to the financial sector. AIG FP was betting (whether by intent or accident) that spreads would not widen and that the firm would thus earn the coupon on the CDS. The bet simply went wrong. As with LTCM, there is far more to the story than just a spread position (including, as with LTCM, leverage and the human component that led to the positions), but recognizing the large directional nature of AIG's positions makes the source of the losses easier to understand. It does not completely explain the incident, but it does shed valuable light on it.

****

---

[61]The interest rate risk of an FRN is close to zero because coupons change with the level of rates. The credit spread risk of an FRN will be roughly the same as the spread risk of a fixed-rate bond (technically, a fixed-rate bond with coupons fixed at the forward floating rate resets). For a fixed-rate bond, the spread risk and the interest rate risk will be close to the same. In other words, to find the credit spread risk of an FRN, we simply need to calculate the interest rate risk of a fixed-coupon bond with its coupon roughly equal to the average floating coupon, which will be the fixed coupon of a par bond with the same maturity.

[62]Spreads went back down to roughly 250 bps by early 2010 (figures from Bloomberg). Not all of AIG's positions would have been five years, nor would they all have been financials, but this analysis gives an order-of-magnitude estimate for the kinds of spread movements seen during this period.

Organizational Structure

It is critically important to address the question of what role and organizational structure are best for risk management and risk measurement. This question is closely tied to corporate governance (and regulatory) issues. I will review these issues but not delve into them in detail. The topic is important and should not be glossed over, but it is outside my particular expertise. Furthermore, there is a substantial literature on corporate governance that readers can access.

Two references are particularly valuable. Crouhy, Galai, and Mark (2001, ch. 3) cover a broad range of issues concerned with risk management in a bank. They start with the importance of defining best practices, in terms of policies, measurement methodologies, and supporting data and infrastructure. They also discuss defining risk management roles and responsibilities, limits, and limit monitoring. Crouhy, Galai, and Mark (2006, ch. 4) focus more on the corporate governance aspect and on defining and devolving authority from the board of directors down through the organization.

I will discuss the issues of organizational structure and corporate governance from the perspective of a large publicly traded firm, owned by shareholders whose interests are represented by a board of directors. I will assume that the firm has a senior management committee responsible for major strategic decisions. Most or all the discussion that follows could also be translated in an obvious manner to a smaller or privately held firm—for example, by substituting the owner for the board or the CEO for the senior management committee.

I will start with the role of the board of directors and senior management, following Crouhy, Galai, and Mark (2006, ch. 4). Starting with the board and senior management has to be correct if we truly believe that managing risk is a central function of a financial firm. Crouhy, Gailai, and Mark (2006) specify the role of the board as understanding and ratifying the business strategy and then overseeing management, holding management accountable. The board is not there to manage the business but rather to clearly define the goals of the business and then hold management accountable for reaching those goals. Although this view runs contrary to the view of a director at a large financial group who claimed that "A board can't be a risk manager" (Guerrera and Larsen 2008), in fact the board must manage risk in the same way it manages profits, audit, or any other aspect of the business—not operational management but understanding, oversight, and strategic governance.

For practical execution of the strategic and oversight roles, a board will often delegate specific responsibility to committees. I will consider as an example an archetypal financial firm with two committees of particular importance for risk—the risk management committee and the audit committee. Not all firms will have both, but the roles and responsibilities described must be met in one form or another.

The risk management committee will have responsibility for ratifying risk policies and procedures and for monitoring the effective implementation of these policies and procedures. As Crouhy, Galai, and Mark (2006) state, the committee "is responsible for independently reviewing the identification, measurement, monitoring, and controlling of credit, market, and liquidity risks, including the adequacy of policy guidelines and systems" (p. 94). One area where I diverge from Crouhy, Galai, and Mark slightly (by degree, not qualitatively) is in the level of delegation or devolution of responsibility. I believe that risk is so central to managing a financial firm that the board should retain primary responsibility for risk. The risk committee is invaluable as a forum for developing expertise and advice, but the board itself should take full responsibility for key strategic risk decisions.

An inherent contradiction exists, however, between the board's responsibility to carry out oversight and strategic governance, on the one hand, and to select truly independent nonexecutive directors, on the other. Critical understanding and insight into the complex risks encountered by financial firms will generally be acquired through experience in the financial industry. Nonexecutive directors from outside the industry will often lack the critical skills and experience to properly hold managers and executives accountable—that is, to ask the right questions and understand the answers. Crouhy, Galai, and Mark (2006, p. 92) propose an interesting solution, establishing a "risk advisory director." This person would be a member of the board (not necessarily a voting member) specializing in risk. The role would be to support board members in risk committee and audit committee meetings, both informing board members with respect to best practice risk management policies, procedures, and methodologies and also providing an educational perspective on the risks embedded in the firm's business.

Most large financial firms have an audit committee that is responsible for ensuring the accuracy of the firm's financial and regulatory reporting and also compliance with legal, regulatory, and other key standards. The audit committee has an important role in "providing independent verification for the board on whether the bank is actually doing what it says it is doing" (Crouhy, Galai, and Mark 2006, p. 91). There is a subtle difference between this role and the role of the risk management committee. The audit committee is rightly concerned with risk processes and procedures. The audit committee focuses more on the quality and integrity of the processes and systems, the risk committee more on the substance.

Crouhy, Galai, and Mark (2006, p. 95) rightly place responsibility for developing and approving business plans that implement the firm's strategic goals with the firm's senior management. Risk decisions will usually be delegated to the senior risk committee of the firm. Because risk taking is so inextricably linked with profit opportunities, the risk committee must include the firm's CEO and senior heads of business units, in addition to the chief risk officer (CRO), chief financial officer, treasurer, and head of compliance.

Regarding the organizational structure within the firm itself, the standard view is laid out most clearly in Crouhy, Galai, and Mark (2006). A CRO and "risk management group" are established, independent of the business or trading units. The senior risk committee delegates to the CRO responsibility for risk policies, methodologies, and infrastructure. The CRO is "responsible for independent monitoring of limits [and] may order positions reduced for market, credit, or operational concerns" (p. 97).

I have a subtly but importantly different view, one that is somewhat at variance with accepted wisdom in the risk management industry. I do believe there must be an independent risk monitoring and risk measuring unit, but I also believe that ultimate authority for risk decisions must remain with the managers making trading decisions. Risk is a core component of trading and portfolio management that cannot be dissociated from managing profits, so the management of risk must remain with the managers of the business units. It must ultimately reside with the CEO and senior management committee and devolve down through the chain of management to individual trading units.

Decisions about cutting positions are rightly the responsibility of those managers with the authority to make trading decisions. To my mind, there is a fundamental conflict in asking a CRO to be responsible for cutting positions without giving that CRO the ultimate authority to make trading decisions. The CRO either has the authority to take real trading decisions, in which case he or she is not independent, or the CRO is independent of trading, in which case he or she cannot have real authority.

This view is at variance with the accepted wisdom that proposes a CRO who is independent and who also has the authority to make trading decisions. I believe that the accepted wisdom embeds an inherent contradiction between independence and authority. I also believe that the accepted wisdom can perilously shift responsibility from managers and may lull managers into a false sense that risk is not their concern because it is being managed elsewhere in the organization.

Nonetheless, independence of risk monitoring and risk measurement is critical. Firms already have a paradigm for this approach in the role that audit and finance units play in measuring and monitoring profits. Nobody would suggest that traders or portfolio managers be responsible for producing the P&L statements of the firm. These are produced by an independent finance unit and subject to careful auditing. Areas throughout the organization rely on this P&L and recognize the importance of having verifiable, independent numbers. Risk should be thought of in the same way—information crucial to the organization that must be independently produced and verifiable.

My view of the organizational structure of a risk group is summarized in **Figure 3.4.** The center of the figure, the core down the middle, shows the primary responsibility for managing risk.[63] Managing P&L and other aspects of the organization devolves from the board of directors to senior management (the CEO and senior management committee) and eventually down to individual trading units and business lines. The remaining key items are as follows:

- **Finance unit:** Develops valuation policy, ensures integrity of P&L, advises board and senior management on P&L and accounting issues.

- **Risk unit:** Develops risk policies, develops risk reports, ensures integrity of risk reports, advises board and senior management on risk issues.

- **Operations/middle office:** Books and settles trades, prepares P&L and risk reports, and delivers P&L and risk reports throughout the organization.

This structure gives primary responsibility for managing risk to the managers who have the authority and responsibility to make decisions. At the same time, it emphasizes the role of the risk unit in designing risk policies and advising all levels of the organization on risk matters, from the board down through individual business units. The responsibility for actually running reports, both P&L and risk reports, is given to the operations/middle office group. Risk and P&L reporting are so closely linked that it makes sense to have one operational group responsible for both, instead of finance producing one set (P&L) and risk producing another (risk).

The board and senior managers should rely on the risk unit for advice and direction, but the board and senior management must take responsibility for being informed and educated about risk. It is also important to understand that the risk unit's role of advising the board and senior management includes the responsibility to alert the board and senior management when there are problems with respect to risk, just as the finance unit would with respect to profits.

---

[63]This organizational layout differs from, for example, Crouhy, Galai, and Mark (2006, Figure 4.2) in emphasizing the central role for the board and senior management in monitoring and enforcing risk guidelines, with the risk unit playing a supporting role in ensuring integrity of risk reporting, developing risk policy, advising, and so on.

Figure 3.4. Functions and Responsibilities for Risks and P&L

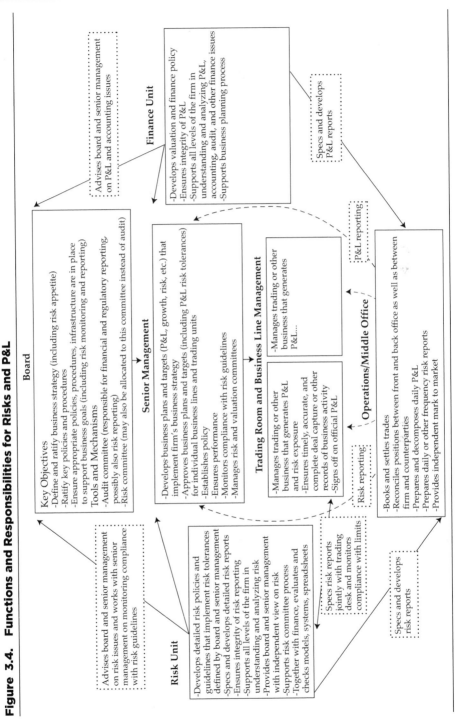

One final issue to discuss is the use and implementation of limits. There can be a wide variety of limits. For market risk, limits may consist of restrictions or specification of the authorized business and allowed securities to be traded, VaR limits within individual business units and overall for a portfolio or firm, restrictions on types of positions and maximum size of positions, concentration limits that stop traders from putting all their risk in one instrument or one market, stop-loss limits that act as a safety valve and early warning system when losses start to mount, and inventory age limits that ensure examination of illiquid positions or those with unrecognized losses. For credit risk, limits may involve the allowed number of defaults before a business or portfolio requires special attention or controls on the allowed downward migration of credit quality within a loan or other portfolio. For the overall business, there may be limits on the liquidity exposure taken on by the firm.

Limits are an important way of tying the firm's risk appetite, articulated at the board and senior management level, to strategies and behavior at the trading unit or business unit level. Limits are important at the business planning stage because they force managers to think carefully about the scale and scope of a new business, in terms of the level of limits and the risk areas across which limits must be granted. Limits are important for ongoing businesses for two reasons. First, they tie the business activity back to the firm's overall risk appetite and to the decision of how to distribute the risk across business lines. Second, limits force managers to compare periodically (say, daily, weekly, or monthly) the risk actually taken in the business with what was intended.

Crouhy, Galai, and Mark (2006) have a discussion of limits, and Marrison (2002, ch. 11) has a particularly clear discussion of the different types of limits and principles for setting limits.

Brief Overview of Regulatory Issues

Regulation is important not only because firms must operate within the rules set by regulators but also because banking regulation has been a major driver of innovation and adoption of risk management procedures at many institutions. Two problems, however, make it difficult to provide a complete treatment here. First, it is outside my particular expertise. Second, and more importantly, the topic is changing rapidly and dramatically; anything written here will be quickly out of date. The response to the global financial crisis of 2008–2009 has already changed the regulatory landscape and will continue to do so for many years to come. I will only provide some background, with references for further exploration.

Many texts cover bank regulation, and although these treatments are not current, they do provide background on the conceptual foundations and history of banking regulation. Crouhy, Galai, and Mark (2006) discuss banking regulation and the Basel Accords in chapter 3 and mid-2000s legislative requirements in the United States regarding corporate governance (the Sarbanes–Oxley Act of 2002) in chapter 4. Marrison (2002, ch. 23) also covers banking regulations.

Globally, the Basel Committee on Banking Supervision (BCBS) is the primary multilateral regulatory forum for commercial banking. The committee was established in 1974 by the central bank governors of the Group of Ten (G–10) countries. Although the committee itself does not possess formal supervisory authority, it is composed of representatives from central banks and national banking regulators (such as the Bank of England and the Federal Reserve Board) from 28 countries (as of 2010). The BCBS is often referred to as the "BIS Committee" because the committee meets under the auspices and in the offices of the Bank for International Settlements in Basel, Switzerland. Technically, the BIS and the Basel Committee are separate. The original 1988 BCBS accord, history on the committee, valuable research, and current information can be found at the BIS website.[64]

The most important regulatory requirement for banks is in regard to capital holdings. Regulatory capital is money that is available for covering unanticipated losses. It acts as a buffer or safety net when losses occur, either because assets fall below the level of liabilities or because assets cannot be liquidated quickly. In the 1980s, global regulatory developments accelerated because of concern about the level and quality of capital held by banks in different jurisdictions, with a particular focus on the low level of available capital held by Japanese banks relative to their lending portfolios. The low capital of Japanese banks was believed to give them an unfair competitive advantage.

Although capital is the most important regulatory requirement, two difficulties arise in defining regulatory capital. The first is deciding what level of capital is sufficient. The second is defining what actually counts as capital. Regarding the appropriate level of capital, the problem is determining how much a bank might lose in adverse circumstances, which, in turn, depends on determining the type and amount of assets a bank holds. Neither of these problems is easy to solve, and the issue is compounded by the necessity to have a set of standards that are relatively straightforward and that can be applied equitably across many jurisdictions using standardized accounting measures that are available in all countries.

Early global standards regarding assets were simple. Bank assets were put into broad risk categories, providing guidance as to the amount of capital that had to be reserved against the possibility that the asset would be impaired. Some assets were counted at 100 percent of face value (e.g., a loan to a private

---

[64]See www.bis.org/bcbs.

company, which was considered to be at risk for the whole of the loan amount), and others were given a lower risk weighting (e.g., 0 percent for cash because cash has no credit risk and is immediately available or 50 percent for housing mortgages). All assets were added up (taking the appropriate risk weighting into account), and these were the bank's total *risk-weighted assets*. Banks were then required to hold capital equal to a percentage of the risk-weighted assets.

Defining the capital is where the second difficulty arises because defining exactly what counts as capital, and how good that capital is, can be hard. It is widely accepted that equity and reserves are the highest-quality form of capital. Equity and reserves—investment in the business provided by outside investors or retained earnings that will disappear in the case of losses—clearly provide a buffer against losses. Other sources of capital—say, undeclared profits—may not be available to cover losses in the same manner and thus may not provide as good a buffer.

Much of the development of global regulation since the 1980s has focused on these three aspects: first, which assets contribute how much to risk-weighted assets; second, what is the appropriate capital ratio; and, third, what counts as capital.

Originally, only the credit risk of assets was taken into account, with no inclusion of market risk (price risk from sources other than default, such as the overall movement of interest rates). New standards published in 1996 and implemented in 1998 sought to include market risk. The rules for risk weighting of assets, however, were still quite crude. The so-called Basel II rules published in 2004 sought to update capital adequacy standards by providing more flexibility but also more precision in the ways that the total risk of assets and total capital are calculated. The details are less important than recognizing that there has been a process for trying to improve how capital requirements are calculated.

The global financial crisis of 2008–2009 highlighted deficiencies in the global regulatory framework, and regulators have responded with Basel III. The process started with a broad framework published in September 2009 and has continued through 2011. Focus has expanded beyond bank-level regulation (setting bank-level capital requirements, for example) to managing systemwide risks, so-called macroprudential regulation.

Managing the Unanticipated

The ultimate goal for risk management is to build a robust yet flexible organization and set of processes. We need to recognize that quantitative risk measurement tools often fail to capture just those unanticipated events that pose the most risk to an organization. The art of risk management is in building a culture and organization that can respond to and withstand these unanticipated events.

Managing risk for crises, tail events, or disasters requires combining all types of risk—market risk, credit risk, operational risk, liquidity risk, and others. Generally, crises or disasters result from the confluence of multiple events and causes. Examples are the collapse of Barings in 1995 (and also the same firm's collapse in 1890) and the Société Générale trading loss in January 2008.

Risk management is about managing all types of risk together—building a flexible and robust process and organization. The organization must have the flexibility to identify and respond to risks that were not important or recognized in the past and the robustness to withstand unforeseen circumstances. Importantly, it also must incorporate the ability to capitalize on new opportunities.

Examining risk and risk management in other arenas can provide useful insights and comparisons: insight into the difference between measuring and managing risk and comparison with methods for managing risk. Consider the risks in ski mountaineering or backcountry skiing, of which there are many. There is the risk of injury in the wilderness as well as the risk of encountering a crevasse, icefall, or rockfall—as with any mountaineering—but one of the primary risks is exposure to avalanches. Avalanches are catastrophic events that are virtually impossible to forecast with precision or detail.

Ski mountaineering risks and rewards have many parallels with financial risks and rewards. Participating in the financial markets can be rewarding and lucrative; ski mountaineering can be highly enjoyable, combining the challenge of climbing big mountains with the thrill of downhill skiing—all in a beautiful wilderness environment. Financial markets are difficult to predict, and it can be all too easy to take on exposure that suddenly turns bad and leads to ruinous losses; avalanches are also hard to predict, and it is all too easy to stray onto avalanche terrain and trigger a deadly slide.

Managing avalanche risk has a few basic components, and these components have close parallels in managing financial risk:

Learning about avalanches in general—When and how do they occur?[65] The analogy in the financial world would be gaining expertise in a new financial market, product, or activity before jumping in.

Learning about specific conditions on a particular day and basing decisions on this information—First, is today a high or low avalanche risk day? Then, using this information combined with one's own or the group's risk tolerance, one must decide whether to go out. In financial risk management, this component would be analogous to learning the specific exposures in the portfolio and then deciding whether to continue, expand, or contract the activity.

---

[65] A common problem for beginner backcountry skiers is ignorance of the risks they are taking. One day there might be little risk from avalanche and another day, great exposure, but in neither case does the beginner even know that he or she is exposed.

Creating damage control strategies—What processes and procedures will mitigate the consequences of disaster when and if it strikes? For example, backcountry skiers should go in a group with every member carrying the tools for group self-rescue—a beacon, probe, and shovel. An avalanche beacon is a small radio transceiver that can be used by group members who are not buried to locate a buried companion, and the probe and shovel are necessary to dig the companion out. A beacon reduces the consequences of being caught and buried by an avalanche: Having a beacon gives a reasonable chance, maybe 50–80 percent, of being recovered alive; without a beacon, the chance is effectively zero. In addition, safe travel rituals can minimize the effect of an avalanche if it does occur. These damage control strategies are the final component of managing avalanche risk. For financial risk management, this component is analogous to building a robust and flexible organization that can effectively respond to unexpected shocks.

The comparison with backcountry travel in avalanche terrain highlights some important issues that carry over to financial risk management. First is the importance of knowledge and attention to quantitative measurement. Veteran backcountry skiers spend time and effort learning about general and specific conditions and pay considerable attention to quantitative details on weather, snowpack, and so forth. (Those who do not take the time to do so tend not to grow into veterans.) Managers in the financial industry should also spend time and effort to learn quantitative techniques and then use the information acquired with those tools.

Second is the importance of using the knowledge to make specific decisions, combining quantitative knowledge with experience, judgment, and people skills. In almost all avalanche accidents, the avalanche is triggered by the victim or a member of his or her party. Avalanche accidents usually result from explicit or implicit decisions made by skiers. Decision making requires skill and judgment and the management of one's own and others' emotions and behavior. Group dynamics are one of the most important issues in backcountry decision making. The same is true in managing financial risk. Quantitative measurement is valuable but must be put to good use in making informed decisions. Financial accidents generally do not simply occur but result from implicit or explicit decisions made by managers. Managers must combine the quantitative information and knowledge with experience, judgment, and people skills.

Third, both avalanches and financial accidents or crises are tail events— that is, they happen rarely and the exact timing, size, and location cannot be predicted with any degree of certainty. Nonetheless, the conditions that produce events and the distribution of events are amenable to study. One can say with some confidence that certain situations are more likely to generate an event than others. (A 38-degree slope the day after a two-foot snowfall is likely to avalanche, and for financial events, a firm with $100 million of S&P 500 exposure is more likely to have severe losses than a firm with $10 million of less risky 10-year bonds.)

Finally, there is an apparent paradox that appears in dealing with both avalanches and financial accidents: With better measurement and management of risk, objective exposure may actually increase. As skiers acquire more skill and tools to manage avalanche risk, they often take on more objective exposure. The analogy in the financial arena is that a firm that is better able to measure and manage the risks it faces may take on greater objective exposure, undertaking trades and activities that it would shy away from undertaking in the absence of such tools and skills.

Upon further consideration, however, this is not paradoxical at all. A skier without knowledge or damage control strategies *should* take little objective exposure; he or she should go out only on low-risk days and then only on moderate slopes. Doing so is safe but not very much fun because steep slopes in fresh powder are the most exciting. With knowledge and damage control strategies, a skier will take more objective exposure—go out more often, in higher risk conditions, and on steeper slopes. Going out in higher risk conditions and on steeper slopes means taking on more objective danger, but with proper knowledge, experience, recovery tools, and decision making, the skier can reduce the risk of getting caught in an avalanche or other adverse situations and also reduce the consequences if he or she does get caught. Most importantly, the steeper slopes and better snow conditions mean better skiing and a big increase in utility, and with proper management of the risks, it can be accomplished without a disproportionate increase in adverse consequences.

Similarly, a financial firm that can better measure, control, and respond to risks may be able to undertake activities that have both greater profit potential and greater objective exposure without facing a disproportionate increase in the probability of losses.

Investment management always trades off risk and return. Managing risk is not minimizing risk but rather managing the trade-off between risk and return. Good risk management allows the following possibilities:

- Same return with lower risk.

- Higher return with same risk.

Generally, the result will be some of both—higher return and lower risk. But in some situations, the objective exposure increases. For a financial firm, internal management of exposures might be improved in such a way that larger positions could be taken on with the same probability of loss (more exposure leading to the same risk). This might come about, say, by more timely reporting of positions and exposures so that better information on portfolio exposures is made available, allowing better management of portfolio diversification. The result would be a decrease in "risk" in the sense of the likelihood of loss or the impact of losses on the firm but an increase in "risk" in the sense of larger individual positions and larger profit potential.

This increase in exposure with increased risk management sophistication should not really be surprising. It is simply part of the realization that managing risk goes hand in hand with managing profits and returns. Risk management is not about minimizing risk but, rather, about optimizing the trade-off between risk and return.

Avalanches and financial accidents differ, however, in two important respects. First is the frequency of events. Avalanches occur frequently—many, many times during a season—so that veteran backcountry travelers (those who know enough and wish to survive) are constantly reminded that avalanches do occur. In contrast, severe financial events are spaced years apart; individual and collective memory thus fades, leading to complacency and denial.

Second is the asymmetry of payoffs. The penalty for a mistake in avalanche terrain is injury or death; the penalty in financial markets is losing one's job. The reward on the upside in financial markets can be quite high, so the asymmetry—substantial reward and modest penalty—creates incentive problems.

Maybe the most important lesson to learn from comparing financial risk with avalanche risk is the importance of the "human factor": the confluence of emotion, group dynamics, difficult decision making under uncertainty, and other factors that we humans are always subject to. The final and most important chapter in the popular avalanche text *Staying Alive in Avalanche Terrain* (Tremper 2008) is simply titled "The Human Factor." In investigating accident after accident, avalanche professionals have found that human decision making was critical: Victims either did not notice vital clues or, as is often the case, ignored important flags.

Tremper explains:

> There are two kinds of avalanche accidents. First, an estimated two-thirds of fatalities are caused by simple ignorance, and through education, ignorance is relatively easy to cure. The second kind of accident is the subject of this chapter—when the victim(s) knew about the hazard but proceeded anyway. They either simply didn't notice the problem, or more commonly, they overestimated their ability to deal with it. . . . Smart people regularly do stupid things. (p. 279)

Exactly the same holds for financial accidents and disasters. Ignorance is relatively easy to cure. The goal of quantitative risk measurement, and the subject of the balance of this book, is to educate and inform: to cure ignorance. Ignorance may be caused by a lack of understanding and education, and it is also caused by a lack of information and data—the inability to measure what is happening in a firm. Risk measurement is aimed at addressing these problems. As such, risk measurement has huge benefits. The fact that two-thirds of avalanche fatalities are the result of ignorance probably carries over to the financial arena: Many financial accidents (as we will see in Chapter 4) result from simple mistakes, lack of knowledge, misinformation, or lack of data—in short, financial ignorance that can be cured.

But, as with avalanches, there is a second kind of financial accident—those that are the result of the human factor. Making decisions under uncertainty is hard. Thinking about uncertainty is difficult. Group dynamics, ego, and outside pressures all conspire to cloud our judgment. To paraphrase Tremper, we should be able to practice evidence-based decision making and critically analyze the facts. We should arrive at the right decision automatically if we just have enough information. In reality, it often does not work out that way. Information, education, data—alone these are not sufficient, which brings us back to risk management. Risk management is managing people, managing process, managing data. It is also about managing ourselves—managing our ego, our arrogance, our stubbornness, our mistakes. It is not about fancy quantitative techniques but about making good decisions in the face of uncertainty, scanty information, and competing demands.

Tremper's chapter on "The Human Factor" has interesting ideas, many taken from other areas that deal with risky decision making. One point is the importance of regular accurate feedback, which is relatively easy for avalanches because avalanches occur regularly and publicly. It is more difficult for financial disasters because they occur less frequently and less publicly. Nonetheless, feedback is important and reminds us that things can and do go wrong. Examples of financial disasters can help us be a little more humble in the face of events we cannot control.

A second area Tremper focuses on is the mental shortcuts or heuristics that we often use in making decisions and how these can lead us astray. This point is related to the issue of heuristics and cognitive biases in probabilistic thinking discussed in Chapter 2 of this text. The heuristics discussed in Chapter 2 are related more particularly to the assessment of probabilities, whereas these heuristics can better be thought of as decision-making shortcuts that often lead us toward errors.

The most important of these heuristics, which carry over naturally to financial risk taking, are as follows:

- **Familiarity:** We feel more comfortable with what is familiar, which can bias our decision making even in the face of objective evidence. This tendency is particularly a problem when disasters occur infrequently because we can become lulled into thinking that because nothing bad has happened yet, it is unlikely that it will. Tremper points out that snow is stable about 95 percent of the time. If we ski a particular slope regularly, it will feel familiar, but we probably have not seen it when it is cranky. The slope will feel familiar, we will feel that we know it well, but that does not make it any less dangerous.

- **Commitment:** When we are committed to a goal, it is hard to change in the presence of new evidence; indeed, it is sometimes even hard to recognize that there is new evidence. Success in finance requires dedication and perseverance, commitment to goals, and optimism. But commitment can also blind us to changing circumstances. The balance between persevering to achieve existing goals and responding to changing circumstances is difficult.

- **Social proof or the herding instinct:** We look to others for clues to appropriate behavior and tend to follow a crowd. This phenomenon has two components. The first is related to the problem of familiarity just discussed. We often look to the experience of others to judge the safety and profitability of unknown activities. When others are doing something and not suffering untoward consequences, we gain confidence that it is safe, sometimes even against our better judgment. The second component is the pressure not to be left behind. When everyone else is making money, it is hard to resist, even if one should know better. Isaac Newton offers a famous example: He invested relatively early in the South Sea Bubble but sold out (on 20 April 1720, at a profit), stating that he "can calculate the motions of the heavenly bodies, but not the madness of people." Unfortunately, he was subsequently caught in the mania during the summer and lost far more than his original profit.[66]

- **Belief and belief inertia:** We often miss evidence that is contrary to our beliefs, and our beliefs change slowly in response to new evidence. This point is best summed up by a quote from Josh Billings: "It ain't so much the things we don't know that get us into trouble. It's the things we know that just ain't so."

---

[66] See Kindleberger (1989, p. 38).

Unfortunately, decision making is hard. It is hard whether the decisions involve avalanches, medical diagnoses, or risk management in a financial firm. There is no way to avoid this problem. Facts, education, and careful thinking are all necessary for good decision making, but unfortunately, they are not sufficient.

Strategy

Managing risk, like managing any aspect of business, is hard. But the task is made easier by having a well-planned strategy. A good risk management strategy is simple to state, if often difficult to carry out:

- Learn about the risks in general; learn about the business and the people.
- Learn about specific exposures and risks; learn about the details of the portfolio.
- Manage people, process, organization; focus on group dynamics, the human factor.
- Implement damage control strategies to minimize the impact when and if disaster strikes.

4. Financial Risk Events

Benefits of Financial Disaster Stories

Stories of financial disasters hold a certain unseemly interest, even providing an element of schadenfreude for those in the financial markets. Nonetheless, there are real and substantive benefits to telling and hearing stories of financial disaster. First is the value of regular feedback on the size, impact, and frequency of financial incidents. This feedback helps to remind us that things can go badly; importantly, it can remind us during good times, when we tend to forget past disasters and think that nothing bad can possibly happen. This effect helps protect against what Andrew Haldane, head of financial stability at the Bank of England, has described as "disaster myopia": the tendency for the memory of disasters to fade with time.[67] It is the "regular accurate feedback" that Tremper recommends as necessary for good avalanche decision making. It also serves "pour encourager les autres"—to encourage those who have not suffered disaster to behave responsibly.[68]

The second benefit is very practical: learning how and why disasters occur. We learn through mistakes, but mistakes are costly. In finance, a mistake can lead to losing a job or bankruptcy; in avalanches and climbing, a mistake can lead to injury or death. As Mary Yates, the widow of a professional avalanche forecaster, said, "We are imperfect beings. No matter what you know or how you operate 95 percent of your life, you're not a perfect person. Sometimes these imperfections have big consequences."[69] Learning from mistakes can help you identify when and how to make better decisions, and studying others' mistakes can reduce the cost of learning. I think this is an important reason why avalanche accident reports are one of the most popular sections of avalanche websites and why the American Alpine Club's annual *Accidents in North American Mountaineering* is perennially popular. Yes, there is a voyeuristic appeal, but reviewing others' mistakes imparts invaluable lessons on what to do and what not to do at far lower cost than making the mistakes oneself.

---

[67]See Valencia (2010).

[68]The full phrase from Voltaire's *Candide* is "Dans ce pays-ci, il est bon de tuer de temps en temps un amiral pour encourager les autres." ("In this country [England], it is wise to kill an admiral from time to time to encourage the others.") The original reference was to the execution of Admiral John Byng in 1757. It is used nowadays to refer to punishment or execution whose primary purpose is to set an example, without close regard to actual culpability.

[69]From Tremper (2008, p. 279). Mary Yates's husband, along with three others, was killed in an avalanche they triggered in the La Sal Mountains of southern Utah.

Systemic vs. Idiosyncratic Risk

As discussed in Chapter 1, an important distinction exists between idiosyncratic risk and systemic risk. Idiosyncratic risk arises from within a firm and is generally under the control of the firm and its managers. Systemic risk is shared across firms and is often the result of misplaced government intervention, inappropriate economic policies, or misaligned macroeconomic incentives.

The distinction between idiosyncratic and systemic risks is important because in the aftermath of a systemic crisis, they often become conflated in discussions of the crisis, such as that of 2007–2009. Overall, this book focuses on idiosyncratic risk, but this chapter discusses examples of both idiosyncratic and systemic risk. We will see that systemic risk has been and continues to be a feature of banking and finance for both developed and developing economies. Importantly, the costs of systemic events dwarf those of idiosyncratic events by orders of magnitude. From a societal and macroeconomic perspective, systemic risk events are by far the more important.

The distinction between idiosyncratic and systemic disasters is also important because the sources and solutions for the two are quite different. The tools and techniques in this book are directed toward measuring, managing, and mitigating idiosyncratic risk but are largely ineffective against systemic risk. Identifying and measuring systemic risk resides more in the realm of macroeconomics than in quantitative finance. An analogy might be useful. Learning to swim is an effective individual strategy to mitigate drowning risk for someone at the town pool or visiting the beach. But for someone on the Titanic, the ability to swim was useful but not sufficient. A systemic solution including monitoring iceberg flows, having an adequate number of lifeboats and life belts on the ship, and arranging rescue by nearby ships was necessary (but sadly missing for the Titanic). Similarly, when macroeconomic imbalances alter costs, rewards, and incentives, an individual firm's risk management actions will not solve the macroeconomic problems.[70]

---

[70]Regarding the risks of systemic events, the story of Goldman Sachs provides a useful cautionary tale. As related in Nocera (2009), during 2007 Goldman did not suffer the kinds of losses on mortgage-backed securities that other firms did. The reason was that Goldman had the good sense (and good luck) to identify that there were risks in the mortgage market that it was not comfortable with. As a result, Goldman reduced some mortgage exposures and hedged others. Note, however, that although Goldman did not suffer losses on the scale that Bear Stearns, Merrill Lynch, and Lehman Brothers did during the crisis, it still suffered in the general collapse. Ironically, Goldman was later pilloried in the U.S. Congress for shorting the mortgage market, the very action that mitigated its losses and that prudent idiosyncratic risk management principles would recommend.

Idiosyncratic Financial Events

Financial and trading disasters are often discussed under the rubric "rogue trading." Like many myths, this one contains some truth but only partial truth. We will see, through examining a variety of events, that many financial disasters are not characterized by rogue trading. Trading disasters occur for a variety of reasons. Sometimes the cause is a rogue trader, as in the case of Barings Bank's 1995 collapse or AIB/Allfirst Financial's losses, but many events have resulted from legitimate trading activity gone wrong or a commercial or hedging activity that developed into outright speculation.

Table 4.1 shows a list of financial events over the years, focusing on events resulting from losses caused by trading in financial markets. It does not cover incidents that are primarily fraudulent rather than trading related, so it does not include Bernard Madoff's fraud. The list is long and, from my experience, reasonably comprehensive regarding the types of financial disasters, but it is not complete. The list clearly does not include events that are not publicly reported, and many fund managers, family trusts, and hedge funds are secretive and loath to reveal losses. For present purposes, Table 4.1 is sufficient; it both shows the scope of losses and includes losses from a wide variety of sources.

Table 4.1 includes few entries relating to the 2008–09 crisis, and for this reason, it may seem out of date. In fact, the absence of recent events is intentional because Table 4.1 is intended to focus on *idiosyncratic* trading disasters and not *systemic* or *macroeconomic* financial crises. There have been huge losses across the global financial system relating to the recent financial crisis, but these losses are generally associated with the systemic financial crisis and are not purely idiosyncratic risk events. To focus more clearly on purely idiosyncratic events, Table 4.1 does not include most of the recent events. I will return to the costs of systemic crises later in this chapter.

Before turning to the table itself, caveats regarding the quoted loss amounts are necessary. These are estimates, often provided by the firm that suffered the loss and after a malefactor has left. Reconstructing trading activity after the fact is always difficult and sometimes is open to different interpretations. Even for simple exchange-traded instruments, it is surprisingly difficult, and financial disasters often involve complex OTC instruments for which pricing is hard, compounded with fraud and intentionally concealed prices and trades. Different accounting and mark-to-market standards across jurisdictions mean that different events may have different standards applied. Sometimes the "loss" that is publicly reported includes restatements for prior incorrectly reported profits

Table 4.1. Trading Losses

Company Name	Original Currency Nominal (billion)	USD Nominal (billion)	Loss 2007 (billion)	Loss Relative to 2007 GDP (billion)	Year of Loss	Instrument
Long-Term Capital Management	USD 4.60	$4.60	$5.85	$7.36	1998	Interest rate and equity derivatives
Société Générale	EUR 4.90	7.22	6.95	7.03	2008	European index futures
Amaranth Advisors	USD 6.50	6.50	6.69	6.83	2006	Gas futures
Sumitomo Corporation	JPY 285.00	2.62	3.46	4.71	1996	Copper futures
Orange County	USD 1.81	1.81	2.53	3.60	1994	Interest rate derivatives
Showa Shell Sekiyu	JPY 166.00	1.49	2.14	3.16	1993	FX trading
Kashima Oil	JPY 153.00	1.50	2.09	2.98	1994	FX trading
Metallgesellschaft	USD 1.30	1.30	1.87	2.74	1993	Oil futures
Barings Bank	GBP 0.83	1.31	1.78	2.48	1995	Nikkei futures
Aracruz Celulose	BRL 4.62	2.52	2.43	2.46	2008	FX speculation
Daiwa Bank	USD 1.10	1.10	1.50	2.09	1995	Bonds
CITIC Pacific	HKD 14.70	1.89	1.82	1.84	2008	FX trading
BAWAG	EUR 1.40	1.29	1.56	1.83	2000	FX trading
Bankhaus Herstatt	DEM 0.47	0.18	0.76	1.71	1974	FX trading
Union Bank of Switzerland	CHF 1.40	0.97	1.23	1.55	1998	Equity derivatives
Askin Capital Management	USD 0.60	0.60	0.84	1.19	1994	Mortgage-backed securities
Morgan Grenfell & Co.	GBP 0.40	0.66	0.85	1.11	1997	Shares
Groupe Caisse d'Epargne	EUR 0.75	1.10	1.06	1.08	2008	Derivatives
Sadia	BRL 2.00	1.09	1.05	1.06	2008	FX speculation
AIB/Allfirst Financial	USD 0.69	0.69	0.80	0.91	2002	FX options
State of West Virginia	USD 0.28	0.28	0.51	0.83	1987	Fixed-income and interest rate derivatives
Merrill Lynch	USD 0.28	0.28	0.51	0.83	1987	Mortgage (IO and PO[a]) trading
WestLB	EUR 0.60	0.82	0.82	0.82	2007	Common and preferred shares
China Aviation Oil (Singapore)	USD 0.55	0.55	0.60	0.65	2004	Oil futures and options
Bank of Montreal	CAD 0.68	0.64	0.64	0.64	2007	Natural gas derivatives
Manhattan Investment Fund	USD 0.40	0.40	0.48	0.57	2000	Short IT stocks during the internet bubble
Hypo Group Alpe Adria	EUR 0.30	0.37	0.41	0.44	2004	FX trading
Codelco	USD 0.21	0.21	0.30	0.44	1993	Copper futures
Dexia Bank	EUR 0.30	0.27	0.31	0.37	2001	Corporate bonds

(continued)

Table 4.1. Trading Losses (continued)

Company Name	Original Currency Nominal (billion)	USD Nominal (billion)	Loss 2007 (billion)	Loss Relative to 2007 GDP (billion)	Year of Loss	Instrument
National Australia Bank	AUD 0.36	0.31	0.34	0.36	2004	FX trading
Calyon	EUR 0.25	0.34	0.34	0.34	2007	Credit derivatives
Procter & Gamble	USD 0.16	0.16	0.22	0.31	1994	Interest rate derivatives
NatWest Markets	GBP 0.09	0.15	0.19	0.25	1997	Interest rate options
Kidder, Peabody & Co.	USD 0.08	0.08	0.10	0.15	1994	Government bonds
MF Global Holdings	USD 0.14	0.14	0.13	0.14	2008	Wheat futures

Notes: Derived from a list of "trading losses" that originated on Wikipedia, with calculations, additions, and verification from published reports by the author. "USD Nominal" is the original currency converted to U.S. dollars at the exchange rate for the year listed as "Year of Loss" using the annual exchange rate from *Foreign Exchange Rates (Annual), Federal Reserve Statistical Release G.5A,* available at www.federalreserve.gov/releases/g5a/. The "Loss 2007" is the dollar nominal converted to 2007 dollars using the annual average CPI for the "Year of Loss." The "Loss Relative to 2007 GDP" is the dollar nominal loss converted to a 2007 amount using the change in U.S. nominal GDP. This adjusts for both inflation and, roughly, growth in the economy. Note that the "Year of Loss" is a rough estimate of the year of the loss; some losses were accumulated over many years, so the conversions to U.S. nominal and 2007 equivalents are only approximate. Losses associated with the systemic financial crisis of 2008–2009 have been excluded. AUD = Australian dollar, BRL = Brazilian real, CAD = Canadian dollar, CHF = Swiss franc, DEM = German mark (replaced by the euro), EUR = euro, GBP = British pound, HKD = Hong Kong dollar, JPY = Japanese yen, USD = U.S. dollar.

[a]IO = interest only; PO = principal only.

Source: Sources by company are listed in the Supplemental Information in the Research Foundation of CFA Institute section of www.cfapubs.org.

---

rather than simply the economic loss from trading.[71] Finally, a firm and the managers that have suffered a loss may have both the motivation and the opportunity to overstate or understate the loss, saying it is larger than it really is to make predecessors look foolish or venal and to flatter future results or smaller than it really is to minimize the culpability of incumbent managers and the damage to the firm.

One final issue regarding the amounts in Table 4.1 needs to be discussed. A dollar lost in 1974 would be equivalent to more than 1 dollar today. Inflation is an obvious factor; a dollar in 1974 could buy more goods or services than it

---

[71]Kidder, Peabody & Co.'s 1994 loss resulting from U.S. Treasury bond trading is a case in point. The "loss" is reported by some sources as $350 million. This amount was actually a write-down by Kidder or Kidder's parent, General Electric Company, which reflected both trading losses and the restatement of previously reported, but fictitious, profits. According to U.S. SEC documents, the actual loss caused by trading was $75 million.

can today. In addition, the market and the economy have grown over time so that a dollar in 1974, even after adjustment for ordinary (consumer price) inflation, represented a larger proportion of the total market or the total economy; a dollar could buy a larger proportion of the total goods and services produced. Table 4.1 shows both an adjustment in the nominal amounts for inflation (using the U.S. CPI) and a rough adjustment for the size of the economy using U.S. nominal GDP growth. This latter adjustment is only approximate but gives a better idea of the relative importance of losses in different years than one would get by adjusting for inflation alone.[72]

Thus, Table 4.1 shows the events, with the original currency amount, the original converted to U.S. dollars (at the average FX rate for the approximate year of loss), the U.S. dollar amount in 2007 dollars, and the U.S. dollar amount adjusted so that it is proportionate to 2007 U.S. nominal GDP (i.e., adjusted for changes in both inflation and, roughly, the size of the economy). The events are sorted by the size of the loss relative to 2007 nominal GDP.

Categorization and Discussion of Losses. Table 4.1 is interesting in itself and highlights the importance of financial disasters over the years. The name "Herstatt," for example, has entered the language as a particular form of cross-currency settlement risk—that which results from differing times for currency transfers.[73]

We can, however, do more than simply admire the size of the losses in Table 4.1. We can use the events to understand more about the sources and circumstances of financial disasters and losses. I have attempted to provide additional information on each event, shown in **Table 4.2,** concerning

- Whether the event involved fraud.

- If there was fraud, whether it primarily involved fraudulent trading—that is, actively hiding trades from supervisors or accountants, creating false trading entries, and so on. I mean this to be distinct from simply trading in excess of limits, which often involves taking larger positions than authorized but not actively hiding that fact.

---

[72] As an example, the Herstatt loss in 1974 was $180 million at the time. Adjusting for U.S. CPI inflation (320.6 percent from 1974 to 2007) brings it to $760 million in 2007. Adjusting for growth in U.S. nominal GDP (838.8 percent, which adjusts for both inflation and growth in the economy), the loss is equivalent to roughly $1,710 million in 2007.

[73] Note that "Herstatt risk" refers to the circumstances under which Herstatt was closed rather than the trading loss that caused Herstatt's collapse.

Table 4.2. Trading Losses, with Additional Characteristics

A. Involving Fraud
Fraud = Yes and Fraudulent Trading = Yes

Company	Loss Relative to 2007 GDP (billion)	Fraud	Fraudulent Trading	Fraud Originated to Cover Up Problem	Normal Trading, Hedging, or Commercial Activity Gone Wrong	Trading in Excess of Limits	Primary Activity Finance or Investing	Years over which Losses Accumulated	Failure to Segregate Functions	Lax Trading Supervision or Mgmt/Control Problem	Note
Société Générale	$7.03	Yes	Yes	Special	No	Yes	Yes	2	Unknown	Yes	Fraud seems to have originated to hide outsized profits.
Sumitoma Corp.	4.71	Yes	Yes	Yes	No	Yes	No	13	Unknown	Yes	Fraud originated with off-the-books trading, then continued in an attempt to recover losses—apparently not for personal gain (apart from keeping job).
Barings Bank	2.48	Yes	Yes	No	No	Yes	Yes	3	Yes	Yes	Fraud was for personal gain (higher bonus).
Daiwa Bank	2.09	Yes	Yes	Yes	No	Yes	Yes	11	Yes	Yes	Fraud started with small ($200,000) loss, then continued to hide and try to recover losses.

(continued)

Table 4.2.   Trading Losses, with Additional Characteristics (continued)

Company	Loss Relative to 2007 GDP (billion)	Fraud	Fraudulent Trading	Fraud Originated to Cover Up Problem	Normal Trading, Hedging, or Commercial Activity Gone Wrong	Trading in Excess of Limits	Primary Activity Finance or Investing	Years over which Losses Accumulated	Failure to Segregate Functions	Lax Trading Supervision or Mgmt/ Control Problem	Note
AIB/Allfirst Financial	$0.91	Yes	Yes	No	No	Yes	Yes	5	Yes	Yes	Fraud was for personal gain (higher bonus).
Bank of Montreal	0.64	Yes	Yes	No	No	Unknown	Yes	2	No	Probably no	Fraud was for personal gain (higher bonus).
Codelco	0.44	Yes	Yes	Yes	No	Yes	No	<1	Unknown	Yes	Mistaken buy vs. sell led to $30 million loss, then trader tried to recover and lost more.
National Australia Bank	0.36	Yes	Yes	Yes	Unknown	Yes	Yes	1 to 2	Unknown	Unknown	Fraud originated to cover an AUD5 million loss, then losses grew.
Kidder, Peabody & Co.	0.15	Yes	Yes	No	No	No	Yes	3	No	Unknown	Generated fraudulent profits by taking advantage of accounting system flaws.

(continued)

Table 4.2. Trading Losses, with Additional Characteristics (continued)

Fraud = Yes and Fraudulent Trading = No

Company	Loss Relative to 2007 GDP (billion)	Fraud	Fraudulent Trading	Fraud Originated to Cover Up Problem	Normal Trading, Hedging, or Commercial Activity Gone Wrong	Trading in Excess of Limits	Primary Activity Finance or Investing	Years over which Losses Accumulated	Failure to Segregate Functions	Lax Trading Supervision or Mgmt/ Control Problem	Note
Showa Shell Sekiyu	$3.16	Yes	No	Yes	Yes	Unknown	No	Many	No	No	Losses were hidden for years, apparently to avoid embarrassment.
Kashima Oil	2.98	Yes	No	Yes	Yes	Unknown	No	6	No	No	Losses were hidden for years, apparently to avoid embarrassment.
CITIC Pacific	1.84	Yes	No	Yes	Yes	Yes	No	1	No	Yes	There was apparently fraud to cover up a mistaken hedging transaction.
BAWAG	1.83	Yes	No	Yes	Yes	Probably yes	Yes	2 to 8	Unknown	Maybe	Losses hidden (fraudulently) from 2000 to 2006.
Morgan Grenfell	1.11	Yes	No	No	Yes	Yes	Yes	2	Unknown	Unknown	Fraud to circumvent regulatory rules on holding concentrated position in a single firm. Not fraud to hide trades or for personal gain. *(continued)*

©2011 The Research Foundation of CFA Institute

Table 4.2. Trading Losses, with Additional Characteristics (continued)

Company	Loss Relative to 2007 GDP (billion)	Fraud	Fraudulent Trading	Fraud Originated to Cover Up Problem	Normal Trading, Hedging, or Commercial Activity Gone Wrong	Trading in Excess of Limits	Primary Activity Finance or Investing	Years over which Losses Accumulated	Failure to Segregate Functions	Lax Trading Supervision or Mgmt/Control Problem	Note
State of West Virginia	$0.83	Yes	No	Yes	Yes	No	Yes	<1	Unknown	Unknown	Losses from poor investment strategy covered up for a period, but no fraud in generating losses.
China Aviation Oil (Singapore)	0.65	Yes	No	Yes	Maybe	Unknown	No	1 to 2	Unknown	Probably no	Speculation in oil futures and options, with fraud to hide losses from investors.
Manhattan Investment Fund	0.57	Yes	No	Yes	Yes	No	Yes	3	Unknown	No	Fraud to cover losses made through an otherwise legitimate strategy to short technology stocks during the technology bubble.
Hypo Group Alpe Adria	0.44	Yes	No	Yes	Probably	Unknown	Yes	2	Unknown	Unknown	Fraud to cover losses from a currency swap.

(continued)

Table 4.2. Trading Losses, with Additional Characteristics (continued)

Company	Loss Relative to 2007 GDP (billion)	Fraud	Fraudulent Trading	Fraud Originated to Cover Up Problem	Normal Trading, Hedging, or Commercial Activity Gone Wrong	Trading in Excess of Limits	Primary Activity Finance or Investing	Years over which Losses Accumulated	Failure to Segregate Functions	Lax Trading Supervision or Mgmt/Control Problem	Note
NatWest Markets	$0.25	Yes	No	Yes	Yes	Probably no	Yes	2	Partial	Yes	Interest rate options were mismarked, apparently in error to start, then fraudulently to conceal losses.
Fraud = Other and Fraudulent Trading = NA											
MF Global	0.14	Possible	NA	NA	Yes	Yes	Yes	<1	No	Yes	Trade exceeded authorized position size.
Dexia Bank	0.37	Un-known	NA	NA	Yes	Unknown	Yes	1 to 2	Unknown	Unknown	Bond trade "ignored internal control procedures and invested in risky investments."
B. Not Involving Fraud											
Long-Term Capital Management	$7.36	No	NA	NA	Yes	No	Yes	<1	No	No	Large positions in swap spreads, equity volatility, yield curve arbitrage, stocks, etc.
Amaranth Advisors	6.83	No	NA	NA	Yes	No	Yes	<1	No	No	Large position in natural gas futures. (continued)

Table 4.2. Trading Losses, with Additional Characteristics (continued)

Company	Loss Relative to 2007 GDP (billion)	Fraud	Fraudulent Trading	Fraud Originated to Cover Up Problem	Normal Trading, Hedging, or Commercial Activity Gone Wrong	Trading in Excess of Limits	Primary Activity Finance or Investing	Years over which Losses Accumulated	Failure to Segregate Functions	Lax Trading Supervision or Mgmt/Control Problem	Note
Orange County	$3.60	No	NA	NA	Yes	No	Yes	1	No	No	County investment pool, leveraged, badly hurt when rates rose in 1994.
Metallgesellschaft	2.74	No	NA	NA	Yes	No	Yes	1	No	No	Hedging strategy that went wrong.
Aracruz Celulose	2.46	No	NA	NA	Yes	Unknown	No	1	No	Unknown	Speculative FX trading, growing out of hedging commercial transactions.
Bankhaus Herstatt	1.71	No	NA	NA	Yes	Probably yes	Yes	1 to 2	Unknown	Yes	FX speculation, possibly outside of limits.
Union Bank of Switzerland	1.55	No	NA	NA	Yes	No	Yes	1 to 3	No	Yes	Mispricing of embedded options led to losses when Japanese bank shares fell.
Askin Capital Management	1.19	No	NA	NA	Yes	No	Yes	1	No	No	Investment in mortgage-related products.

(continued)

Table 4.2. Trading Losses, with Additional Characteristics (continued)

Company	Loss Relative to 2007 GDP (billion)	Fraud	Fraudulent Trading	Fraud Originated to Cover Up Problem	Normal Trading, Hedging, or Commercial Activity Gone Wrong	Trading in Excess of Limits	Primary Activity Finance or Investing	Years over which Losses Accumulated	Failure to Segregate Functions	Lax Trading Supervision or Mgmt/ Control Problem	Note
Groupe Caisse d'Epargne	$1.08	No	NA	NA	Yes	Yes	Yes	<1	No	Maybe	Large positions in equity futures, said to exceed limits.
Sadia	1.06	No	NA	NA	Yes	Unknown	No	1	No	No	Speculative FX trading, growing out of hedging commercial transactions.
Merrill Lynch	0.83	No	NA	NA	Yes	Yes	Yes	1	No	Yes	Trading in mortgage IO/PO strips, partly beyond authorized limits, caused losses when rates spiked up.
WestLB	0.82	No	NA	NA	Yes	Probably no	Yes	1	No	Maybe	Proprietary trading, primarily spreads between common and preferred shares.
Calyon	0.34	No	NA	NA	Yes	Yes	Yes	<1	No	Maybe	Large positions in index-based CDSs, said to be in excess of authorized limits.

(continued)

Table 4.2. Trading Losses, with Additional Characteristics (continued)

Company	Loss Relative to 2007 GDP (billion)	Fraud	Fraudulent Trading	Fraud Originated to Cover Up Problem	Normal Trading, Hedging, or Commercial Activity Gone Wrong	Trading in Excess of Limits	Primary Activity Finance or Investing	Years over which Losses Accumulated	Failure to Segregate Functions	Lax Trading Supervision or Mgmt/ Control Problem	Note
Procter & Gamble	$0.31	No	NA	NA	Maybe	Yes	No	<1	No	Unknown	Speculation in highly leveraged swaps related to interest rates and FX.

Notes: See notes to Table 4.1. Data on additional characteristics are based on reading of published reports (see the Supplemental Information in the Research Foundation of CFA Institute section of www.cfapubs.org for sources) and the author's judgment.

- If there was fraud, whether it was primarily to hide losses that had originated from sources other than fraud. An example is Codelco, where a computer entry led to a wrong-way-round trade that lost $30 million. Subsequent fraudulent trading appears to have been an attempt to make back the original loss.

- Whether the underlying company or business was involved in (primarily) banking, finance, or investment activity.

- Whether the event involved legitimate trading, hedging, or commercial activity that went wrong in some way. For example, Amaranth Advisors' losses in natural gas futures trading were a result of Amaranth's legitimate business activity, even if one might argue, at least in retrospect, that the size and exact form of the position taking may have been foolish. As another example, Aracruz Celulose was a Brazilian pulp producer that lost money in FX speculation. The speculation seems to have started as a commercially reasonable strategy to hedge the FX exposure resulting from export earnings, a strategy that grew into leveraged speculation.

- Years over which the losses accumulated.

- Whether there was a failure to segregate activities (particularly trading and back-office).

- Whether there was lax trading supervision or other management/control problems.

The information shown in Table 4.2 is, to some extent, subjective. The data are based on a reading of published reports of the incidents and reflect my judgment. When the exact nature or circumstance of a loss is not clear from reports, I have tried to note that in the table. I have used my best judgment in sorting events into the various categories; sources are given in the online Supplemental Information so that others can make their own assessment.

Table 4.3 lists the events, again sorted by the size of the loss relative to 2007 GDP, with a longer description of each event.

Fraud. Fraud is an important distinguishing characteristic for the events listed in Table 4.1. There are 35 events in total, and 19 (54 percent) involved fraud in one way or another. Some very large losses have involved fraud (Société Générale, Barings, Sumitomo Corporation, Showa Shell Sekiyu), but by the same token, some of the larger losses have not involved fraud (Long-Term Capital Management, Amaranth Advisors, Orange County). Panel A of Table 4.2 shows events in which fraud appears to have been involved, and Panel B shows those for which fraud does not seem to have been important.

Table 4.3. Short Description of Trading Losses

Company Name	Loss Relative to 2007 GDP (billion)	Instruments	Year of Loss	Short Description
Long-Term Capital Management	$7.36	Interest rate and equity derivatives	1998	LTCM had highly leveraged positions in a variety of markets (swap spreads, equity volatility, yield curve arbitrage, stocks, etc.). None of these on their own in a smaller size or at a different time would have been bad positions but together were toxic. After Russia's 1998 debt default, large market moves generated losses for LTCM. Furthermore, because of the large size and illiquid nature of many trades, LTCM was caught in a liquidity crisis.
Société Générale	7.03	European index futures	2008	Jérôme Kerviel was a trader in equity cash/futures arbitrage. Starting in 2006, he put on outright positions, which became very large (up to €49.9 billion). By the end of 2007, Kerviel had made a profit of €1.4 billion. Kerviel used fictitious trades to hide the size of the profits. During early 2008, the positions started losing substantial amounts. The bank closed out positions. Managers were alleged to have been aware of the size of the positions but to have ignored the risk when the trades were profitable, but these allegations were disputed.
Amaranth Advisors	6.83	Gas futures	2006	Amaranth was a hedge fund initially focused on convertible arbitrage. Its energy desk, dominated by a single trader, undertook spread trades in natural gas—among them that March/April spreads would widen (March up because of heating demand, April down with warm weather and lower demand). Similar trades had been profitable before. Nonetheless, position size was very large, relative to the market and relative to Amaranth's capital. Eventually, the spreads moved against Amaranth, and the hedge fund had to close because of the size of losses.
Sumitomo Corporation	4.71	Copper futures	1996	Trading in copper by a single trader was carried out far beyond authorized trading limits over a number of years, with fraudulent reporting and hiding of trades. The original trading apparently started in 1985 with off-the-books trading, and then fraudulent trading continued in attempt to recover original losses.

(continued)

Table 4.3. Short Description of Trading Losses (continued)

Company Name	Loss Relative to 2007 GDP (billion)	Instruments	Year of Loss	Short Description
Orange County	$3.60	Interest rate derivatives	1994	Robert Citron, as treasurer of Orange County, California, managed about $7.5 billion in capital and leveraged it with an additional $12.5 billion using reverse repos. He bought bonds but also exotics, such as inverse floaters. Basically, he was funding short and investing long. When short rates went up in 1994 (curve inverted), the county lost substantial sums and declared bankruptcy.
Showa Shell Sekiyu	3.16	FX trading	1993	Speculation in forward FX led to losses that accumulated over many years because of a lack of mark-to-market and clear accounting rules. It is likely, but not absolutely clear to me, that this started as a commercially reasonable strategy to hedge FX trade receipts or liabilities and then grew into outright speculation.
Kashima Oil	2.98	FX trading	1994	Speculation in forward FX led to losses that accumulated over many years because of a lack of mark-to-market and clear accounting rules. It is likely, but not absolutely clear to me, that this started as a commercially reasonable strategy to hedge FX trade receipts or liabilities and then grew into outright speculation.
Metallgesellschaft	2.74	Oil futures	1993	Strategy to hedge long-dated fixed-price oil delivery contracts using short-dated futures and OTC swaps (essentially buying a stack of near-contract futures). Although questionable, the strategy is not fatally flawed but provides only a partial hedge. It is subject to basis risk (if the spread between the short-dated futures price and long-dated contract price moves), liquidity risk (if the near-contract futures price falls, generating realized losses that will only be recouped over time as the long-term contracts mature), and counterparty credit risk (if long-dated contract price falls, counterparties may renege on contracts, generating credit losses). Metallgesellschaft apparently suffered primarily from liquidity risk, with basis risk contributing. Different accounting treatment of hedge gains and losses between the United States and Germany also contributed.

(continued)

Table 4.3.   Short Description of Trading Losses (continued)

Company Name	Loss Relative to 2007 GDP (billion)	Instruments	Year of Loss	Short Description
Barings Bank	$2.48	Nikkei futures	1995	Nick Leeson was a trader/manager who was supposed to be arbitraging Osaka vs. SIMEX futures. He had both trading and operational responsibility. Starting in 1992, he took outright positions and fraudulently hid losses in an "error account" 88888. Reported profits were large through 1994 (with true, offsetting losses hidden in the error account). Positions grew in the first two months of 1995; losses and consequent margin calls from futures exchanges grew so large that the fraud could not be maintained after the Kobe earthquake struck, and Leeson fled on 23 February 1995. Barings collapsed under the weight of the losses.
Aracruz Celulose	2.46	FX speculation	2008	A commercially reasonable strategy to hedge FX trade receipts grew into a large speculative activity. This worked as long as the BRL did not depreciate substantially, but when it did in late 2008, the trade generated large losses.
Daiwa Bank	2.09	Bonds	1995	A bond trader held both trading and back-office responsibilities in Daiwa Bank's New York branch. Over a period of 11 years, he accumulated $1.1 billion of losses (not for personal gain), which he hid by fraudulently selling securities held in custody for the bank and customers. The trader confessed on 13 July 1995. Management at the branch was very poor, and senior managers misled bank examiners and regulators, both before the confession and more actively after. The bank's U.S. license was revoked, and Daiwa was expelled from the United States.
CITIC Pacific	1.84	FX trading	2008	This Hong Kong–based firm was seemingly attempting to hedge a prospective AUD1.6 billion acquisition, but for reasons I cannot determine, the hedge was levered to AUD9 billion. There were claims of trading without authorization and lax supervision.

(continued)

Table 4.3. Short Description of Trading Losses (continued)

Company Name	Loss Relative to 2007 GDP (billion)	Instruments	Year of Loss	Short Description
BAWAG	$1.83	FX trading	2000	BAWAG was an Austrian bank alleged to have invested in a hedge fund (with connections to senior bank officials) to speculate in financial markets (FX in particular). The hedge fund made substantial losses in yen FX trades, and the bank conspired to hide the losses for roughly six years. BAWAG was mixed up in the 2005 Refco fraud, which brought the earlier trading losses to light, but the Refco scandal appears to have been separate from these FX losses.
Bankhaus Herstatt	1.71	FX trading	1974	Herstatt speculated in FX trading and built up substantial losses. The name "Herstatt" is now used for a type of settlement risk, after the circumstances of Herstatt's closing. German authorities closed the bank early (New York time) on 26 June 1974. Counterparty banks had transferred DEM moneys to Herstatt for settlement of FX trades, but Herstatt was closed by authorities before Herstatt transferred USD moneys in payment, and the counterparties faced losses. This nearly caused the collapse of the payment system. Since then, settlement procedures have been changed to remove the intraday delay for settlement of FX trades.
Union Bank of Switzerland	1.55	Equity derivatives	1998	The equity derivatives trading desk had very large positions in Japanese bank convertible preference shares. It did not properly hedge or value the embedded put options, and when Japanese bank shares fell precipitously (after Yamaichi Securities Co. went under in November 1997), it lost large amounts. This event is believed to have precipitated the merger of UBS and SBC in 1998. The loss is often quoted as CHF625 million, the amount UBS wrote off prior to the merger, but it should also include the CHF760 million write-off after the merger. The equity derivatives desk apparently operated without the same risk management controls as other parts of the firm.

(continued)

Table 4.3. Short Description of Trading Losses (continued)

Company Name	Loss Relative to 2007 GDP (billion)	Instruments	Year of Loss	Short Description
Askin Capital Management	$1.19	Mortgage-backed securities	1994	Askin Capital Management invested in PO strips of CMOs (collateralized mortgage obligations). POs are very sensitive to rises in interest rate—when rates rise, principal repayments slow and POs fall in value. In 1994, rates rose dramatically, prepayments fell, the POs lost value, and Askin was caught in a liquidity crisis and had to liquidate all funds. This led to the closure of Askin's hedge funds—Granite Partners, Granite Corporation, and Quartz Hedge Fund—with the loss of virtually all assets.
Morgan Grenfell	1.11	Shares	1997	Firm purchased highly speculative stocks; some fraud involved to circumvent rules restricting a fund holding concentrated positions in a single company.
Groupe Caisse d'Epargne	1.08	Derivatives	2008	The event involved trading by a small group of equity derivatives traders at a proprietary trading unit of Caisse Nationale des Caisses d'Epargne (the holding company of Groupe Caisse d'Epargne). Losses eventually reported as €750 million. Traders were said to exceed limits.
Sadia	1.06	FX speculation	2008	A commercially reasonable strategy to hedge FX trade receipts grew into a large speculative activity. This worked as long as the BRL did not depreciate substantially, but when it did in late 2008, the trade generated large losses.
AIB/Allfirst Financial	0.91	FX trading	2002	John Rusnak was an FX trader at Allied Financial (a U.S. subsidiary of Allied Irish Banks) who accumulated $691 million in losses. He claimed to make money by running a large options book that was hedged in the cash markets. In 1997, he started to lose money in outright yen forward positions and created fake options to hide those losses. He managed to enter the fake options into the back-office system. Rusnak manipulated prices used to value positions and circumvented limits. The fraud was not uncovered until 2002.

(continued)

Table 4.3. Short Description of Trading Losses (continued)

Company Name	Loss Relative to 2007 GDP (billion)	Instruments	Year of Loss	Short Description
State of West Virginia	$0.83	Fixed-income and interest rate derivatives	1987	A consolidated fund that pooled short-term assets of local governments invested short-term funds in long-term bonds with substantial leverage. When a sharp rise in long-term rates occurred in April 1987, the strategy resulted in large losses (30-year Treasury rates went from 7.46 percent at the beginning of March to 8.45 percent at the end of April). Losses were fraudulently hidden and eventually disclosed in December 1988.
Merrill Lynch	0.83	Mortgages (IOs and POs) trading	1987	A trader in mortgage IO/PO strips exceeded trading authorization and created a large pool of IOs and POs. Merrill sold the IOs, but the POs were apparently overpriced, and Merrill held onto them. (On 8 April, Merrill underwrote $925 million of strips but only sold the IOs. The trader, Howard A. Rubin, then created another $800 million [beyond authority] and again sold the IOs. Rates went up sometime around 10 April.) When the rate spiked, the value of the POs fell. Merrill eventually traded out, taking a $275 million loss.
WestLB	0.82	Common and preferred shares	2007	WestLB was a German state-run bank. Losses were in proprietary trading, primarily in spreads between common and preferred shares. (Gains from trading in bonds and currencies partially offset the equity losses.) Note that in subsequent years, because of the systemic financial crises, WestLB has run into substantial problems related to investments and its loan book.
China Aviation Oil (Singapore)	0.65	Oil futures and options	2004	China Aviation Oil is a Singapore-based company that has a monopoly of China's jet fuel market. Managers at the firm speculated on movements in the price of oil and then tried to hide the losses from investors.
Bank of Montreal	0.64	Natural gas derivatives	2007	David Lee overvalued BMO's natural gas options by mismarking positions for which prices were not available. He colluded with an outside broker to have them provide these mismarked positions to the bank's risk management group.

(continued)

Table 4.3. Short Description of Trading Losses (continued)

Company Name	Loss Relative to 2007 GDP (billion)	Instruments	Year of Loss	Short Description
Manhattan Investment Fund	$0.57	Short IT stocks during the internet bubble	2000	Michael Berger was an Austrian investment manager (operating in the United States) who started Manhattan Investment Fund, a hedge fund, in 1996. The strategy was shorting technology stocks. Unfortunately for Berger, who was right in fundamentals but wrong in timing, the technology bubble continued to inflate through 2000. By 1999, trading losses had accumulated to more than $300 million (according to the U.S. SEC). Berger forged documents and fraudulently reported gains to investors throughout the period 1996–2000. Berger pled guilty to fraud in 2000 but subsequently fled the United States.
Hypo Group Alpe Adria	0.44	FX trading	2004	There were €300 million losses from a currency swap in 2004 with subsequent fraud to cover the losses. The 2004 trading losses were minor, however, relative to the losses in the 2007–09 financial crisis (2009 after-tax losses: €1.6 billion). The bank was nationalized in December 2009 to avoid a collapse. As of early 2010, problems are ongoing.
Codelco	0.44	Copper futures	1993	Trader for Chilean state copper company entered a mistaken futures buy instead of a sell into a computer system, which led to a $30 million loss. The trader then took large positions in copper but also silver and gold futures, and the loss grew to $210 million.
Dexia Bank	0.37	Corporate bonds	2001	There is little information on this event, but apparently a bond trader "ignored internal control procedures and invested in risky investments." In any case, this was overshadowed by losses related to municipal and bond insurance in the 2007–09 financial crisis. Losses for 2008 were €3.3 billion, and the bank required state aid from Belgium, France, and Luxembourg.
National Australia Bank	0.36	FX trading	2004	FX trader lost AUD5 million in 2003 and fraudulently claimed AUD37 million profit to cover up. During 2004, trading (fraudulently concealed) generated a total of AUD360 million in losses.

(continued)

Table 4.3. Short Description of Trading Losses (continued)

Company Name	Loss Relative to 2007 GDP (billion)	Instruments	Year of Loss	Short Description
Calyon	$0.34	Credit derivatives	2007	Calyon was a U.S.-based subsidiary of Crédit Agricole. Losses appear to have been from trading in index-based CDSs (credit default swaps) that were said to be in excess of the unit's authorized limits. The trader involved and five superiors were fired.
Procter & Gamble	0.31	Interest rate derivatives	1994	This event involved speculation in highly leveraged swaps related to interest rates and FX.
NatWest Markets	0.25	Interest rate options	1997	Initially, exchange-traded DEM options were mismarked as a result of not accounting properly for the volatility smile, apparently in error rather than fraudulently. Subsequently, the trader fraudulently manipulated marks in the swaption book to hide the original losses. There was poor segregation of responsibilities with the trader supplying at least some of the implied volatility marks.
Kidder, Peabody & Co.	0.15	Government bonds	1994	Joseph Jett, a Kidder Peabody bond trader, generated fraudulent profits by taking advantage of accounting system flaws. The accounting system ignored the difference between spot and forward prices. A trader could exploit this problem and generate phantom "profits" by selling U.S. Treasury strips forward and buying the bond (reconstituting the bond). The loss is often quoted as $350 million or $250 million, but that is the write-off that Kidder Peabody and GE had to take to adjust for earlier reported "phantom" profits. The real loss seems to have been more like $75 million according to the SEC.
MF Global Holdings	0.14	Wheat futures	2008	A trader exceeded authorized position size on wheat contracts. The trade entry system that should have blocked the trade did not do so.

Notes: See notes to Table 4.1. The description of the event is based on reading of published reports (see the Supplemental Information in the Research Foundation of CFA Institute section of www.cfapubs.org for sources) and the author's judgment.

We usually think of fraud as motivated by personal enrichment—the celebrated "rogue trader."[74] Barings might be the best-known case, where Nick Leeson reportedly hid losing trades, inflated his group's trading profits, and earned large personal bonuses. In addition to Barings, the events at AIB/Allfirst; Kidder, Peabody & Co.; and Bank of Montreal appear to have involved fraud for personal gain.

Although fraud for personal enrichment jumps to mind first, it does not appear to be the most common source of fraud. I have found it useful when examining the events in Table 4.2, Panel A, to consider the following classifications of fraud:

- Primarily involving actively fraudulent trading, divided into
  - Fraud for personal enrichment.
  - Fraud to make back losses or some other motivation that is not primarily personal enrichment.
- Not primarily fraudulent trading, usually to hide losses that have occurred by other means.

Before turning to examination of specific cases, we should note an important philosophical point regarding distinctions between different forms of fraud. On the one hand, in the eyes of the law, in the effect on shareholders or investors or fellow workers, and in the size of losses, there is little distinction among different motivations for fraud. The judge in the National Australia Bank case stated it succinctly: "You and your team saw yourselves as . . . justified in your criminal conduct by asserting that your principal motives were to make money for the bank (not for yourselves). That is simply no excuse."[75] Fraud is fraud, and there is no excuse.

On the other hand, to combat and protect against fraud, we need a more nuanced approach. Understanding the origin of and motivation for fraud, understanding the modalities of fraud, is one step toward designing organizations, processes, and procedures that are not vulnerable to fraud. For example, we will see that most frauds are undertaken to cover up other problems, which implies that measures to reduce errors that might grow into fraudulent events will be one strategy to minimize the incidence of fraud.

▨ *Fraudulent trading for personal enrichment.* In some cases, the primary motivation for or origin of the fraudulent trading appears to be personal gain. These are the cases that most closely fit our idea of rogue trading: hiding trades,

---

[74]By personal gain or enrichment, I mean direct gain over and above retaining one's job and a more-or-less standard salary; personal enrichment would, for example, take place through a large bonus that would not have been paid absent the fraud.

[75]Miletic (2005).

creating false trade entries, and so on, in the pursuit of a promotion, a larger bonus, or other direct reward. Barings, AIB/Allfirst, Kidder Peabody, and Bank of Montreal most closely fit this paradigm. Interestingly, this category does not seem to cover the majority of fraud cases, or even the majority of fraudulent trading cases.

■ *Fraudulent trading for other reasons (usually to cover losses).* Other cases involve fraudulent trading, but the intent was usually to cover a (relatively) small loss. Daiwa Bank, Codelco, Sumitomo, and National Australia Bank fall into this category. Codelco is a nice example. A trader for the Chilean state copper company was trading copper futures (as part of his normal job) and apparently entered a buy instead of a sell into a computer system. This wrong-way trade generated a $30 million loss. To try to make back the loss, the trader took unauthorized positions in copper, silver, and gold and grew the loss to almost $210 million. Unfortunately, the evidence of Table 4.2, Panel A (and my own personal experience, cleaning up after such an incident and not as a perpetrator), shows that this pattern is all too common: An otherwise innocent mistake leads to a loss that then leads to a fraudulent cover-up of losses, often with further trading that magnifies the loss.

Daiwa is another example—and one of the most egregious. The fraud apparently started as an attempt to hide a $200,000 loss early in the career of a bond trader in New York, with the fraud continuing to save and protect reputation. The fraud was apparently not for personal benefit but, rather, on behalf and for the benefit of the bank. The fraud continued for 11 years. Management at the branch was very poor, and senior managers misled bank examiners and regulators, both before the trader's confession and more actively after. The bank's U.S. license was revoked, and Daiwa was expelled from the United States.

Of course, one must view the statements of perpetrators who say that they did not act for personal enrichment skeptically, but in the Daiwa case (and other cases), there is reasonable evidence that offenders did not benefit directly, apart from the obvious benefit of retaining a job and more or less standard salary.[76]

Société Générale is a special case. It could be considered both as a case of trading for personal enrichment and as an odd case of cover-up. Published reports indicate that Jérôme Kerviel, the trader involved, originally hid trades and created false entries to hide excessive profits, not hide losses.

---

[76]In the case of Toshihide Iguchi and Daiwa's losses on bond trading, even the U.S. prosecutor said as much (*New York Times*, 27 September 1995: www.nytimes.com/1995/09/27/business/an-unusual-path-to-big-time-trading.html). In the case of NatWest Markets' loss on mismarking swaption volatilities, the regulator (the Securities and Futures Authority) concluded afterwards that the event as a whole was not inspired by the pursuit of personal gain.

■ *Fraud other than directly fraudulent trading.* Ten events shown in Table 4.2, Panel A, involved fraud but not fraudulent trading, at least in terms of a single trader executing and hiding trades against his or her employer's interest: Showa Shell Sekiyu, Kashima Oil Co., CITIC Pacific, BAWAG, Morgan Grenfell & Co., the state of West Virginia, Hypo Group Alpe Adria, and NatWest Markets. For all except Morgan Grenfell, the fraud involved covering up losses that were generated in some other way, usually to avoid revealing the losses to shareholders or regulators. Most or all of the losses were generated in relatively standard business.[77]

Morgan Grenfell was an exception: The fraud involved setting up dummy companies to avoid regulatory restrictions on a fund holding large concentrations in a single company. Investment in the companies was not illegal or fraudulent per se except for the regulatory prohibition on the concentrations, although the investments themselves appear to have been based on very poor judgment.

■ *Origin of fraud.* Most of the cases of fraud shown in Table 4.2, Panel A, were motivated more by attempts to cover up a problem than by the goal of personal enrichment. Four out of nineteen (Barings, AIB/Allfirst, Bank of Montreal, Kidder Peabody, plus possibly Société Générale) were primarily motivated by personal gain. In contrast, 13 out of 19 were primarily motivated by trying to cover up a problem or trading loss.

Various policies and practices are needed to avert fraud no matter what its origin:[78]

- Separation of front-office and back-office (trade processing and P&L reporting) responsibilities.
- Mark-to-market accounting and timely reporting of P&L, with P&L disseminated up the management hierarchy.
- Effective risk measurement and reporting architecture.
- Strong business line supervisory controls.
- Firm understanding by senior management of the business and products traded.

These policies and practices ensure that fraud is hard to execute (e.g., separation of front-office and back-office functions makes it hard to forge trade tickets) and that mistakes and unusual P&L get recognized early (mark-to-market

---

[77]BAWAG may be an exception. BAWAG apparently invested in a hedge fund that undertook trading outside of BAWAG's authorized investment rules, although it seems that senior BAWAG managers may have directed the hedge fund to do so.

[78]See Wilmer Cutler Pickering Hale and Dorr (2008) for a discussion of lessons learned from trading loss events. The report focuses on rogue traders and five of the events discussed here (Daiwa, Barings, AIB/Allfirst, Kidder Peabody, Société Générale).

accounting ensures problems are recognized). High-quality information and transparency are the first defense against fraud, but availability of information alone is not sufficient: Managers must understand and be able to use the information.

As argued earlier, however, understanding the origin of or motivation for fraud is also important for developing strategies to combat it. Certain strategies are particularly effective against fraud motivated by personal gain:

- Ensuring that incentive systems do not encourage excessive risk.

- Monitoring and scrutinizing successful traders as much as (or more than) unsuccessful traders.

- Ensuring that traders take regular vacations. (It is hard to maintain a fraud when someone is out of the office.)

- Setting up a culture of compliance and responsible risk taking, starting at the top with the board and senior management.

These strategies and practices are well accepted, but there are others, not as often highlighted, that are particularly important to avert fraud that originates in trying to hide losses resulting from other sources:

- Designing systems and processes to make it easy for traders and back-office personnel to do the right thing and hard to do the wrong thing.

- Investing in people and infrastructure to streamline and automate operational procedures to reduce operational errors.

- Setting up a culture that encourages employees to own up to mistakes.

Financial markets can be a complex, fast-moving, and confusing environment. Automation, checklists, and well-designed systems and procedures can smooth both front-office and back-office activity and make it easier to do the right thing. For example, an option-pricing screen that accepts an entry of "101.16" as a U.S. Treasury price of 101 16/32 can lead to confusion between (decimal) $101.16 and $101.50; this is a minor error for an option strike when it is far out of the money but potentially serious when the option is at the money.

Table 4.4 summarizes the total number of events shown in Tables 4.1, 4.2, and 4.3, categorized by whether there was fraud or not and whether the event involved legitimate business activity that went wrong for one reason or another. The categorization by fraud was just discussed; the categorization by legitimate business activity that went wrong is discussed next.

Normal Business Activity Gone Wrong. It might seem odd to think of financial disasters as being the result of normal business, but that is the case for many events. Table 4.2, Panel B, shows events for which fraud was not a primary issue. These events constitute 14 out of 35 (plus 2 for which I could not determine whether fraud was involved) events. When we also consider

Table 4.4. Summary of Events, Categorized by Fraud and Legitimate Business Activity

Fraud Present	Number	Legitimate Business Activity	Number
Yes fraud	19	Trading/commercial origin	23
Fraudulent trading	9	Trading	18
Personal enrichment	4	No fraud	11
Other reasons	5	Yes fraud	5
Not fraudulent trading	10	Uncertain	2
Fraud to cover problems	13	Commercial activity, led to speculation/fraud	5
No fraud	14	Not trading/commercial origin	8
Uncertain if fraud present	2	Uncertain origin	4
Total	35	Total	35

Note: These counts summarize the data shown in Table 4.2.

events that did include fraud, we find that the majority of events were the result of or originated in legitimate trading, hedging, or commercial activity. In total, 23 out of 35 events originated in normal business activity that went wrong (with 4 events unknown or uncertain).

The meaning of "normal trading, hedging, or commercial activity that went wrong" needs a little clarification. It can be divided into three rough categories:

- Legitimate trading or hedging that was simply ill judged, not fraudulent.
- Legitimate trading or hedging that involved fraud tangentially.
- Speculation that started from a legitimate commercial activity.

The meaning of these categories is best explained by considering the cases that fall under them.

■ *Legitimate trading or hedging that was simply ill judged, not fraudulent (11 cases).* This category includes LTCM, Amaranth Advisors, Orange County, Groupe Caisse d'Epargne, Askin Capital Management, WestLB, Bankhaus Herstatt, Merrill Lynch, Calyon, Union Bank of Switzerland, and Metallgesellschaft. Virtually all of these were financial or investment firms that were undertaking business they were intended to and with at least some expertise in their area. (Metallgesellschaft, although not a financial firm, is included because its hedging program was a significant part of the business strategy rather than an ancillary activity.) After the fact, one can argue that their positions were inappropriate, too large, even irresponsible, but that argument is always easier to make after rather than before. LTCM, for example, was a hedge fund with large positions in a variety of markets, and the positions were particularly large in swap spreads and equity volatility. The fund was highly leveraged and lost virtually all its capital, but there was no malfeasance or wrongdoing. In some cases, there was trading in excess of limits (Group Caisse d'Epargne, Merrill Lynch, Calyon, and probably Bankhaus Herstatt), although not what I would judge as outright fraud. Metallgesellschaft was a case of a commercial firm hedging its business activity.

■ *Legitimate trading or hedging that involved fraud tangentially (five cases).* This category covers financial or investment firms that were involved in legitimate business but fraud was involved to cover up losses or some other problem. That is, the fraud was not central to the loss. This category includes BAWAG, West Virginia, Manhattan Investment Fund, NatWest Markets, and Morgan Grenfell. West Virginia is a good example. The loss was the result of investing short-term funds (from a fund that pooled short-term assets of local governments) in long-term bonds with substantial leverage. (The situation, by the way, was remarkably similar to Orange County's. The substantive difference is that in the Orange County case, there was no cover-up after the losses.) Manhattan Investment Fund was a famous fraud, but the loss itself appears to have resulted simply from a strategy to short technology stocks during the tech bubble (a strategy that was ultimately correct but, in this case, executed too early).

■ *Speculation that started from a legitimate commercial activity (five cases).* This is an interesting and important category—nonfinancial firms that undertook speculative or other trading that led to large losses. It includes Aracruz, Sadia, Showa Shell Sekiyu, Kashima Oil, CITIC Pacific, and possibly China Aviation Oil Corporation. Aracruz and Sadia were Brazilian companies that apparently moved from legitimate hedging of export earnings to leveraged speculation and are discussed more later. Showa Shell Sekiyu and Kashima Oil were two Japanese companies that speculated in FX, with the speculative activity probably originating in hedging FX payments related to oil imports. These two cases are particularly important because they highlight the importance of marking to market and recognizing losses early. Press reports indicate that Kashima Oil's losses accumulated over six years (and Showa Shell Sekiyu's over an unspecified but comparable period). Under Japanese accounting rules of the time, the losses could be rolled over and effectively hidden from shareholders. CITIC's losses appear to have originated in an attempt to hedge an acquisition in a foreign currency, but the hedge was highly levered for some reason. Some of these cases involved fraud (Showa Shell Sekiyu, Kashima Oil, CITIC Pacific, China Aviation Oil), and others did not (Aracruz, Sadia).

The first category, legitimate trading, is particularly important when considering risk management for financial institutions. Ten of the eleven cases (excluding Metallgesellschaft) involve financial or investment firms undertaking normal financial or investment activity. These events raise some fundamental questions about managing risk. Fraud is easy to categorize as illegal and unethical (even if the fraud itself can be difficult to identify), and there is no question that fraudulent activities should be prohibited. For legitimate financial activity, in contrast, there is no good way to distinguish between "good" activity that leads to profits and "bad" activity that leads to losses.

The bottom line is that there is no unambiguously "good" versus "bad" financial activity. Some investments or trading strategies are better than others, but trading and investing is risky and involves taking positions that may or may not work out, which is what makes managing risk, like managing any other part of a business, difficult and challenging.

Note that some frauds listed in Table 4.2, Panel A, originated in legitimate trading activity (Sumitomo, Daiwa, National Australia Bank, and Codelco), but I do not include these as "normal business" because fraud was the central component of the event.

The columns "Failure to Segregate Functions" and "Lax Trading Supervision or Management/Control Problem" show that the nonfraudulent losses in Table 4.2, Panel B, for "financial institutions" are not predominantly the result of operational or supervisory problems. (This finding is naturally in contrast to cases of fraudulent trading, in which failure to segregate functions or supervisory problems are usually present.) Among these 10 cases (excluding Metallgesellschaft), there were no cases of failure to segregate front- and back-office functions. In four cases (LTCM, Amaranth, Orange County, and Askin Capital Management), lax supervision or management/control issues did not appear to be an issue. For Bankhous Herstatt and UBS, the trading activity (FX trading for Herstatt, equity derivatives related to Japanese bank convertible preference shares for UBS) was not supervised with the same rigor or integrated as fully as other activities at the bank. For Merrill Lynch's mortgage trading, the trader reportedly exceeded trading authorizations. The other three (Caisse d'Epargne, WestLB, and Calyon) may have involved lax trading supervision or other control issues.

When we turn to nonfinancial institutions (those firms for which "Primary Activity Finance or Investing" is no), we also find evidence of financial disasters that originated in normal business practices. Aracruz and Sadia speculated in the FX markets and lost large amounts, but according to a banker familiar with the Brazilian markets, this trading was relatively common and originated from standard business practices. Both firms had large export businesses and thus generated revenues in dollars versus costs in Brazilian reals. Standard business practice would be to hedge future export receipts by selling dollars forward. For many years, this trade was also a profitable speculative strategy because of the differential between Brazilian real and U.S. dollar interest rates. High Brazilian and low U.S. interest rates meant that forward FX rates implied depreciation of the real, but in fact, the real was relatively stable for a long period. This situation led many firms to move from hedging future export earnings to leveraged speculation.[79] The real depreciated dramatically starting in August 2008, which led to large trading losses. Although this depreciation did not last long, the losses were large enough that the firms were forced to close out and crystallize their losses.

Among nonfinancial institutions, even those events that did involve fraud usually originated in some way from a normal business activity. Showa Shell Sekiyu's and Kashima Oil's events probably originated in hedging import or export earnings, CITIC Pacific's event appears to have been a hedging transaction that was the wrong size, and China Aviation Oil may have started hedging jet fuel purchases.

Other Characteristics. In addition to fraud and normal business activity, two other characteristics need to be discussed.

▓ *Years over which fraud accumulated.* Events involving fraud generally also involve longer periods over which losses accumulate, which is natural because the goal of fraud is to hide losses and delay the day of reckoning. We might also think that losses over a longer period would be larger because there would be more time for losses to accumulate, but the largest-loss events in Table 4.2 (LTCM, Société Générale, and Amaranth) were actually losses over a short period. There are competing influences: Longer means more time for losses to accumulate, but larger losses come to light faster because they threaten the existence of the institution. In fact, of the three largest events, two resulted in the collapse of the institution (LTCM and Amaranth).

▓ *Failure to segregate and lax supervision.* "Failure to segregate functions" refers to the failure to separate trading and back-office or record-keeping functions, with Nick Leeson's responsibility for both trading and back-office at Barings being probably the best-known example. Although this fault has been highly publicized, it does not appear to have been a substantial factor in

---

[79] An alternative strategy, one that had the same economic impact, was for a Brazilian company to borrow in dollars (paying low U.S. interest rates) and pay the debt back out of future earnings in reals. This strategy worked well as long as the real did not depreciate substantially; if it did, it would leave the borrower with substantial foreign currency liabilities and FX losses.

most events—only 3 out of 22 (with 13 unknown or difficult to determine). One reason may be the emphasis segregation of responsibilities has been given in regulations and best practice guidelines: In recent years, firms have learned to close this gap.

"Lax trading supervision or management/control problem" refers to failure by managers to properly supervise traders or otherwise exercise control. This issue has been a factor in many events (12 out of 21, with 8 unknown and 6 difficult to determine). I have included under this rubric a wide range of problems, from the extraordinary (the behavior of Daiwa managers that eventually led to Daiwa's expulsion from the U.S. banking market) to the all too common (the failure of managers to fully understand or appreciate the risk of products or businesses that subordinates were undertaking, as appears to have been contributing factors with Union Bank of Switzerland and Merrill Lynch in 1987).

Summary. *Fraud* is a part of many financial disasters, but often it is used to cover up after losses rather than being involved in the original loss. *Nonfraud* events are almost as common as fraud-related events. Losses resulting from *normal business* characterize many events. Some of the largest, in fact, were simply bad judgment or bad luck, not involving fraud or the exceeding of trading limits or mandates. LTCM, Amaranth, Union Bank of Switzerland, and Askin Capital all seem to fall in this category.

Lax trading supervision or other *management/control problems* contributed to many incidents. Failure to separate trading and back-office functions, however, has not been as prevalent, possibly because it is such a well-recognized problem.

Lessons Learned. One valuable product of reviewing financial disasters is to learn lessons on how to better manage a firm. (And it is important to recognize that issues contributing to financial disasters are often general management issues rather than specific risk issues.) The short paper "Rogue Traders: Lies, Losses, and Lessons Learned" (Wilmer Cutler Pickering Hale and Dorr 2008) provides an excellent summary of the topic and reviews a few of the episodes considered here. The discussion is focused specifically on rogue traders (unauthorized trading involving fraud—Daiwa, Barings, AIB/Allfirst, Kidder Peabody, and Société Générale), but it is quite useful generally. Of note, the appendix provides a "lessons learned" checklist (p. 10):

A. Setting the right tone from the top: Senior management and boards must encourage a culture of compliance and responsible risk taking.

B. Senior managers must understand the complexities of the products their firms trade.

C. Strong business line supervisory controls are essential.

    D. Successful traders may require more, not less, scrutiny.

    E. Management should ensure that incentive systems do not encourage excessive risk.

    F. Vacations are a good thing [because they force somebody else to manage the positions, shedding light on any nefarious activity].

    G. Risk managers should be encouraged to challenge traders' valuations.

    H. Operations, risk management, and compliance reporting lines should be separate from the business lines.

    I. Dual or matrix reporting lines must be clear.

    J. Strong back-office controls are as essential as front-office controls.

    K. Effective risk management architecture is critical.

Systemic Financial Events

When we move from idiosyncratic to systemic financial events, we move from small potatoes to real money; although idiosyncratic losses may be measured in hundreds of millions of dollars, systemic losses are measured in hundreds of billions.

Systemic financial events come in a variety of forms: hyperinflation and currency crashes, government debt default or restructuring, and banking crises. This section touches only the surface. A wide literature covers the topic: Mackay (1932), originally published in 1841, provides an entertaining look at the South Sea Bubble in England, the Mississippi scheme in France, and the tulip mania in Holland. Kindleberger (1989) is a classic work on asset manias and crashes, and Reinhart and Rogoff (2009) is a comprehensive and instructive compendium of financial crises across 800 years and more than 60 countries.

Table 4.5 shows what Reinhart and Rogoff call the "big five" crises in advanced countries from World War II through mid-2000 (i.e., prior to the current, 2007–2009, financial crisis). Reinhart and Rogoff briefly discuss the bailout costs of financial crises. They point out that the estimates vary widely and, more importantly, that the true costs extend beyond the commonly quoted bailout costs to cover the fiscal impact of reduced tax revenue and other fiscal stimulus costs. Whatever the true costs, however, they are large. Table 4.5 shows that the 1984–91 U.S. savings and loan (S&L) crisis cost somewhere between 2.4 percent and 3.2 percent of GDP. Stated in terms of 2007 GDP (to be comparable with the losses quoted in Table 4.1), it would be roughly $340 billion to $450 billion. Compared with this amount, the individual company losses are small.

If we turn to the current, 2007–2009, financial crisis, the costs are similarly huge. Consider just Fannie Mae and Freddie Mac, which were taken over by the government in late 2008 as the subprime housing crises exploded. Fannie Mae reportedly lost $136.8 billion in the two-and-a-half years from the fourth quarter

Table 4.5. Selection of Systemic Banking Crises for Developed Countries (prior to 2007)

Country	Estimated Bailout		Note
	Upper	Lower	
Spain, 1977–1985	16.8%	5.6%	Apparently a persistent economic slump, the aftereffect of OPEC's oil price rise in the mid-1970s, and the transition to democracy led to a financial crisis—"52 banks (of 110), representing 20 percent of banking system deposits, were experiencing solvency problems."
United States (S&L crisis), 1984–1991	3.2	2.4	Financial deregulation and the aftereffects of Regulation Q led to overextension by many S&Ls. "More than 1,400 S&L's and 1,300 banks failed."
Norway, 1987–1993	4.0	2.0	"Financial deregulation undertaken during 1984–1987 led to a credit boom . . . accompanied by a boom in both residential and nonresidential real estate." Problems at small banks began in 1988. "The turmoil reached systemic proportions by October 1991, when the second and fourth largest banks had lost a considerable amount of equity."
Sweden, 1991–1994	6.4	3.6	A financial and real estate bubble developed in the 1980s. A variety of factors (led by the 1990 global slowdown) caused the bubble to burst. "Overall, 5 of the 6 largest banks, with more than 70 percent of banking system assets, experienced difficulties."
Japan, 1992–1997	24.0	8.0	A stock market and real estate bubble burst around 1990. Banks suffered from sharp declines in stock market and real estate prices.

Notes: These are the "big five" crises of developed countries from World War II through mid-2000 mentioned in Reinhart and Rogoff (2009, p. 164). The "Estimated Bailout" columns show costs as percentage of GDP (Table 10.9). The "Note" column is based on Laeven and Valencia (2008) and is supplemented with the current author's comments.

Sources: Based on Reinhart and Rogoff (2009) and Laeven and Valencia (2008).

of 2007 through the first quarter of 2010. As of May 2010, the U.S. government has provided $145 billion in support to Fannie Mae and Freddie Mac.[80] The Congressional Budget Office projects that the total cost may reach $389 billion.[81] Note that this is only a fraction of the cost for the overall U.S. financial meltdown, and the United States is only a part of the overall global damage.

Fannie Mae and Freddie Mac are also important because they are examples of the systemic nature of the incentives, costs, and policy decisions that contribute to systemic crises. Fannie and Freddie have suffered such large losses as much because they were following their congressional mandate—to subsidize the U.S. residential housing market and expand access and affordability—as because they made specific management or risk mistakes. For decades, investors assumed that an implicit U.S. guarantee (now made explicit) stood behind Fannie and Freddie paper, and investors provided funding at rates better than those other financial institutions could access. This situation skewed costs and incentives in the mortgage market, contributing to Fannie's and Freddie's large holdings and large losses and also contributing to the overall residential real estate bubble. The skewed incentives were and continue to be government policy, and these skewed incentives contributed to a systemic crisis whose costs overshadow any idiosyncratic disaster.

A number of firms that were involved in idiosyncratic events listed in Table 4.1 were also caught in the systemic crisis of 2007–2009. The losses resulting from systemic problems were many times the losses caused by idiosyncratic events.

As an example, Hypo Group Alpe Adria shows up in Table 4.1 as losing €300 million in 2004 because of a currency swap (with subsequent fraud to hide the extent of the loss). This amount pales next to Hypo's recent credit and other losses. In December 2009, the bank was taken over and rescued by the Republic of Austria. The after-tax loss for 2009 was €1,600 million, and as of early 2010, the problems were continuing. As another example, Dexia Bank suffered an idiosyncratic loss of €300 million in 2001, but losses for 2008 were €3,300 million and required state aid from Belgium, France, and Luxembourg.

---

[80] As of May 2010, according to the *New York Times* (Applebaum 2010) and Bloomberg (10 May 2010).

[81] Data as of June 2010; see www.cbo.gov/ftpdocs/108xx/doc10878/01-13-FannieFreddie.pdf.

5. Measuring Risk

What Is Risk Measurement?

This chapter is a guide to quantitative risk measurement. The topic is often referred to as "risk management," but we should remember that, as the prior chapters have argued, risk management is not about elegant quantitative techniques but, rather, is the everyday work of actually managing an organization and the risks it faces. Managing risk requires much more than simple measurement. Although measurement is necessary in a financial environment, measurement alone is not sufficient for risk management.

The quantitative tools and techniques that fall under the rubric "quantitative risk measurement" can substantially improve the management of financial firms, but the technical nature of the field can present a barrier to their effective use. The nature of the barrier is twofold. First, some of the techniques are indeed complex and can take time and effort to master even for technically trained users. Second, and often more importantly, the techniques are frequently presented as complex, arcane, and in some way mysterious. In fact, risk measurement is very simple.

The essence of risk measurement is to provide a realistic view of what could happen in the future, most particularly what could happen to the firm's profit and loss. This activity is not predicting the *specifics* of the future, such as "the firm will earn $500,000" or "it will lose $20,000," but rather providing informed judgments about the range or distribution of possible outcomes. Predicting the future in detail is not possible; learning about the range of future possibilities is not only possible but also something we do every day in all aspects of our life. We cannot predict the precise weather tomorrow, but if we are in Chicago in January, we can say with a high degree of confidence that the temperature will be between −10° and +50° F. In Honolulu, we can say with similar confidence that the temperature will *not* be within that range. Likewise, we cannot predict next year's P&L, but we can say how likely it might be to lose $100,000 versus $10 million.

Chapters 2 and 3 argued that managing risk requires understanding and living with uncertainty and randomness. It is not easy to move from thinking that "this portfolio will earn 5 percent next year" to "this portfolio will most likely earn 5 percent, but there is some chance it will earn 0 percent and even some small chance it will lose 10 percent." It is even harder to assign realistic probabilities to these events—say, a 1-in-50 chance the portfolio will lose 10 percent or more. But simply stated, that is the goal of "quantitative risk measurement"—to think carefully, in a systematic and organized way, about future uncertain outcomes and then communicate that information in a way that improves the management of the firm.

In short, quantitative risk measurement simply aims to arrive at, and then communicate, an assessment of the possible future P&L. Although a great deal of elaborate language and mathematics may be required to make this goal a reality, in the end, it all comes down to quantifying the range or distribution of possible future outcomes and communicating this information in a useful way. Throughout this chapter, I will try to emphasize this simple underlying idea. I may or may not succeed in making the explanations clear, but the reader should never forget that the underlying idea is simple, even if the techniques used are sometimes complex.

Typology of Financial Risks

Risk is the possibility of a realized P&L different from an expected or anticipated P&L, and in this sense, there is no distinction between different types of risk. Market risk, credit risk, and operational risk each entail the possibility of gains or losses different from expected. Nonetheless, the sources, circumstances, and results of risk in different parts of the business are so different that there is a real benefit in distinguishing between different risks within a financial organization. In addition, these risks are often considered separately in practice, so it is important to understand some of the nomenclature applied to each.

I distinguish among five major categories of risk:

* Market risk,
* Credit risk,
* Liquidity risk,
* Operational risk, and
* Other (legal and regulatory, business, strategic, reputational).

Market and credit risk are discussed in detail later in separate sections. They have the most space because they are often the largest in terms of potential losses but also because they are the most amenable to mathematical analysis and thus have been the most studied. The areas of liquidity, operational, and other risks, however, should not be downplayed simply because they are less amenable to analysis with sophisticated mathematical tools; for example, many serious financial mishaps can be traced to operational issues.

Market risk is the first thing that comes to mind for financial institutions—price risk associated with traded securities, assets, and financial instruments. Prices can go down as well as up, often in the worst way at the worst possible time. Stock markets provide the quintessential example of market risk: the Dow Jones index lost 23 percent on Black Monday (19 October 1987); the S&P 500 went down by 37 percent in 2008 and then up by about 26 percent in 2009; the Dow Jones lost 89 percent between 1929 and 1932 and did not recover to its highest 1929 level until 1954.[82]

Market risk is often categorized according to the underlying market instrument: equity price risk, interest rate (or fixed-income) risk, foreign exchange (FX) risk. These distinctions can be useful for institutional reasons because instruments within a market often behave in a similar way or have similar conventions, but these categorizations can also obscure similarities. From a P&L perspective, a dollar (or pound or euro) earned from equities is the same as a dollar earned from FX. The important distinguishing characteristic is how likely gains are versus losses, not the name put on the security. In measuring and managing risk, we must often look below the surface to arrive at a deeper understanding of the sources of risk.

Credit risk "is the risk that the value of a portfolio changes due to unexpected changes in the credit quality of issuers or trading partners" (McNeil, Frey, and Embrechts 2005, p. 327). Credit risk ultimately arises from defaults—either immediate or projected non-repayment of promised amounts.

Credit is an interesting case because credit can often be considered a market risk itself. A corporate bond is an example: The credit quality of the issuing company will determine the market demand for, and thus the market price of, the bond itself. Although credit risk is usually classified separately from market risk, the line between them is increasingly fuzzy, and in some cases, it can be more fruitful to consider credit as yet another market risk.

One distinction between market and credit risk might be that when a security is priced and traded in the market (as in a corporate bond or a credit default swap), it is market risk; when it is not traded (as for some bank loans or in trade settlement), it is nonmarket credit risk.

In the end, the distinction between market and credit risk is difficult to make, but credit risk arises in so many and such varied forms that it is worth considering on its own. The modeling of credit risk is often dramatically different from that of market risk. Market risk modeling usually relies on observed market prices, whereas the distribution of losses for credit risk often must be constructed from the underlying processes generating defaults. Furthermore, the horizon for credit risk is generally longer—more often measured in months or years than the days or weeks of market risk.

---

[82]See Marrison (2002, p. 4) for these plus additional examples.

Liquidity risk is very important and is one of the more difficult risks to conceptualize and measure. Liquidity risk actually comprises two distinct concepts—asset liquidity and funding liquidity. These two can interact, but it is necessary to keep them conceptually distinct, and it is unfortunate that they both go under the rubric of liquidity risk.

Funding liquidity risk, also called "cash flow risk," refers to the ability to raise or retain the debt required for financing leveraged positions, meeting margin calls, or paying fund redemptions. This issue is particularly critical for leveraged portfolios using short-term debt instruments—such as repos—that are subject to margin calls.

Asset liquidity risk refers to the ability to buy or sell in the necessary size at the prevailing market price in a timely fashion. Asset liquidity will differ, sometimes dramatically, across instruments and market conditions and at different times. Some markets—for G–7 government bonds or currencies, for example—are so deep and developed that most trades can be executed at any time with minimal impact. Other markets—for an esoteric derivative instrument or local currency emerging market bond, for example—may be active during normal times but effectively shut during market disruption.

Funding and asset liquidity risk can interact in a lethal combination. Adverse price movements, or even a turn in market sentiment, may induce margin calls or redemptions, putting pressure on funding liquidity. If the portfolio does not have sufficient cash or sources of new funding, the manager will have to sell assets. If the positions are large relative to normal market transactions or concentrated in illiquid securities, poor asset liquidity may mean that sales can be done only at very disadvantageous prices. The fall in prices may trigger further margin calls, then further asset sales, leading into a "death spiral."

A homeowner might face both funding and liquidity risk (and their interaction) when weighing whether to refinance or sell. Funding liquidity is whether one can get a mortgage, and asset liquidity is whether one can sell the house. The two problems are separate, but in tough times, they can become intertwined. For example, if a homeowner needs money, he or she can either sell the house or remortgage. If this person needs money during a financial crisis, maybe the house will not sell. If the person's credit is also bad and thus no mortgage is available, then the problem suddenly becomes serious.

Jorion (2007) summarizes it well:

> Funding liquidity risk arises when financing cannot be maintained owing to creditor or investor demands. The resulting need for cash may require selling assets. Asset liquidity risk arises when a forced liquidation of assets creates unfavorable price movements. Thus liquidity considerations should be viewed in the context of both the assets and the liabilities of the financial institution....

During episodes of systemic risk . . . liquidity evaporates. . . . Liquidity risk probably is the weakest spot of market risk management systems. (p. 333)

Operational risk is crucial but difficult to measure. Operational risk is important because operational failures appear central to many financial disasters. I would argue that given the current state of understanding, the focus should be more on managing than on measuring operational risk. We may not be able to measure it very well, but it is so critical that it cannot be ignored and must be managed nonetheless.

Even defining operational risk is difficult and in flux. The general industry consensus (incorporating guidance from Basel regulators) defines "Operational risk [as] the risk of loss resulting from inadequate or failed processes, people and systems or from external events" (Jorion 2007, p. 495). This definition is a balance between older narrow definitions (risk arising from operations or trade processing) and overly broad definitions that include everything that is not market or credit risk.

Quantitative measurement and statistical analysis of "inadequate or failed processes, people and systems" is difficult. Nonetheless, there can be substantial returns to a disciplined approach, even if it is somewhat more qualitative than that applied to market or credit risk. The Basel Committee on Banking Supervision (2003) outlines a framework for measuring operational risk that looks particularly useful.

Much can be accomplished in controlling operational risks by improving processes and procedures to reduce the frequency and severity of errors, reduce costs, and improve productivity. One primary goal should be to make processes such that it is easy for people to do the right thing and hard to do the wrong thing.[83] Furthermore, improved processes and procedures can both control operational risk and increase profits by reducing costs—for example, by making costs insensitive to trade volumes.

Other risks I group together. These other risks include such things as legal and regulatory risk, general business risk, strategic risk, and reputational risk. These risks are clearly important, but I will not discuss them in detail.

---

[83] An example of a procedure that makes it easy to do the right thing and hard to do the wrong thing would be having a bank custodian hold foundation or pension fund assets. This arrangement makes it virtually impossible for the portfolio manager to abscond with the institution's funds. The manager could give unauthorized instructions to trade, but that would only result in security x being sold and security y being bought, with only very indirect benefits to the manager, if any.

Introduction to Quantitative Risk Measurement

In Chapter 2, I discussed the definition of risk. The conclusion was that risk itself is a difficult and slippery concept, but for the purpose of financial risk management, I would define risk as *the possibility of P&L being different from what is expected or anticipated; risk is uncertainty or randomness measured by the distribution of future P&L.* The distribution or density function describes the probability of different possible outcomes.

As an example, consider two activities: the first a $10 coin toss bet (win $10 on heads, lose $10 on tails) and the second a hypothetical yield curve strategy with many possible outcomes. When graphed, these distributions would look like **Figure 5.1**. Panel A shows the two possible outcomes from the coin toss, each with probability one-half. It is a very simple distribution or density because it has only two outcomes, each with the same probability. Panel B of Figure 5.1 shows the P&L generated by a yield curve trade. It is more complicated because there are many possible outcomes—some large profits, some large losses, but mostly close to zero. The trade itself is complicated, but the graph of the outcomes is relatively straightforward—a large range of possible outcomes, having higher probability for results around zero profit and lower probability in the tails (large profit or large loss). This is the general shape of a distribution (density function) we would usually expect to see in financial applications.

The distribution function contains all the "objective" information about the random outcomes; it tells us the probability of high profits versus large losses versus average performance. Quantitative risk measurement is really nothing more than learning about and understanding the P&L distribution. If we knew everything about the P&L distribution, we would know virtually everything there is to know about the risk of the particular activity. We would not know what profit we would make tomorrow—after all, the future is always

Figure 5.1. P&L from Coin Toss Bet and Hypothetical Yield Curve Strategy

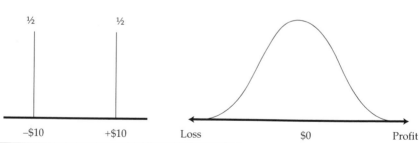

©2011 The Research Foundation of CFA Institute

uncertain—but we could determine how likely it is that we could make a given profit. The distribution would not remove our uncertainty, but it would put bounds on that uncertainty. In fact, this is the most we can ask for because the future is always uncertain and contingent.

If we "know" the P&L distribution, we know virtually everything there is to know about the risk of the particular activity. By "knowing" the distribution, I actually mean more than just having a graph, such as Figure 5.1; we need to understand the sources of risk, what generates the distribution. Nonetheless, the distribution itself, as in Figure 5.1, is the first, and most important, step.

It is easy to say that risk measurement is merely determining the distribution of P&L, but determining the distribution can be very hard to actually do. Practical and theoretical problems make risk measurement difficult, often extremely difficult. The coin toss example is simple: There are two outcomes and only two, and we know the probability of those outcomes. For the yield curve strategy, there will be many potential outcomes. Just determining the range of possibilities may be difficult. And coming up with reasonable estimates of probabilities is even more difficult. Unlike a coin toss bet, we generally do not *know* the probabilities for a financial trade or portfolio. Maybe we can arrive at good estimates for the probabilities, but we will never know the probabilities for certain.

How Much Higher Will Interest Rates Be Tomorrow?

To see how difficult it can be to determine the probabilities for financial matters, and even the range of possible outcomes, consider the following: Is it reasonable to think that one-week interest rates will rise by 5 percentage points (i.e., 500 bps) in just two days? Certainly not. Unless, that is, you are sitting in London on 15 September 1992, the day before "Black Wednesday," when the British government took sterling out of the exchange rate mechanism and George Soros made his reputed $1 billion profit betting against sterling. One-week rates went from just below 10 percent on the 15th to 15 percent on the 17th, then back to 9.19 percent on the 23rd. It was certainly an interesting time to trade the U.K. markets, but determining the range of possible outcomes for the next day's markets was difficult.

Summary Measures: Volatility (Standard Deviation) and VaR.

Although the P&L distribution shown in Figure 5.1 provides a full description of risk, it is rare that we will use the full distribution in practice. Usually, we will use summary measures that tell us things about the distribution—because the full distribution is too difficult to measure, or because it is too complicated to easily grasp, or because we simply want a convenient way to summarize the distribution.

In statistics, the first two features of a distribution that one focuses on are the *location*, on the one hand, and *scale* or *dispersion*, on the other. Location quantifies the central tendency or some typical value, and scale or dispersion quantifies the spread of possible values around the central value. For risk, the most important characteristic is the dispersion or spread of the distribution, primarily because the dispersion of P&L is large relative to the typical value.

The summary measures that we use are often called "risk measures": numbers that summarize important characteristics of the distribution. We must remember, however, that although summary measures are extraordinarily useful, they are to some degree arbitrary, more useful in some circumstances and less useful in others. "Risk" itself is not a precise concept and depends on investor preferences; different investors may view the risk of the same investment differently. Because the property we are trying to measure ("risk") is somewhat vague, the summary measures themselves will, of necessity, also be somewhat arbitrary. The statistician Cramer's remarks regarding location and scale measures are appropriate here: "Each measure has advantages and disadvantages of its own, and a measure which renders excellent service in one case may be more or less useless in another" (Cramer 1974, pp. 181–182). Using these quantitative measures requires common sense, experience, and judgment.

The most familiar measures of location and scale are the mean and standard deviation (commonly called "volatility" and denoted σ in finance). An example of a distribution and its mean and standard deviation are shown for a hypothetical yield curve strategy in **Figure 5.2**. Panel A shows a lower dispersion (less spread out) distribution, and Panel B shows a higher dispersion (more spread out) distribution. The mean is zero for both, but the standard deviation is higher for the distribution in Panel B.

The standard deviation (volatility) is one dispersion measure relevant for risk measurement. The standard deviation is well known from statistics and is widely used, but it is by no means the only summary measure we could use. Value at risk, or VaR, is another popular summary measure. The VaR is simply a quantile—that is, the point on the horizontal axis so that some fixed fraction of the distribution is below that point. The concept is easiest to explain graphically, and **Figure 5.3** shows the 5 percent quantile. The point Y is chosen so that the area to the left of Y is 5 percent of the total area representing the distribution. The distance Y from the mean is the 5 percent VaR. VaR, like the standard deviation, is just one particular summary measure of dispersion of the distribution.

Figure 5.2. Location and Scale (Standard Deviation) for P&L from Hypothetical Yield Curve Strategy

A. Low Dispersion (small standard deviation)

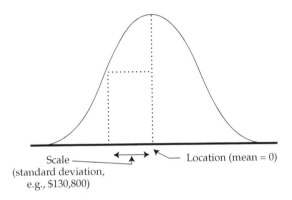

Scale ——— (standard deviation, e.g., $130,800)   Location (mean = 0)

B. Higher Dispersion (larger standard deviation)

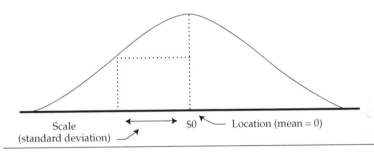

Scale (standard deviation) $0   Location (mean = 0)

Volatility (standard deviation) is defined as the average of squared deviations from the mean. That is, for every possible profit, we calculate the distance from the mean, square that distance, and take the average of the squares (finally taking the square root):

$$\text{Volatility} = \sqrt{\text{Average}(\text{Profit} - \text{Mean})^2}.$$

The volatility is effectively an average of deviations from the mean. The greater the dispersion around the mean, the larger the volatility will be.

VaR is a quantile of the distribution and is summarized graphically in Figure 5.3. A quantile is characterized by two numbers: first, a probability level Z defined by the user, and second, a resulting level of profit or loss Y. The definition for VaR_Z is as follows: *the P&L level Y such that there is a probability Z that the P&L will be worse than Y and a probability 1 − Z that it will be better*

Figure 5.3. Five Percent VaR for P&L from Hypothetical Yield Curve Strategy

A. Low Dispersion (small VaR)

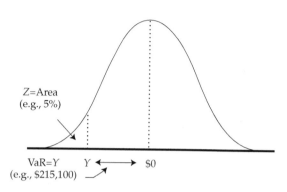

Z=Area
(e.g., 5%)

VaR=Y   Y ⟵⟶ $0
(e.g., $215,100)

B. Higher Dispersion (larger VaR)

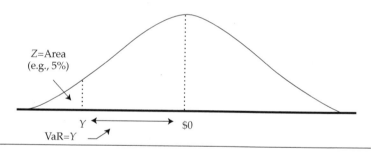

Z=Area
(e.g., 5%)

Y ⟵⟶ $0
VaR=Y

than Y. The P&L is measured over some fixed time horizon (for example, one day). In Figure 5.3, we can see that the $VaR_{5\%}$ is the point on the horizontal axis chosen so that the probability, the area under the curve below Y, is 5 percent. The idea behind VaR is simple: The level of loss is specified in such a way that a worse loss happens with a predefined probability.[84]

The volatility (standard deviation) and the VaR each summarize the dispersion of the distribution in their own way. For nice, symmetrical, well-behaved distributions, such as those shown in Figures 5.2 and 5.3, they can be used almost interchangeably. In Figure 5.2, we could ask what is the probability

---

[84]In the literature, the probability level chosen can be either the probability that loss will be worse than Y (my Z) or the probability that loss will be better than Y (my 1 – Z). Jorion (2007), for example, uses 1 – Z. For clarity, I will generally quote both Z and 1 – Z as in "5 percent/95 percent VaR."

that the P&L is less than the standard deviation—what is the probability to the left of -1σ? For a normal (Gaussian) distribution, the probability will be 15.9 percent. In other words, we could think of the volatility as the 15.9 percent/ 84.1 percent VaR. Alternatively, we can note that for a normal (Gaussian) distribution, the probability to the left of -1.64σ is 5 percent so that -1.64σ is the 5 percent/95 percent VaR. For a normal distribution, volatility and VaR are direct transforms of each other and thus we can move easily from volatility to VaR and back, and in this sense they can be used interchangeably.[85]

It is important to remember that volatility and VaR are merely summary measures and that each may be more useful or less depending on circumstances. There is nothing magical about either one, although we might sometimes be tempted to think so. They merely summarize the distribution, albeit in somewhat different ways—either by looking at an average of deviations from the mean (volatility) or at a point on the tail of the distribution (VaR). Indeed, for well-behaved symmetrical distributions, they can be used almost interchangeably, and for a normal (Gaussian) distribution, we can easily convert from one to the other.

For any summary measure, the underlying P&L distribution (say, the one shown in Figure 5.2 or 5.3) is measured for some given time horizon (say, one day). The P&L will then be the P&L over one day, and the volatility or VaR calculated from the distribution will also be for one day. Alternatively, the P&L might be for, say, one week or 10 days, in which case the volatility and VaR would be for one week or 10 days. It is extraordinarily useful to have a simple rule to translate from 1-day volatility and VaR to one-week or 10-day volatility and VaR. The standard way to go from one time period to another is to scale by the square root of the time:

$$\text{Volatility}(1\text{ week}) = \text{Volatility}(1\text{ day}) \times \sqrt{5} \quad [\text{there are 5 business days in a week}]$$

$$\text{Volatility}(10\text{ days}) = \text{Volatility}(1\text{ day}) \times \sqrt{10} \quad [10\text{ days vs. 1 day}].$$

This time translation or time scaling is widely used and reasonably reliable, but it should be taken as a useful rule of thumb rather than a mathematical law because it assumes return independence across time, which is reasonably realistic but may not be absolutely correct.

---

[85] A third summary measure, which I will only mention here and is more fully discussed in Coleman (forthcoming), is expected shortfall. For most cases, the expected shortfall is just the average loss conditional on the loss being worse than the VaR: *Expected shortfall* = $E[Loss|Loss < Y]$. In Figure 5.3, VaR is the point Y, and the expected shortfall is the average of all losses Y and worse. In other words, the expected shortfall takes account not just of the point Y but also of how much worse losses could be.

Normal Distribution. The normal distribution is commonly used to represent P&L distributions. The normal distribution is well known and easy to work with, and in many respects it works well. It is not perfect, and indeed we will see later that it misses some important aspects of observed P&L distributions, but the normal is so useful and so widely used that we will start with it.

The normal distribution is a bell-shaped symmetrical distribution. It is characterized by two parameters, the mean and the standard deviation. The mean gives the location—where the distribution is centered. The standard deviation gives the scale—the spread or dispersion. For most risk measurement purposes, we are primarily concerned with the dispersion as measured by the standard deviation (or volatility) and will ignore the mean or assume it is zero.[86] **Figure 5.4** shows a stylized version of the normal probability density function.

We are most interested in the probability that an observation will be within a certain distance of the mean, say ±1σ or ±2σ. The probability that an observation will be within ±2σ is 95 percent, and the probability it will be below −2σ is 2.5 percent.[87] If the P&L is normally distributed, then we can say that the probability the P&L will be below −2σ is 2.5 percent. The probability it will be below −1σ is about 16 percent.

Figure 5.4. Normal Distribution

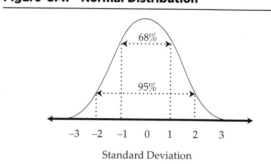

<hr>

[86]In many cases, the mean is so small relative to the volatility that we can ignore it. For the S&P 500 Index, the daily standard deviation is roughly 1.2 percent and the average daily return is only 0.03 percent (calculated from Ibbotson Associates data for 1926–2007, which show that the annualized mean and standard deviation for monthly capital appreciation returns are 7.41 percent and 19.15 percent, respectively).
[87]The probability it will be outside of ±2σ is 95 percent, and symmetry ensures there is a 2.5 percent probability it will be below −2σ and a 2.5 percent probability it will be above +2σ.

©2011 The Research Foundation of CFA Institute

Comments regarding VaR and Other Summary Measures.

There are many critiques of volatility and VaR, many that are not justified. Some commentators have said that VaR is useless and even a fraud. In my experience, these views often fall at one of two extremes:

- Pro-VaR: It is the silver bullet that answers all risk measurement questions.

- Anti-VaR: It is at best useless, more often misleading or worse.

As often happens, the truth is closer to a Hegelian synthesis of the two views: VaR (and quantitative risk measurement more generally) can provide useful information but has definite limitations. When properly understood and appropriately applied, VaR provides information and insight, but when VaR is misapplied or misunderstood, it can certainly be misleading.

VaR is often referred to as the "worst-case loss" or "statistically worst-case loss." This is a horribly misleading term and misleading idea. By definition, there is a probability that losses will be worse than the VaR. Furthermore, no matter what value one might choose as the "statistically worst-case loss," sometime, somewhere, it will be worse. In reality, VaR is best thought of as measuring outcomes that, although out of the ordinary, are still reasonably likely and not "worst-case" possibilities. The most reasonable statement I have seen comes from the excellent paper by Litterman (1996, footnote 1): "We think of this [VaR measured as one-day, once-per-year or $Z = 1/250$] not as a 'worst case,' but rather as a regularly occurring event with which we should be comfortable" (p. 74).

VaR is a measure of the tail of the distribution. Because there is large variability and uncertainty in tail events, VaR must be used with special caution, particularly when the probability Z is low. The lower the probability Z—say, going from 5 percent/95 percent to 0.1 percent/99.9 percent—the more careful one should be. Tail events are (by their nature) rare and thus hard to measure, and the farther out one goes in the tail, the more rare they become. It is easy to see how and why this is the case. Consider one year's worth of daily data. Roughly speaking, the 5 percent/95 percent VaR corresponds to the 12th-worst daily P&L out of the year (the 12th lowest out of 250 days). In a sense, one has 12 observations and so can be somewhat confident in estimating the 5 percent/95 percent VaR from one year's data. Consider instead the 0.4 percent/99.6 percent VaR, which corresponds roughly to the worst of the 250 days, or the 0.1 percent/99.9 percent, which is "worse than" the worst day. It should be obvious that trying to get an estimate of either of these using one year's worth of daily data is going to be imprecise. When moving from the 5 percent/95 percent VaR to the 0.1 percent/99.9 percent VaR, the reliability of any estimate will go down; one should have less confidence in the VaR estimate and should use it far more cautiously.

Any estimate of volatility or VaR is based on how the portfolio would have behaved under certain historical conditions. Such a historically based number may not predict how the portfolio will behave in the future. As a result, VaR and volatility are often criticized as "backward looking," but this criticism misses the point. Understanding how the portfolio would have behaved under past circumstances provides valuable information and insight. Understanding the past is the first step toward understanding what might happen in the future; as George Santayana said, "Those who cannot remember the past are condemned to repeat it."

Volatility and VaR each have their strengths and weaknesses. Volatility uses all the observations (a good thing). It is particularly useful when the distribution is symmetrical, the focus is mostly on the central part of the distribution, and the extremes in the tails are either well behaved or not of primary interest. Volatility will be less useful for a nonsymmetrical (skewed) distribution or if the focus is particularly on the tails of the distribution. For example, consider a distribution such as that shown in **Figure 5.5**, which is nonsymmetrical and has a fat left tail. The volatility will be an average of all deviations, including the relatively moderate positive upper tail together with the small number of much more extreme losses in the left part of the tail. In this case, the volatility may not provide a good representation of the left tail; that is, volatility may understate the risk of large losses.

VaR focuses specifically on the tails of the distribution, a good thing. VaR is popular as a risk measure precisely because it provides a succinct summary of large losses (tail events) in a manner that is simple to understand and explain. The units are P&L in terms of dollars or returns, exactly the units that a trader, manager, or investor would use. The idea of VaR, that 5 percent of the time one should expect to see losses at the level of the $VaR_{5\%}$ or worse, is easy to explain. As Jorion (2007) says: "[VaR's] greatest advantage is that it summarizes risk in a single, easy-to-understand number" (p. 105).

Figure 5.5. Nonsymmetrical Distribution with Fat Tail

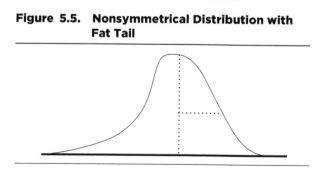

Unfortunately, this simplicity is also VaR's greatest weakness. Risk can never be fully summarized by a single number. There is always a strong temptation to take such a number as the final word when, in reality, it should be only a start toward a deeper understanding of the variability and uncertainty inherent in future outcomes. A temptation exists when using VaR to fall into the "illusion of certainty," even believing that losses will be no worse than the VaR. Furthermore, as mentioned earlier, tail events are particularly hard to measure, which makes VaR for small Z (far out in the tail) difficult to measure and any estimates inherently imprecise.

A benefit of VaR is that it will capture the asymmetry of a distribution such as the one in Figure 5.5. VaR focuses on the lower tail, but there will be distributions for which VaR is not ideal. Consider **Figure 5.6**: The distribution in Panel A has a thin lower tail below the VaR versus Panel B, in which the tail extends far out to the left. The VaR is the same in both, but there is more risk of extreme losses with the distribution in Panel B. (In this case, the expected shortfall may give a better representation of the risk.) The point here is not to argue that either volatility or VaR is particularly flawed but, rather, to point out that with any risk measure one must use caution, applying judgment and common sense. Volatility or VaR will tell us something about the distribution, but as with any summary measure, it may hide as well as reveal information.

Standard Trading Conditions vs. Extreme Events. Both volatility and VaR are widely used in the finance industry. There are two related but somewhat divergent uses for these measures, and highlighting these two uses can clarify how and why we use them. Volatility and VaR are used for one or both purposes:

- To standardize, aggregate, and analyze risk across disparate assets (or securities, trades, portfolios) under standard or usual trading conditions.
- To measure "tail risk" or extreme events.

Risk measurement often focuses on the latter—tail events—but it is equally important to focus on risk under standard or usual trading conditions. Standardizing and analyzing risk across disparate assets and large portfolios provides information necessary for understanding and managing risk and P&L under standard trading conditions, which are, by definition, most of the time. Furthermore, analyzing risk under usual trading conditions will provide valuable clues to performance under more extreme conditions.

The standardization and aggregation of risk across disparate assets and portfolios provided much of the original impetus for the development and adoption of VaR at J.P. Morgan in the late 1980s and early 1990s. Dennis Weatherstone, J.P. Morgan's chairman, needed to understand risk across the

Figure 5.6. Two Distributions with Same VaR but Different Tails

A. Distribution with Thin Tail, Small Expected Shortfall

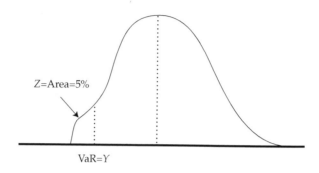

Z=Area=5%

VaR=Y

B. Distribution with Fat Tail, Large Expected Shortfall

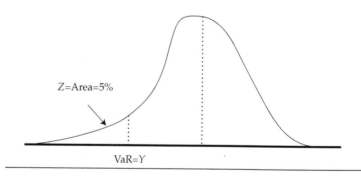

Z=Area=5%

VaR=Y

various divisions and products of the bank.[88] Weatherstone came from the FX trading desk and had a good intuitive grasp of risk, but he needed some way to quickly and easily compare risks that he was not so intimately familiar with. VaR and volatility provided the tools he needed.

To see how and why volatility and VaR can aid in comparing and understanding disparate assets, consider two trades: owning $20 million of a 10-year U.S. Treasury bond (the on-the-run as of January 2009, which was the 3.75 percent on 15 November 2018) versus a €7 million long futures position in the CAC 40 index (when the $:€ was 1.30 so that €7 million corresponded to $9.10 million). These are the positions considered in Chapter 1. They are, however, very different positions: The first is a straightforward purchase of a simple bond

---

[88] See, for example, Nocera (2009).

denominated in U.S. dollars, and the second is a derivatives position in a euro-denominated equity index with no up-front investment. One is a traditional security, the other a derivative security; one is fixed income, the other equity. Which is more risky? How can we compare and aggregate the risk of these two quite disparate trades? We cannot look at the nominal amount invested because the bond is a $20 million investment and the futures position involves roughly zero investment. They are in different currencies and different asset classes. Furthermore, any trader or manager with extensive experience in one would not be likely to have deep familiarity with the other, so relying just on experience and common sense will likely not work.

Both trades, however, have one common denominator: the P&L. Money is money, profits are profits, and losses are directly comparable between the two. (One must, of course, remember to express both in the same currency, either dollars or euros.) **Figure 5.7** shows the P&L distributions for these two trades, both expressed in dollars. The distribution for the U.S. bond in Panel A is narrower (less dispersed) than for the CAC index in Panel B. The daily volatility for the bond is $130,800, and for the CAC index futures, it is $230,800.[89] This figure provides an easy and direct comparison between the two. Panel C shows the two distributions overlaid, and we can say that the CAC futures position is more risky because the distribution is more dispersed (and both are centered around zero).

These distributions are relatively well behaved (not too far from normal or Gaussian), and for comparison of everyday behavior, the volatilities give a very good idea of the relative riskiness of the two positions. The CAC futures position is more risky because it has higher volatility, $230,800 versus $130,800 for the bond.[90] We could equally well use the VaR, something like the 5 percent/95 percent VaR, which is not too far out in the tails, and we would get the same answer.[91] By no means does this analysis tell us everything we need to know about the positions, but it is an enormous step toward fuller knowledge. And it certainly tells us more than simply knowing that it is $20 million in bonds versus €7 million in futures.

---

[89]We will not worry for the moment how these are calculated; just take it on faith that these numbers are, more or less, correct. How volatility and VaR are calculated is discussed in a later section.

[90]The CAC futures are more risky when holding $20 million of the bond and €7 million of the futures. If we held $40 million of the bond, the bond position would be more risky—scaling (size of positions) is all important.

[91]The 5 percent/95 percent VaR for the bond is about $214,500, and for the CAC position, it is about $379,000.

Figure 5.7.   P&L Distribution for Bond and Equity Futures Compared

A. P&L Distribution for Bond (standard deviation $130,800)

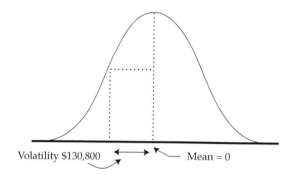

B. P&L Distribution for Equity Futures (standard deviation $230,800)

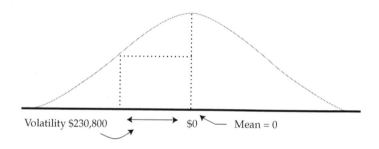

C. P&L Distributions for Bond and Equity Futures

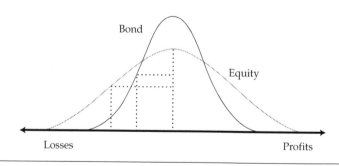

Volatility and VaR are also good as tools for aggregating disparate risks into an overall number. We could ask for the P&L distribution for a portfolio of the two trades combined: $20 million of U.S. bonds plus €7 million of CAC index futures. Although these assets are very different, money is money and we can combine the P&L distributions to get an aggregate P&L for the portfolio. Combining the P&Ls may not be easy, and later I will discuss exactly how it is done using the volatility and VaR, but what matters for now is that the distribution of the overall P&L is what we really care about. How dispersed is the P&L for the combined portfolio? What is the volatility or VaR for the combined portfolio? This analysis will give us a good idea of the risk for the combined portfolio and the risk relative to the individual assets.

When we do the calculations, we find that the volatility for the combined portfolio is about $297,000, which is more than either asset alone ($130,800 for the bond and $230,800 for the equity index) but less than the sum of the two assets on their own ($361,600). We would expect that the combined portfolio is less risky than the sum of the two assets on their own because U.S. bonds and French equities should provide some diversification benefit. Some days when bonds go down, equities go up, and vice versa, so that the two assets combined provide some diversification. The portfolio volatility is $297,000 versus $361,600 for the sum of the assets individually, which gives us a measure of the degree of diversification.

We can see that volatility and VaR are extraordinarily useful for comparing and aggregating the risk of disparate assets, but we must never forget that these are not substitutes for true understanding of risks. Consider Weatherstone and J.P. Morgan again: "Weatherstone had been a trader himself; he understood both the limits and the value of VaR. It told him things he hadn't known before. He could use it to help him make judgments" (Nocera 2009). But VaR alone was not the answer. In general, volatility and VaR are valuable tools for comparing across products, but they are no substitute for good judgment and true understanding.

We have been considering the comparison and aggregation of risk under standard trading conditions, but VaR is as often used for the second purpose—measuring extreme or tail events. In this context, VaR is sometimes referred to as the "statistically worst-case loss," but as I argued earlier, this is a horribly misleading idea. VaR should not be viewed as a "worst-case loss" but rather as a periodically occurring event that we should be comfortable with. We should think of VaR as providing a scale for the possible loss, not a maximum-loss or worst-case scenario. We also must remember that, by their nature, tail events are rare, so measuring tail events is inherently difficult and open to large errors and uncertainty. As a result, when applied in this second sense, VaR must be used cautiously and any conclusions treated with care. I will have more to say about measuring tail events in later sections.

These two uses of summary risk measures can never be precisely separated, but the conceptual differentiation clarifies some of the uses, benefits, and limitations of volatility and VaR. For usual or normal trading conditions, there are standard statistical and quantitative techniques, and the interpretation of results is relatively straightforward. Using volatility and assuming normality or linearity of the portfolio are often acceptable when considering the central part of the distribution, meaning that simple and computationally efficient techniques can be used. Measuring tail events, in contrast, is delicate, and the appropriate statistical and quantitative techniques are often difficult. In the tails, normality is generally not an appropriate assumption and more complex statistical assumptions and more sophisticated quantitative, numerical, and computational techniques must be applied. The inherent variability of tail events is generally higher than for the central part of the distribution, and uncertainty caused by estimation error and model error is larger. As a result, the estimation of VaR or other summary measures for tail events is inherently more difficult, and the use and interpretation of results more problematic.

Methods for Estimating Volatility and VaR

The basic idea behind estimating volatility and VaR is very simple: Measure the P&L distribution by looking at the past, and assume that it will be more or less the same in the future. Although this is simple to say, many details make it difficult in practice. Three approaches are commonly used in the industry: *parametric*, *historical simulation*, and *Monte Carlo*.

Each method has pros and cons, and within the risk measurement community, the debates can be heated. In the end, however, there is no best method that works in all situations. Properly applied in appropriate circumstances, each has its own place.

The three methods share a number of features. First, it is useful to think of the P&L (changes in portfolio value) as resulting from two components:

- External market risk factors
- Positions—that is, the firm's holdings and the security characteristics that determine the sensitivity to risk factors

Decomposing P&L in this way is useful for a couple of reasons. First, the distinction separates components that are external to the firm (market risk factors) from components that are under the control of the firm (positions). Market risk factors are generally independent of a firm's actions, and *distributions* of these factors generally do not change dramatically over short periods (such as days or weeks).[92] Regarding positions, a firm chooses whether and how much of a security to buy or sell. Furthermore, a firm's holdings can change frequently. It is thus quite fruitful to treat market risk factors and security holdings separately.

The second reason for distinguishing risk factors from positions is that multiple securities will often depend on the same market risk factors. For example, different bonds all depend on yields or the yield curve in the same way, and different equities may all have a beta to the same equity index (say, the S&P 500). When considering a portfolio with many holdings, this observation not only simplifies calculations but also clarifies the manner in which the portfolio risk depends on market risks.

The three methods differ in how they treat the distributions of external market risk factors and how changes in market risk factors are translated into changes in portfolio value.

There is considerable debate on the pros and cons of alternate methods, but we should never forget that we can only *estimate* volatility and VaR; we will never have the "true" value. Indeed, I would argue that there is no "true" value because there is no fixed and unchanging P&L distribution. We are not in a repeated game of chance; tomorrow's P&L is in some respects a one-time event (like tomorrow's weather). The world evolves, and there is no fixed unchanging probability distribution that we could label as the "true" distribution. We are not in the realm of pure frequency-type probability. We can look at history to measure what the distribution has been in the past. We can do our best to estimate what the distribution of tomorrow's P&L will be, but the future will always hold surprises for us. The alternative methods for obtaining volatility and VaR are simply alternative estimation strategies and should be judged by their usefulness. In different circumstances and for different portfolios, one will be better than another, but there is no single approach that always works.

The three methods share a number of features. As mentioned earlier, it is useful to think of the P&L (changes in portfolio value) as resulting from two components:

- External market risk factors
- Position holdings and security characteristics that determine the sensitivity to risk factors

---

[92] I say "generally" because sometimes it seems that the market moves almost overnight from tranquil to panic mode.

The decomposition is very useful, but that is not to say that it is always easy to actually measure and use these components. Take the most basic question: What is the position or asset holding? We might think this question is simple because it just means, for example, do we hold $20 million or $30 million of the bond? Surely this is an easy question. But in a large organization with many trading desks taking positions—positions that may change frequently during a day and with disparate systems for booking and settling those trades that may not talk to each other in real time—simply reconciling, summing, and netting the holdings may not be trivial.[93] For more complex products, we add to this problem the difficulty of modeling the asset sensitivity to risk factors and estimating the volatility of risk factors, and we begin to see why estimating portfolio volatility and VaR is difficult in practice.

Exhibit 5.1 lays out in tabular format some of the differences and similarities, and some of the strengths and weaknesses, for the three alternative approaches.[94]

One important detail that I want to mention is the relationship between volatility and VaR for the parametric or normal approach. For the parametric approach, we generally estimate the volatility instead of the VaR directly. Because we assume that the P&L distribution is normal (Gaussian), however, it is easy to derive the VaR from the volatility. We can calculate the level of losses Y corresponding to any chosen probability Z by simply looking the answer up in a table for the normal distribution. **Figure 5.8** helps explain the idea. Panel A shows a normal distribution and the volatility (standard deviation). Panel B shows the same normal distribution but with the 5 percent/95 percent VaR drawn in. The VaR is farther out on the left tail than the volatility, but the 5 percent/95 percent VaR is always the same multiplicative factor: 1.64 times the volatility. For the normal distribution, the 5 percent VaR (called the 5 percent quantile in statistics) is always 1.64 times farther out than the volatility. That is, the 5 percent/95 percent VaR is 1.64 standard deviations from the mean, and the volatility is, by definition, one standard deviation from the mean. The 1 percent/99 percent VaR is 2.33 standard deviations from the mean, or 2.33 × volatility. Thus, when the volatility estimate is $130,800 (and crucially, the distribution is assumed to be normal), the 5 percent/95 percent VaR is 1.64 × 130,800 or $215,100 and the 1 percent/99 percent VaR is $304,800.

---

[93] Experience has taught me that simply getting reliable data on holdings can be a substantive hurdle in implementing a first-class risk measurement system.

[94] See Coleman (forthcoming) for more detail on these three approaches.

Exhibit 5.1. Comparison of Parametric, Historical Simulation, and Monte Carlo Approaches

Item	Parametric	Historical Simulation	Monte Carlo
Market risk factors	Parametric distribution (almost always normal) Estimate variance–covariance (volatility) using historical data	Empirical (historical) distribution from chosen past period	Parametric distribution (often but not necessarily normal) Estimate parameters usually from historical data Generate Monte Carlo realizations of market risk factors
Security sensitivity/ revaluation	Linear sensitivity (for normal risk factors, simply matrix multiply variance–covariance by delta)	Usually full revaluation of securities using historical values of risk factors	Usually full revaluation of securities using simulated values of risk factors
Speed of computation	Good	Fair	Poor
Ability to capture nonlinearity	Poor	Good	Good
Ability to capture nonnormality	Poor	Good	Fair
Pros	Simple, quick, relatively transparent	Captures nonnormality of historical risk factor distribution Captures nonlinearity of security sensitivity	Captures nonlinearity of security sensitivity well
Cons	Normality assumption for market risk factors Linearity for security sensitivity These may not be appropriate for some purposes	Computationally more difficult than parametric. Results may be sensitive to historical period in a less transparent manner than parametric or Monte Carlo. Potentially larger sampling variability.	Computationally difficult. Usually does not capture non-normality.

Figure 5.8. Volatility and VaR for Normal Distribution

A. Volatility (standard deviation)

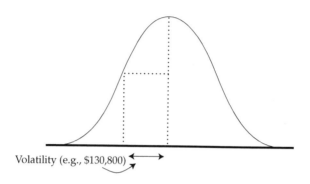

B. VaR

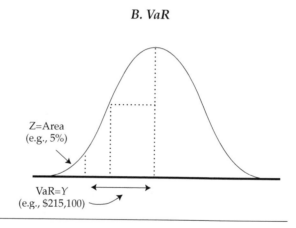

Techniques and Tools for Tail Events

The most difficult and vexing problem in quantitative risk measurement is trying to quantify tail or extreme events. Tail events are important because large losses are particularly significant and VaR is often used to quantify the likelihood of large losses. The probability level Z is chosen low, say 1 percent or 0.1 percent, to produce a low probability that losses will be worse than the VaR and a high probability that they will be better. **Figure 5.9** shows how a low level for Z implies that the VaR measures the left-hand tail of the distribution. Using VaR in this manner requires focusing on the tail of the distribution.

Measuring tail events is difficult for two fundamental reasons. First, tail or extreme events are by their nature rare and thus difficult to measure. By

Figure 5.9. VaR for Low Probability Level Z

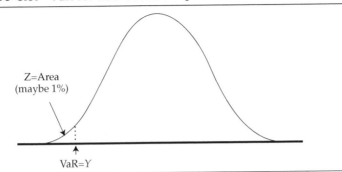

Z=Area
(maybe 1%)

VaR=Y

definition, we do not see many rare events, so it is difficult to make reliable measurements of them and to form judgments about them. Second, because of the scanty evidence, we are often pushed toward making assumptions about the tails of distributions (extreme events), but simple and common assumptions are often not appropriate. Most importantly, the assumption of normality is often not very good far out in the tails. Although rare events are rare, they do occur, and measurements across different periods, markets, and securities show that in many cases extreme events occur more often than they would if the P&L behaved according to the normal distribution in the tails. This does not mean the normal distribution is a bad choice when looking at the central part of the distribution, but it does provide evidence that it can be a poor approximation when examining extreme events.

One example, among many, of the non-normal nature of extreme events is given in the beginning sections of Beirlant, Schoutens, and Segers (2005). They look at the number of large negative returns for the Dow Jones Industrial Average for the period 1954–2004. There were 10 log returns of −5.82 percent or worse (out of 51 years, or roughly 12,500 days), shown in **Table 5.1**. Let us assume that the volatility (standard deviation) of log returns is 25 percent annualized, or 1.58 percent daily.[95] Using this estimate for volatility, we can calculate how many standard deviations away from the mean each move is, which is also shown in Table 5.1 in the column "No. Sigma (Z-score)."

With annualized volatility of 25 percent, a move of −5.82 percent is 3.68σ from the mean. Now we can ask how likely it would be to observe 10 down moves worse than −3.68σ from the mean in 50 years of daily returns *if the distribution were normal*. Even with the high 25 percent estimate of volatility, the probability of a single observation from a normal distribution being −3.68σ

---

[95]Beirlant, Schoutens, and Segers (2005) show that daily volatility estimated over a three-year horizon is usually somewhat less than 25 percent, so 25 percent is a high but not outlandish estimate.

Table 5.1. Ten Largest Down Moves of the Dow, 1954–2004

Date	Close	Log Return	No. Sigma (Z-Score)
19 Oct 1987	1,738.74	−25.63%	−16.22
26 Oct 1987	1,793.93	−8.38	−5.30
27 Oct 1997	7,161.15	−7.45	−4.72
17 Sep 2001	8,920.70	−7.40	−4.68
13 Oct 1989	2,569.26	−7.16	-4.53
8 Jan 1988	1,911.31	−7.10	−4.49
26 Sep 1955	455.56	−6.77	−4.28
31 Aug 1998	7,539.07	−6.58	−4.16
28 May 1962	576.93	−5.88	−3.72
14 Apr 2000	10,305.77	−5.82	−3.68

Source: Based on Beirlant, Schoutens, and Segers (2005, Table 1).

from the mean or worse is tiny—only 0.0117 percent. But we have roughly 12,500 days, so the likelihood of observing one or several such moves in such a long period will be much higher. The probability of observing one or more such moves out of 12,500 days would be roughly 77 percent; two such moves, 43 percent. But the probability of observing 10 or more moves would be minuscule—0.0003 percent.[96] We can continue—for example, asking what is the probability of five or more moves worse than −4.53σ (assuming normality), which turns out to be less than 0.000006 percent. In every case, the probability of observing what is shown in Table 5.1 is minuscule.

We should not get carried away, however. The probabilities implied by a normal distribution do indeed fall off far too quickly given the observations in Table 5.1. The probability of observing 10 moves of −3.68σ or worse is 0.0003 percent, which is miniscule. But the loss levels do not fall off so quickly. For a loss only 20 percent lower, −2.944σ, we are almost sure to observe 10 moves (the probability we will see 10 or more moves of −2.944σ or worse is 99.6 percent). This result seems extraordinary—that the probability of 10 moves of −2.944σ or worse is 0.996 whereas the probability of 10 moves of −3.68σ or worse is 0.000003—but it happens to be true. The probabilities fall off very quickly as the loss levels get worse, but it does not take large changes in loss levels to cause very large falloffs in probability.

---

[96]This result goes back to the case of Bernoulli trials discussed in Chapter 2. We have 12,500 Bernoulli trials (days), with the probability of success (move worse than −3.68σ) being 0.0117 percent. The distribution of multiple successes will be binomial, with the probabilities as quoted in the text.

Figure 5.10 shows the problem with normal tails from a different perspective, showing, on the one hand, the expected frequency of events in the tail (excluding the 1987 crash for now) under the assumption of normality versus, on the other hand, the empirical frequency. The line represents a normal distribution (assuming 12,500 days in total), and the dots show the actual observations. We can see that the normal distribution gives far too few extreme events.

Collecting 51 years of daily data may not be practical for most applications, but it does show us that if we want to consider extreme events, we need to address the issue of fat tails and distributions. Treating the tails as if they are normal leads to thinking such large moves are much less likely than they actually are. (It also leads to guffaws when a trader says, "We are having a 10 standard deviation move every day," when what the trader should really say is that "events are not behaving according to the normal distribution, with more large moves than predicted by normality.")

Figure 5.10. Empirical and Normal Distribution for Tail of Dow Changes, 1954–2004

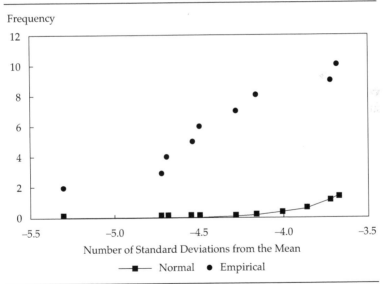

Note: Frequency is the number of days with large down moves (calculated or observed) out of 12,500 days. These observations are from Table 5.2, derived from Beirlant, Schoutens, and Segers (2005, Table 1), but excluding the October 1987 observation (which is far to the left at −16σ).

Broadly speaking, three approaches can be taken when dealing with tail events:

- Simple rules of thumb;
- Alternative but tractable distributional assumptions; or
- Extreme value theory, which focuses on the asymptotics of tail events.

Rules of Thumb. Using simple rules of thumb may not sound sophisticated, but it is, in fact, a sensible strategy. Litterman (1996), speaking about Goldman Sachs, says, "Given the nonnormality of daily returns that we find in most financial markets, we use as a rule-of-thumb the assumption that four-standard-deviation events in financial markets happen approximately once per year" (p. 54). We can interpret this statement probabilistically from three different perspectives (all equivalent but each giving a different viewpoint):

- If daily returns were normal, a once-per-year event would be about 2.7 standard deviations, so Litterman's rule of thumb is to assume that actual once-per-year changes are 1.5 times larger than changes that would occur if events were normally distributed (4.0σ instead of 2.7σ), which seems a significant but not extreme assumption.

- If daily returns were normal, a four-standard-deviation event would have a probability of about 0.0032 percent, which would make it roughly a once-per-125-year event (1/0.000032 = 31,250 days or about 125 years), whereas Litterman's rule of thumb says it is a once-per-1-year event. This seems a much more radical assumption—instead of four-standard-deviation events occurring once every 125 years, they occur once every year.

- If we assume that four-standard-deviation events occur once per year, the probability of a four-standard-deviation event is about 0.39 percent (1/255) instead of 0.003 percent. (This is the same as the second view but stated in probabilities rather than "once-per-x-years.")

This rule of thumb is simple—something that is easily understood and easily communicated—and that simplicity is itself a huge advantage. Primary attention remains focused on measuring the portfolio volatility, or the behavior during standard trading conditions, which is often a difficult task in itself. Collecting portfolio positions, making reasonable judgments about volatility of individual positions, understanding the interaction of various positions and how these affect the overall portfolio volatility—all of these can be extremely difficult tasks. Given the paucity of observations in the tails, a simple rule of thumb, such as "four-standard-deviation events happen once per year," may be as good as more sophisticated, but more complex, approaches.

This simple rule of thumb actually corresponds to what is often done in practice, which is to estimate the volatility of the P&L distribution and then assume that the VaR is larger by a fixed factor. The factor is often determined by assuming that the P&L distribution is normal (giving a factor of 2.7 for a once-per-year event), but here the factor is assumed to be larger by an ad hoc amount (4.0 instead of 2.7). Alternatively, the factor could be chosen by assuming some other distribution (as we will see next) that gives a larger factor than the normal. Conceptually, the approach is to split the problem into two parts—first estimating the scale of the distribution (generally by the standard deviation or volatility) and subsequently focusing on the tail behavior. This strategy can be very fruitful because the scale of the distribution and the tail behavior can often be analyzed separately.[97]

Alternative Distributional Assumptions. Instead of using an ad hoc assumption (such as that four-standard-deviation events occur once per year), we can modify the assumption about the P&L distribution by using some distribution other than the normal. Two distributional assumptions provide fat tails relative to the normal but are still mathematically tractable: the Student's *t*-distribution and a mixture of normals.[98] The important point here is that these distributions are still easy to handle but provide a description of the tails that is often closer to what we observe in financial markets.

We can use this approach for the example of the extreme drops in the Dow Jones quoted earlier. **Figure 5.11** expands from Figure 5.10, showing the expected frequency of events in the tail (excluding the 1987 crash again) for a normal, mixture of normals, and Student's *t*-distribution (in all cases assuming a standard deviation of 25 percent) versus the empirical frequency. As we saw in Figure 5.10, the normal distribution gives far too few extreme events. The mixture of normals and the Student's *t*-distribution, however, give a much more realistic representation of the actual data.

---

[97]Take the simple example of owning $1 million versus $100 million of a U.S. Treasury bond. The scale of the distribution will be very different, but the shape will not change. The tail behavior—for example, the ratio of the VaR to the volatility—will be the same because it is determined by the market risk factor (say, the yield) and not the size of the holding.

[98]"Student" was the pseudonym of William S. Gosset (1876–1937), a Guinness brewing engineer who did not publish under his own name at the company's insistence. Student's *t*-distribution is commonly used in statistics. It is symmetrical and looks very much like the normal in Figure 5.4 except that it has fatter tails than the normal. The exact shape is controlled by the shape parameter or "degrees of freedom," which can range from 1 (very fat tails) up to an arbitrarily large number (when it merges to the normal). A mixture of normals is just as the name implies: a high probability of a normal with a moderate volatility (say 98.75 percent with volatility 24 percent) and a small probability of a normal with a high volatility (say 1.25 percent with volatility 62.5 percent). This distribution will also be symmetrical and look very much like the normal except with fatter tails. These distributions are discussed more fully in Coleman (forthcoming).

Figure 5.11. Empirical and Selected Distributions for Tail of Changes in Dow Jones Index, 1954–2004

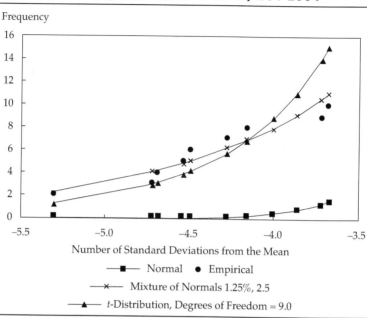

Notes: Frequency is the number of days with large down moves (calculated or observed) out of 12,500 days. The empirical observations are from Table 5.2, derived from Beirlant, Schoutens, and Segers (2005, Table 1), but excluding the October 1987 observation (which is far to the left at −16σ). The "Normal" is a standard normal distribution (standard deviation 1.00). The "Mixture of Normals" is a two-point mixture with α=1.25, β=2.5. (This means 1.25 percent probability of a normal with standard deviation 2.5 × 0.9687 and 98.75 percent probability of a normal with standard deviation 0.9687, giving a distribution with overall standard deviation 1.00. The term 0.9687 is calculated as $1/\sqrt{[0.9875+0.0125\times2.5^2]}$.) The "*t*-distribution" is a standardized *t*-distribution with 9 degrees of freedom multiplied by $1/\sqrt{[9/(9-2)]}$, to give a distribution with standard deviation 1.00.

By using either the mixture of normals or Student's *t*-distribution, we could have some confidence that we would not be horribly off in making statements about extreme events related to changes in the Dow Jones Industrial Average. But we still need to be careful. We have ignored the 1987 crash (which is at −16.22σ). We have chosen the parameters (α = 1.25 and β = 2.5 for the mixture of normals, degrees of freedom = 9 for the Student's *t*) based on a very small number of observations in the tails.[99]

---

[99]In this particular case, we use *v*(degrees of freedom) = 9, but more generally, lower values of *v* on the order of 3–6 appear to match reasonably well with the tails of financial data (see Jorion 2007, p. 130).

©2011 The Research Foundation of CFA Institute

Extreme Value Theory. The third alternative for handling tail or extreme events goes by the name of extreme value theory (EVT), which is the study of the asymptotics of tail events.

Asymptotics in general is the study of probability as the number of events increases. It is the essence of frequency-type probability and has provided the foundation of much of modern probability and statistics. The law of large numbers and the central limit theorem are known to most everyone and are the premier examples of the application of asymptotic methods. They provide tools to study the sum and average of a sequence of random variables as the number of observations gets large. Essentially, they say that the average will ultimately settle down and that it will behave the same no matter what the distribution of the original variables (within some limits). As the number of observations grows, this provides a simple characterization of the average. The beauty and power of the law of large numbers and central limit theorem is that they hold true no matter what the distribution of the underlying random numbers, as long as the random variables do not have too much chance of being too large—for example, if they have finite mean and variance.

The central limit theorem studies the average of a sequence. EVT, in contrast, is an asymptotic theory that examines the maximum (or related characteristics) of a sequence—that is, the tails of a distribution. As such, EVT provides tools and techniques particularly well suited to analyzing VaR and tail events. Just as the average settles down when we increase the number of observations, so the maximum settles down (when suitably normalized, usually by subtracting something that involves n, the number of observations). The central limit theorem says that the average will be normally distributed. EVT says that that the maximum (normalized) will be distributed according to a different distribution, known as the generalized extreme value (GEV) distribution.[100]

The important point is that, within limits, the extremes from any distribution behave in a predictable way when we increase the number of observations (that is, asymptotically). No matter what distribution we start with (again within some limits), the extremes will follow the GEV distribution.

The beauty and power of EVT is that it provides a simple characterization of the tails, analogous to the central limit theorem for the mean, no matter what the distribution of the original random variables (within limits). EVT is mathematically appealing and has considerable intellectual appeal. Unfortunately, in my opinion, the complexity of applying it in practice relegates it to third place as a practical approach for handling tail events.

---

[100]Details can be found in McNeil, Frey, and Embrechts (2005, ch. 7) and in Embrechts, Klüppelberg, Mikosch (2003).

Analyzing Risk

Managing risk requires actually making decisions whether or not to alter the profile of risk. Making such decisions requires knowing not just the level of risk (the dispersion of the P&L distribution) but also the sources of risk in the portfolio and how changes in positions are likely to alter the portfolio risk. Harking back to Chapter 1 and Figure 1.1, we must build the overall portfolio risk from the bottom up, but we also need to drill back down to uncover the sources of the risk.

Litterman (1996) expresses this principle well:

> Volatility and VaR characterize, in slightly different ways, the degree of dispersion in the distribution of gains and losses, and therefore are useful for monitoring risk. They do not, however, provide much guidance for risk management. To manage risk, you have to understand what the sources of risk are in the portfolio and what trades will provide effective ways to reduce risk. Thus, risk management requires additional analysis—in particular, a decomposition of risk, an ability to find potential hedges, and an ability to find simple representations for complex positions. (p. 59)

In this sense, risk management merges into portfolio management. The present section discusses some of the tools and techniques suitable for such portfolio risk analysis. Many of the ideas in this section are based on Litterman (1996). The idea of contribution to risk was developed independently by Garman (1996) and Litterman.[101]

These techniques are most suitable for measuring and understanding risk under standard trading conditions (as opposed to tail events) and under the assumption of linearity. This is not necessarily a weakness of the techniques: Remember that risk must be managed every day, and most trading days are "standard conditions." Furthermore, understanding the portfolio under standard conditions provides the first step to understanding the portfolio under extreme conditions.

A simple approach can provide powerful insights where it is applicable, and many, even most, portfolios are locally linear and amenable to these techniques. Again, Litterman (1996) summarizes the situation well:

> Many risk managers today seem to forget that the key benefit of a simple approach, such as the linear approximation implicit in traditional portfolio analysis, is the powerful insight it can provide in contexts where it is valid.

> With very few exceptions, portfolios will have locally linear exposures about which the application of portfolio risk analysis tools can provide useful information. (p. 53)

---

[101]The marginal contribution is actually just the *beta* of the capital asset pricing model expressed in different units and thus goes back directly to the work of Markowitz, Sharpe, and others.

Triangle Addition. As a guide for understanding how the risks of assets combine to yield the total portfolio risk, volatility and linear approximations are extremely useful. Volatilities add as the sides of a triangle so that the resulting volatility of two combined positions will generally be less than the two alone. Volatility may not be the perfect measure of risk, but the intuition it builds regarding the aggregation of risk is effective, even invaluable.

Consider again the two positions discussed in Chapter 1, the first one a $20 million purchase of a U.S. Treasury (UST) bond and the other a €7 million nominal long position in CAC futures, summarized in **Table 5.2**. The volatility of the U.S. Treasury position on its own is $130,800; the volatility of the CAC futures position on its own is $230,825. What is the volatility of the combined position (+$20 million UST + €7 million CAC)?

Table 5.2. Volatility for Simple Portfolio

Item	Stand-Alone Volatility	Actual Portfolio Volatility	Sum of Stand-Alone Volatility
$20 million UST 10-year bond	$130,800		
€7 million CAC equity futures	$230,825		
UST + CAC		$291,300	$361,625

We can start diagrammatically by laying out volatilities as line segments, the first proportional to $130,800 and the second to $230,825, as shown in **Figure 5.12**. These line segments do not simply add to produce $361,625; the two segments combine as legs of a triangle. For long $20 million of the UST and long €7 million CAC, the triangle is as shown in Panel A, resulting in a combined volatility of $291,300. The key question is, what is the angle between the two legs?

The volatility of a portfolio is calculated from the volatilities of two assets according to

$$\sigma_p = \sqrt{\sigma_1^2 + 2\rho\sigma_1\sigma_2 + \sigma_2^2}. \tag{5.1a}$$

The legs of a triangle combine according to

$$A = \sqrt{B^2 - 2BC\cos\theta + C^2}, \tag{5.1b}$$

155

Figure 5.12. Volatilities as Legs of a Triangle (Vector Addition)

A. Long UST and Long CAC

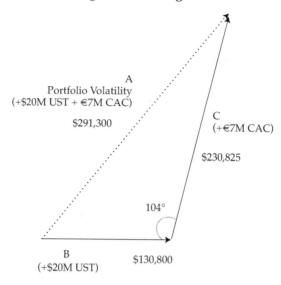

A
Portfolio Volatility
(+$20M UST + €7M CAC)

$291,300

C
(+€7M CAC)

$230,825

104°

B
(+$20M UST)

$130,800

B. Long UST and Short CAC

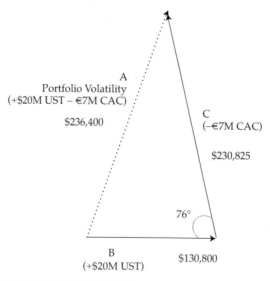

A
Portfolio Volatility
(+$20M UST – €7M CAC)

$236,400

C
(–€7M CAC)

$230,825

76°

B
(+$20M UST)

$130,800

and these two will be equivalent when cosθ = −ρ.[102] For the two positions considered here, ρ = 0.24, so if we are long, θ = 104° and the triangle looks as in Panel A of Figure 5.12. If the correlation were ρ = 1.00, the angle would be θ = 180° and the volatilities would add to $361,625 (the line segments would be collinear).

In contrast, if we are long the UST and short the CAC futures, the correlation is ρ = −0.24 and the angle is 76°, as shown in Panel B of the figure. In this case, the portfolio volatility is only $236,400; the CAC partially hedges the bonds.

Correlation and Risk Reduction Potential. The triangle addition for volatilities can be used to understand the potential for risk reduction and how it varies with the correlation between assets. In Figure 5.12, the combinations considered are +$20 million UST and ±€7 million nominal of CAC futures. Alternatively, we could take the +$20 million UST as fixed and consider the CAC as a hedge, varying the amount of the futures. We could ask by how much the UST volatility can be reduced through hedging—what is the potential for risk reduction? We could calculate the percentage reduction in volatility that we could achieve by optimally hedging the U.S. bond with the CAC futures.

Panel B of Figure 5.12 shows +$20 million UST and −€7 million nominal of CAC, with an angle of θ = 76° between them (cos 76° = 0.24 = −ρ). Hedging the UST with the CAC means keeping the amount of UST fixed (the base line *B*) while varying the amount of the CAC (length of line *C*), with the angle between them determined by the correlation [θ = arccos(−ρ)]. If we wish to minimize the resulting combined volatility (the line *A*), then it should be clear that *A* must make a right angle with *C*, as shown in **Figure 5.13**. But in that case, we have a right triangle with hypotenuse *B*, and *A* = *B*sinθ. The reduction in volatility is *B* − *A*, and the proportional reduction or the risk reduction potential is (*B* − *A*)/*B*:

$$\text{Risk reduction potential} = 1 - A/B = 1 - \sin\theta$$
$$= 1 - \sin\left[\arccos(-\rho)\right]. \tag{5.2a}$$

Deriving this using Equation 5.1a and ρ instead gives

$$\text{Risk reduction potential} = 1 - \sqrt{\left(1 - \rho^2\right)}. \tag{5.2b}$$

---

[102] I know of this analogy between volatilities and triangles from Litterman (1996), but Litterman notes that it may have been used earlier.

Figure 5.13. Triangle Addition and Risk Reduction Potential

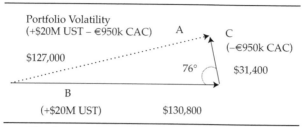

Note: This figure shows side C (the amount of the CAC futures in this case) chosen to provide maximum risk reduction or optimal hedge for side B (U.S. bond in this case).

For the UST and CAC, where the correlation is 0.24, using either Equation 5.2a or 5.2b, we find that the risk reduction potential is only 3 percent. In other words, the UST volatility can be reduced by hedging with CAC futures—but reduced by only 3 percent. Figure 5.13 shows the optimal hedge of the $20 million UST position, with a short position of roughly €950,000 CAC futures (which produces a CAC volatility of $31,400). The portfolio volatility is $127,000, only 3 percent lower than the original UST volatility of $130,800. A risk reduction of 3 percent is very low and means (unsurprisingly) that using CAC futures as a hedge for a U.S. bond would be almost completely ineffective.

Table 5.3 shows the risk reduction potential for various levels of correlation. The low level of risk reduction potential shown in the table is somewhat surprising. It is very low for low correlation (as we saw with the UST and CAC example in Figure 5.13), and even for –0.80 correlation, the risk reduction potential is below 50 percent. As Litterman (1996) points out, "Many traders and portfolio managers may not be aware of how sensitive risk reduction is to the degree of correlation between the returns of the positions being hedged and the hedging instruments" (p. 62).

Table 5.3. Correlation and Risk Reduction Potential

Correlation	Angle θ	Risk Reduction Potential
–0.99	8.1°	85.9%
–0.90	25.8	56.4
–0.80	36.9	40.0
–0.50	60.0	13.4
–0.25	75.5	3.2

Notes: This table shows the solution to Equations 5.2a or 5.2b for various values of the correlation, ρ.

Contribution to Risk. Volatilities and variances do not add, and Equation 5.1 does not, on the face of it, provide a decomposition of portfolio volatility into contributions due to individual assets or groups of assets. Nonetheless, there are two useful ways we can define the contribution a position makes to the volatility or VaR:

- Infinitesimal or marginal—a change in volatility or VaR caused by an infinitesimal change in a position;

- All or nothing—a change in volatility or VaR caused by complete removal of a position.

In my view, the infinitesimal or *marginal contribution to risk*, and the decomposition it provides, is one of the most powerful but underappreciated tools for risk analysis. This contribution to risk provides a useful decomposition of the current risk profile by showing how positions affect the portfolio, thus aiding in the understanding of the portfolio. Positions in a portfolio are usually adjusted little by little rather than by complete removal of a position, and the marginal contribution provides a good estimate of this manipulation for a large portfolio with many small positions. I find the infinitesimal, rather than the all-or-nothing, measure to be the far more useful.

Unfortunately, there is no agreement (but considerable confusion) in the literature regarding nomenclature, and this confusion creates a barrier to better understanding of contribution to risk. Particularly confusing is the fact that RiskMetrics Group uses the term "marginal" for the all-or-nothing measure (even though the term "marginal" is commonly used to denote small changes at the margin and not large finite changes) and uses the term "incremental" for the infinitesimal measure (arguably also at odds with common usage of the term "incremental"). Most of the literature uses the reverse terminology. Nor are texts always clear in their explanation of the formulas or concepts. **Exhibit 5.2** provides a guide to the various terms used by different writers.

The idea of marginal contribution to risk was introduced independently by Litterman (1996) and Garman (1996). I will focus on the marginal contribution to volatility. Note, however, that the concept of contribution to risk is also applicable to all commonly used risk measures (e.g., VaR, expected shortfall).

To start, consider Equation 5.1a for the variance of two assets but now include explicitly the weights of the asset holdings, so that σ_i is the volatility for a unit holding of the position and ω_i is the amount of the holding (measured in dollars, number of bonds, percent of the portfolio—whatever the appropriate unit is). This relationship can be written as

$$\sigma_p^2 = \omega_1^2 \sigma_{11} + 2\omega_1 \omega_2 \sigma_{12} + \omega_2^2 \sigma_{22},$$

Exhibit 5.2. Terms for Contribution to Risk

Source	Infinitesimal	All or Nothing
This book	Marginal contribution or contribution to risk	All-or-nothing contribution to risk
Litterman (1996)	Contribution to risk	
Crouhy, Galai, and Mark (2001)	Delta VaR	Incremental VaR
Marrison (2002)	VaR contribution	
Mina and Xiao/RiskMetrics (2001)	Incremental VaR	Marginal VaR
Jorion (2007)[a]	Marginal VaR and component VaR	Incremental VaR

[a]Unfortunately, Jorion's explication of these ideas is somewhat confusing. His "marginal VaR" (2007, section 7.2.1) is $\partial\sigma_p/\partial\omega_1$ giving terms like $[\omega_1\sigma_{11} + \omega_2\sigma_{12}]$ (instead of $\omega\partial\sigma_p/\partial\omega_1$ giving terms like $[\omega^2{}_1\sigma_{11} + \omega_1\omega_2\sigma_{12}]$) so that his marginal VaR does not add to the total VaR. He subsequently defines "component VaR" (what I call *marginal contribution*) but does not point out its marginal nature and provides a somewhat misleading definition as the approximate change in VaR upon deletion of the asset. See discussion in Coleman (forthcoming).

and the volatility as

$$\sigma_p = \frac{\omega_1^2\sigma_{11} + \omega_1\omega_2\sigma_{12} + \omega_1\omega_2\sigma_{12} + \omega_2^2\sigma_{22}}{\sigma_p}.$$

The second formula suggests a simple ad hoc decomposition of the volatility into constituent parts:

$$MCL_1 = \frac{\omega_1^2\sigma_{11} + \omega_1\omega_2\sigma_{12}}{\sigma_p},$$

with MCL (marginal contribution to volatility, in levels) being defined as that portion attributable to Asset 1; a similar term gives the contribution for Asset 2.[103] The result is that the total volatility is the sum of the two contributions:

$$\sigma_p = \frac{\omega_1^2\sigma_{11} + \omega_1\omega_2\sigma_{12}}{\sigma_p} + \frac{\omega_1\omega_2\sigma_{12} + \omega_2^2\sigma_{22}}{\sigma_p}$$

$$= MCL_1 + MCL_2. \tag{5.3a}$$

---

[103]Marrison (2002, ch. 7) has a nice explication of the marginal contribution (Marrison calls it *VaR contribution*) with clear formulas in both summation and matrix notation. Unfortunately, Marrison does not point out the marginal nature of the measure discussed next (that it gives the infinitesimal change in volatility for an infinitesimal percent change in asset holding), but otherwise the discussion is very useful.

That is, the volatility can be decomposed into additive contributions from the two assets. So far, this is just an ad hoc decomposition of the volatility. The wonderful thing is that we arrive at exactly the same additive decomposition (hence the name marginal contribution) if we take the total differential and consider the change in the volatility resulting from infinitesimal changes in the asset holdings or weights:

$$d\sigma_p = \frac{\omega_1^2 \sigma_{11} + \omega_1 \omega_2 \sigma_{12}}{\sigma_p} \times \frac{d\omega_1}{\omega_1} + \frac{\omega_1 \omega_2 \sigma_{12} + \omega_2^2 \sigma_{11}}{\sigma_p} \times \frac{d\omega_2}{\omega_2}$$

$$d\sigma_p = MCL_1 \frac{d\omega_1}{\omega_1} + MCL_2 \frac{d\omega_2}{\omega_2}.$$

(5.3b)

This is the same decomposition as in Equation 5.3a. Note that the terms MCL_1 and MCL_2 sum to the total volatility and are also the coefficients for decomposing the marginal change in volatility into components due to percentage changes in the two holdings.

If we divide through by another σ_p, we get the percentage change (rather than level change) in volatility:

$$\frac{d\sigma_p}{\sigma_p} = \frac{\omega_1^2 \sigma_{11} + \omega_1 \omega_2 \sigma_{12}}{\sigma_p^2} \times \frac{d\omega_1}{\omega_1} + \frac{\omega_1 \omega_2 \sigma_{12} + \omega_2^2 \sigma_{11}}{\sigma_p^2} \times \frac{d\omega_2}{\omega_2}$$

$$\frac{d\sigma_p}{\sigma_p} = MCP_1 \frac{d\omega_1}{\omega_1} + MCP_2 \frac{d\omega_2}{\omega_2}.$$

(5.3c)

The terms MCP_1 and MCP_2 add to 1.0. This analysis carries over easily to more than two assets. We can call the terms in the decomposition the *marginal contribution (levels)* and *marginal contribution (proportional)*:

$$MCL_i = \frac{\omega_i \left(\sum_j \omega_j \sigma_{ij} \right)}{\sigma_p} \qquad \sum_i MCL_i = \sigma_p$$

(5.4a)

and

$$MCP_i = \frac{\omega_i \left(\sum_j \omega_j \sigma_{ij} \right)}{\sigma_p^2} \qquad \sum_i MCP_i = 1.0.$$

(5.4b)

These terms give the contribution to the change in volatility (levels or proportional) due to an infinitesimal (in practice, a small percentage) change in position.

The derivation of the decomposition of volatility is based on the algebraic definition of the volatility (and variance) and makes no assumptions about the functional form of the P&L distribution. It will hold for any P&L distribution—normal or non-normal. Furthermore, it turns out that we can apply a similar additive and marginal decomposition to *any* risk measure $R(\omega)$ that is linearly homogeneous. In fact, most risk measures used in practice (including volatility, VaR, and expected shortfall but not "probability of shortfall") are linearly homogeneous, so a marginal decomposition can be applied to each of these. It is also important to note that the marginal contribution can be calculated for groups of assets and for subportfolios.[104]

For an example of using marginal contribution, consider the holdings of the UST and the CAC futures discussed earlier and consider a small (infinitesimal) percentage change in each holding. **Table 5.4** shows the result of using Equation 5.4.

The marginal contribution (proportional) of 71.3 percent for the CAC futures shown in Panel A means that the CAC contributes 71.3 percent to the overall portfolio volatility. Multiplying by total volatility gives the marginal contribution in levels of $207,700. I generally find the proportional contribution

Table 5.4. Volatility for Simple Portfolio with Contribution to Risk

			Marginal Contribution	
			Proportional	Level
Item	Volatility per $1M Holding	Position Volatility	$[\omega^2_i \sigma^2_i + \rho\omega_i\sigma_i\omega_j\sigma_j]/ \sigma^2_p$	$[\omega^2_i \sigma^2_i + \rho\omega_i\sigma_i\omega_j\sigma_j]/ \sigma_p$
A. Base case				
+$20M UST 10-year bond	$ 6,540	$130,800	28.70%	$ 83,600
+€7M CAC futures	23,365	230,825	71.30	207,700
Portfolio		291,300	100.00%	$291,300
B. Contribution for short CAC futures				
+$20M UST 10-year bond	$ 6,540	$130,800	17.6%	$ 41,600
−€7M CAC futures	23,365	230,825	82.4	194,800
Portfolio volatility		236,400	100.0%	$236,400
C. Zero contribution for CAC				
+$20M UST 10-year bond	$ 6,540	$130,800	100.0%	$127,000
−€950k CAC futures	23,365	31,440	0.0	0
Portfolio volatility		127,000	100.0%	$127,000

[104]Explicit formulas for marginal volatility contribution by subportfolio are given in Coleman (forthcoming).

more useful, thinking in a two-step process: First, what is the overall portfolio volatility, and second, what do individual positions or components contribute to that overall volatility?

The situation changes when the CAC futures position is *short* €7 million, with the CAC now providing an even larger proportional contribution to the portfolio volatility (although the overall portfolio volatility is lower), as shown in Panel B.

We could also ask, what is the CAC position for which the futures makes no contribution to the volatility? A small short futures starting position will provide a zero marginal contribution to volatility from an infinitesimal change in that position. Specifically, for a holding of –€950,000, small changes in the holdings of the CAC futures will have almost no impact on the portfolio volatility, as shown in Panel C.

The triangle addition of volatilities helps to illustrate what is happening, and the situation is actually the same as that shown in Figure 5.13. The CAC position is chosen so that the resultant portfolio volatility (side *A*) forms a right angle with side *C* (CAC volatility). Triangle addition also helps show how and why such a position has a zero contribution to volatility. Panel A of **Figure 5.14** shows a change in side *C* (CAC volatility—for clarity, a large change rather than infinitesimal). In this case, leg *A* (portfolio volatility) changes in length by

Figure 5.14. Triangle Addition of Volatilities for +$20 Million UST, –€950,000 CAC Futures

A. Change in CAC Volatility (side C)

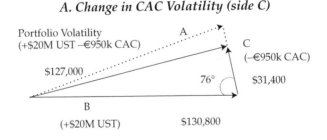

B. Change in UST Volatility (side B)

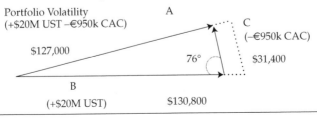

almost nothing. Panel B shows a change in side *B* (U.S. Treasury volatility), and here the length of side *A* changes virtually one for one with side *B*.

The decomposition or marginal contribution to volatility is useful for the insight it provides into how the volatility will change for small changes in a single position, all other positions held fixed. It is particularly useful for large and complex portfolios, exactly the situation where both intuition and such aids as the triangle diagrams (applicable only for two assets) break down.

Best Hedge. A different but equally instructive question to ask is, what would the holding be that would optimally hedge the rest of the portfolio? That is, consider one particular asset and ask what would be the best hedge, using that asset only, for hedging the rest of the portfolio. This problem now involves not an infinitesimal change in the asset but a finite or large change in the asset holding. We can start addressing this question by noting that the marginal contribution to volatility attributable to a particular position may be either positive (adding to the portfolio risk) or negative (lowering the portfolio risk— acting as a hedge). At some point between a positive contribution and a negative contribution, the position will be such that the marginal contribution is zero; this will be the position size that optimally hedges the rest of the portfolio.[105] We can calculate the amount of asset *k* for which the marginal contribution is zero, given no changes in any other asset holdings, which means finding ω_k^* that satisfies the following:

$$MCP_k = \frac{\omega_k \left(\sum_j \omega_j \sigma_{kj} \right)}{\sigma_p^2} = 0$$

$$\Rightarrow \sum_{j \neq k} \omega_j \sigma_{kj} + \omega_k^* \sigma_{kk} = 0.$$

If we solve this equation, we have the "best hedge" using asset *k*:

$$\text{Best hedge} = \omega_k^*$$

$$= -\frac{\sum_{j \neq k} \sigma_{jk} \omega_j}{\sigma_{kk}}.$$

---

[105]Trivially, for a zero position, the marginal contribution will be zero. But there will also generally be a nonzero position such that the marginal contribution is zero, and this position is what we are interested in. It assumes that the position may be long or short (positive or negative). If the position is constrained to be long only, then the best hedge position may not be obtainable; nonetheless, it is useful for the insight it can provide.

The point of zero marginal contribution is the point where portfolio risk is minimized with respect to the size of position k because the marginal contribution is the derivative of the volatility with respect to position. This will be a "best hedge" in the sense of being the position in asset k that minimizes the portfolio volatility (all other positions unchanged).

For the U.S. Treasury and CAC futures example (Figure 5.13 and Table 5.4, Panel C), we vary the size of the CAC position, keeping the $20 million in U.S. Treasury bonds unchanged. The marginal contribution of the CAC is zero when the CAC position is –€950,000. Figure 5.13 shows that the resultant volatility (triangle leg *A*) forms a right angle with the leg representing the CAC volatility. P&Ls for the U.S. Treasury and the CAC are positively correlated, so the CAC best-hedge position is actually a short position, hedging the $20 million long U.S. Treasury position.

The portfolio volatility at the best-hedge position is given by the following:

$$\text{Volatility at asset } k \text{ best-hedge position} = \sigma_p^*(k) = \sqrt{\frac{\omega' \Sigma \omega - \left[(\Sigma \omega)_k\right]^2}{\sigma_{kk}}}. \quad (5.5)$$

Replicating Portfolio. Representing a complex portfolio in terms of a simpler portfolio is very useful as a way of understanding how the complex portfolio behaves and also as a way of communicating to others the general behavior of a portfolio without delving into its full complexity. The idea of a "replicating portfolio" is to provide a simple portfolio that replicates the portfolio in some aspects of its behavior while being less complex than the full portfolio.

We can use the best hedge just discussed to create a simple replicating portfolio. The asset k best hedge (ω_k^*) is that holding of asset k that best hedges the rest of the portfolio. The difference between the actual holding and the best-hedge holding for asset k is a mirror portfolio:

$$\text{Single-asset mirror portfolio using asset } k = MP(k) = \omega_k - \omega_k^*.$$

This is the replicating portfolio that minimizes the portfolio variance when using only asset k. In other words, if we try to replicate the total portfolio with just asset k, then $MP(k) = \omega_k - \omega_k^*$ minimizes the variance and is, therefore, the best replicating portfolio given that we are allowed to hold just one asset.

Using the formulas from the "Best Hedge" section, we can calculate the best hedge using each asset in a portfolio and thus the mirror portfolio for each asset. We can then choose the best mirror portfolio by choosing that asset with the lowest best-hedge volatility. It is natural to call this best mirror portfolio a "replicating portfolio" because it replicates the portfolio best (of all the single assets in the original portfolio).

Such a single-asset replicating portfolio provides a simple representation of how the full portfolio behaves, but it will usually be too simple to be useful on its own. Fortunately, the replicating portfolio idea extends in a straightforward manner to multiple assets to provide a replicating portfolio that is still simple but more informative than using a single asset.[106]

The replicating portfolio using two assets is the two-asset mirror portfolio with the lowest variance. Relatively small replicating portfolios—using 3, 5, or 10 assets—can provide useful information and insight into the full portfolio. The replicating portfolio can serve as a proxy, summary, or approximation of the full portfolio, with the percent variance explained by the replicating portfolio providing a measure of the quality of the approximation. A replicating portfolio composed of liquid and easily tradable assets can also provide an emergency or temporary hedge for quickly reducing the risk of a portfolio.

One straightforward way to calculate the replicating portfolio using n assets is by brute force: Consider all possible combinations of mirror portfolios using assets taken n at a time, calculate the volatility reduction resulting from each combination, and then choose the best one. Such an approach is feasible when the number of assets in the original portfolio, m, and the number of assets in the mirror portfolio, n, are relatively small (say $m < 40$ and $n < 10$), but it becomes tricky when the number of assets in both the replicating portfolio and the original portfolio gets large. Alternatively, for a large portfolio, a strategy analogous to stepwise regression—building up the replicating portfolio assets one at a time—can be used.[107]

The discussion so far has focused on choosing a replicating portfolio from the assets within a portfolio. Alternatively, an externally specified set of assets can be used. The replicating portfolio weights can be chosen by using linear regression analysis.

Risk Reporting

Effective, intelligent, and useful risk reporting is as important as the underlying analysis. Human intuition is not well adapted to recognize and manage randomness. Risks combine within a portfolio in a nonlinear and often highly nonintuitive manner. Even for the simplest case of normal distributions, the volatility (standard deviation) and VaR do not add, so the volatility or VaR of a portfolio is less than the sum of the constituents (because of diversification). Various tools, techniques, and tricks need to be used to uncover the risk for even relatively standard portfolios.

---

[106]Coleman (forthcoming) gives the explicit formulas for multiple-asset mirror portfolios.
[107]This technique is discussed more fully in Coleman (forthcoming).

To illustrate and explain the techniques for analyzing portfolio risk, I will focus on a small portfolio with diverse positions and risks and on a sample risk report that includes the marginal contribution, best hedges, and so on. The intention is not only to explain what the measures are but also to provide insight into how to use them and why they are valuable.

Sample Portfolio. I will consider a portfolio made up of four subportfolios (individual portfolio managers or trading desks):

- Government subportfolio
  - Long $20 million U.S. Treasury, 10 year
  - Long £20 million U.K. gilt, 10 year
  - Short $20 million notional call option on a 5-year U.S. Treasury
- Swaps subportfolio: Long $20 million 10-year swap spread
- Credit subportfolio: Long €15 million corporate bond spread (CDS on France Telecom)
- Equity subportfolio
  - Long €5 million CAC futures
  - Long €5 million French company (France Telecom)

This portfolio is not large in terms of the number of positions, only seven, but it is diverse and complex in terms of products and risk exposure. It is an example where quantitative risk measurement techniques start to bring some transparency to an otherwise complex and opaque situation.

This section discusses market risk (yield, volatility, traded credit spread, equity, FX). The primary focus will be on the sample risk report shown in **Exhibit 5.3.** The report is intended to detail not just the levels but also the sources of the portfolio's risk exposure. In this case, there are only seven positions, and it may be possible to manage such a small portfolio without this risk-reporting technology. But even for this small portfolio, comparing and contrasting exposures across disparate asset classes and currencies is not trivial.

Exhibit 5.3. Sample Portfolio Risk Report

Expected Volatility by Asset Class

Asset Class	Expected Volatility ($)	Contribution	Correlation with Portfolio
Overall	$541,821	100.0%	
FI (bonds + swaps)	272,398	28.1	0.559
Credit	124,915	13.5	0.587
Equity	272,079	37.5	0.746
FX	247,531	20.9	0.457
Volatility	1,518	0.0	0.003

(continued)

Exhibit 5.3. Sample Portfolio Risk Report (continued)

Volatility and 1-out-of-250 VaR

Volatility	$541,821
VaR normal	−1,436,948
VaR 4-sigma rule of thumb	−2,167,285

Top Three Contributors to Risk (volatility)

Contributor	Expected Volatility (1-sigma P&L)	Contribution	Current Position ($M eqv)	Trade to Best Hedge ($M eqv)	% Reduction in Volatility Best Hedge	% Reduction in Volatility Zero Position
EUR EqIndex	230,825	24.5%	$ 9.1	−$12.3	18.2%	16.8%
GBP FX	208,156	17.4	30.9	−36.5	10.9	10.6
GBP Yield10	137,956	16.3	28.0	−70.3	23.1	14.0

Top Three Best Single Hedges

Hedging Instrument	Expected Volatility (1-sigma P&L)	Contribution	Current Position ($M eqv)	Trade to Best Hedge ($M eqv)	% Reduction in Volatility Best Hedge	% Reduction in Volatility Zero Position
GBP Yield10	137,956	16.3%	$28.0	−$70.3	23.1%	14.0%
USD Yield10	128,141	14.7	19.6	−51.5	21.7	12.7
GBP Yield5	151	0.0	0.1	−113.5	21.2	0.0

Best Replicating Portfolios

Item	One Asset	Three Assets
% Variance explained	40.8%	89.0%
% Volatility explained	23.1%	66.9%
Asset Eqv position	GBP Yield10 $70.3M	GBP Yield10 $41.8M
Asset Eqv position		GBP FX $36.5M
Asset Eqv position		EUR EqIn $9.6M

Notes: M = million; eqv = equivalent.

Summary Risk Report. Exhibit 5.3 shows a sample portfolio risk report for this portfolio or trading operation. This report is based on delta-normal or parametric estimation of the volatility and VaR. The report is the top-level report for the portfolio and summarizes the overall exposure and major sources of risk. A good risk-reporting strategy, however, is a little like an onion or a set of Russian nesting dolls: Each layer, when peeled off, reveals the next layer and shows more detail. This is the top layer.[108]

▓ *Volatility.* The first thing to note is the overall volatility: The daily or expected volatility is roughly $540,000, which is to say that the standard deviation of the daily P&L distribution is roughly $540,000. When considering the daily volatility, we are examining everyday trading activity and the central part of the distribution, and we can have some confidence that assuming normality is probably reasonable. We can infer that the daily losses or profits should be more than ±$540,000 about one day out of three (because the probability of a normally distributed variable being below -1σ or above $+1\sigma$ is roughly 30 percent).

The observation on likely P&L immediately provides a scale for possible losses (and gains) for the portfolio and needs to be judged against the size of the portfolio, the investment, or the capital. The size of the portfolio is sometimes easy to determine, sometimes less so. For a traditional, long-only equity portfolio, the size of the portfolio is simply the sum of the notionals of all the positions—the total amount invested. In other cases, it is not so simple. Turn back to the outline of the sample portfolio given earlier and note that it includes both actual securities (such as the $20 million U.S. Treasury) and derivatives (such as the CAC futures). The portfolio investment could be as low as $55 million (the notionals of the U.S. Treasury, the U.K. gilt, and the French equity). But it might be much higher. The sum of all the notionals (counting the derivatives and swap spreads at the notional of the underlying instruments) is roughly $155 million.

If our sample portfolio entailed an investment or capital of only $55 million, then the volatility of $540,000 would imply gains or losses amounting to roughly 1 percent or more of capital every three days—a volatile and risky undertaking. In contrast, if the capital were $500 million, we would expect a mere 0.1 percent or more every three days or roughly 1.7 percent per year (multiplying by $\sqrt{250}$ to annualize)—a ridiculously low-risk venture with probably correspondingly low returns.

---

[108]In Coleman (forthcoming), I discuss more detailed reports that parallel Exhibit 5.3 but zero in on a specific subportfolio.

The daily volatility gives a scale for the portfolio at a point in time, but even more importantly, it provides a reasonably consistent comparison across time. Were the daily volatility to rise to $1 million next week, we could be relatively confident that the risk of the portfolio, at least the risk under standard day-by-day trading conditions, had roughly doubled.

The volatility also provides a reasonably consistent comparison across asset classes. The report shows that the daily volatility for fixed-income products (bonds and swaps) is about $270,000, roughly the same as for equity products. These statistics are the daily volatility of these products considered in isolation: The P&L distribution of fixed-income products alone has a volatility of about $270,000. The similar scale of risk in these two products is valuable information because there is no way to know this information directly from the raw nominal positions: The notional in fixed income ($20 million in U.S. Treasuries, £20 million in U.K. gilts, and $20 million in swap spreads) is many times that in equities (€7 million in CAC futures and €5 million in France Telecom stock).

Volatility by asset class naturally does not sum to the overall volatility: The sum by asset class of $910,000 versus the overall of $540,000 shows the effect of diversification.

■ *VaR.* The next item to note is the daily VaR. The VaR is calculated at a 0.4 percent level. The probability level for VaR is always somewhat arbitrary; 0.4 percent was chosen because it corresponds to roughly one trading day per year (1 out of 250). Such a value should not be considered an unusual event; in Litterman's words (1996), "think of this not as a 'worst case,' but rather as a regularly occurring event with which [one] should be comfortable" (p. 74).

As with the volatility, the VaR provides a scale, in this case the minimum loss one should expect from the worst day in a year. It is important to remember that this is the *minimum* loss, not the average loss or worst loss, that one should expect from the worst trading day in the year; it could be worse. Because of random fluctuations, the actual loss may be worse (or possibly better) and there could be more than one day in a year with losses this bad or worse.

Two values for the VaR are shown. The first is derived from the normality assumption and is just $2.652 \times$ the daily volatility. This value reflects the probability that a normal variable will be 2.652σ below the mean, which is 0.4 percent. The second value is based on Litterman's rule of thumb that a 4σ event occurs roughly once per year so that the VaR is four times the volatility. We could also calculate VaR using other distributional assumptions.

The VaR estimates should be used with care, more care indeed than the volatility. The numbers in these reports are based on assumptions of normality for risk factors and linearity for asset sensitivities (the estimates are delta-normal or parametric). We need to ask whether such assets as those in this portfolio have exhibited fat tails in the past, to what extent nonlinearities are important, and whether and to what extent assets in the portfolio have generated skewed or fat-tailed distributions. For example, the portfolio contains an option, which by its nature has a nonlinear response to underlying yields and will have a skewed distribution. It turns out that in this case, nonlinearities are not large enough to have a substantial effect, but the delicate nature of calculating and using VaR and tail estimates argues for a separate report and more detailed analysis. In the end, I think the four-sigma rule of thumb said to be used at Goldman has much to offer.

■ *Marginal contribution to volatility and correlation.* The marginal contribution to volatility is one of the most useful tools for decomposing and understanding volatility and risk. Exhibit 5.3 shows the proportional (or percentage) marginal contribution—what I called "MCP" earlier—so that contributions add to 100 percent. The marginal contribution by asset class shows that, in a portfolio context, equities actually contribute more to the volatility than does fixed income (37.5 percent versus 28.1 percent), even though on a stand-alone basis they are equally volatile ($272,000 each for fixed income and equities). Because portfolio effects are paramount but often difficult to intuit, the marginal contribution is a better guide to understanding portfolio risk than is the stand-alone volatility.

The correlation of the equity asset class with the full portfolio helps show why equities have a larger contribution. Equities are the most highly correlated with the portfolio, which explains why equities contribute more to the volatility than does fixed income, even though the stand-alone volatilities are the same.

Depending on the size and complexity of the portfolio, examining contribution to risk by individual assets may be useful. For a large and diverse portfolio, there will generally be many assets, and contribution by individual assets should be left to a more detailed next reporting level, below the top-level summary. For a smaller portfolio, an examination of all assets is valuable.

For most any portfolio, however, the top contributors provide useful insight into the portfolio. For this sample portfolio, the top three contributors give a succinct summary of the major risks faced by the portfolio: equity index (CAC), U.K. yields, and sterling FX.[109]

■ *Best single hedges and replicating portfolios.* The marginal contributions show the contribution to risk for the existing portfolio and provide a guide to how the volatility will change for small changes in holdings. But the marginal

---

[109]To my knowledge, Goldman Sachs pioneered the use of reporting top contributors, and it has trademarked the term *Hot Spots* for such a report—see Litterman (1996).

contributions will not be a good guide to the effect of large changes in asset holdings or to what the best hedging assets might be. For this, the best hedges and replicating portfolios are useful.

For any particular asset, the best hedge position is the position that minimizes the expected volatility. This involves a finite, possibly large, change in position. The top best hedge will often differ from the top marginal contributor. For the sample portfolio shown in Exhibit 5.3, the equity index (CAC) is the largest marginal contributor to risk but it is not even in the top three best hedges (it is number five).

The top contributors and the top single hedges measure different characteristics of the portfolio. The top contributor to risk is the top contributor *given the current positions*. It tells us something about the composition of the current portfolio. The best single hedge, in contrast, is the asset that would give the largest reduction in volatility if we bought or sold some large amount. It tells us what would happen for *alternate positions*. We can also treat the best hedge as a mirror or replicating portfolio.

For the sample portfolio in Exhibit 5.3, the EUR equity index (EUR EqIndex) is the top contributor but GBP 10-year yields (the U.K. gilt) is the top best hedge. The U.K. gilt is the best hedge because it is highly correlated with USD 10-year yields (the U.S. Treasury bond) and together they contribute 31 percent of the risk. A hedge using the U.K. gilt (GBP 10-year yields) will hedge both the existing GBP 10-year and the USD 10-year positions.

The top best hedge can be thought of as a replicating portfolio, in the sense that it is the single asset that best replicates the portfolio. For the GBP 10-year yield, the trade from the current holding to the best hedge is a sale of $70.3 million dollars' worth, which means that a buy of $70.3 million of the U.K. gilt would be the best single-asset replicating portfolio. Such a replicating portfolio would explain 23.1 percent of the volatility.

Replicating portfolios can provide a useful proxy or summary of the actual portfolio, but the single-asset portfolio is often too simple. The three-asset portfolio provides a richer summary than the single-asset best hedge and explains far more of the portfolio volatility. The three-asset portfolio explains 66.9 percent of the volatility and provides a valuable summary of the portfolio: It largely behaves like

- Long GBP 10-year yields (10-year U.K. bond, $41.8 million),
- Long GBP FX ($36.5 million of FX exposure caused by holding foreign currency bonds and equities), and
- Long equity index ($9.6 million of CAC).

Credit Risk

I now change gears, from market risk to credit risk. Credit risk is ubiquitous in modern finance. In many ways, analyzing credit risk is no different from analyzing risk arising in any other part of a firm's business—build the distribution of P&L over some horizon and use that distribution to help manage the business activity. Although the underlying idea is simple, particular characteristics of credit risk mean that the techniques for measuring and managing credit risk are often different from and more complex than those for market risk:

- Most credit risks are not traded, and market prices are not available, so the distribution of gains and losses must be constructed from first principles, requiring complex models.

- Public information on the quality and prospects for credit risks is often scarce. This lack of data makes statistical analysis and calibration of models difficult.

- The P&L distribution for credit risks is often skewed, with fat lower tails and a relatively large probability of large losses. Such skewness is difficult to measure but particularly important because the economic capital required to support a portfolio is sensitive specifically to the probability of large losses—the shape of the lower tail drives the economic capital.

- Dependence across risks in a portfolio, which drives the skewness of the credit risk distribution, is difficult to measure with accuracy and hence makes the skewness difficult to measure and model.

For credit risk, the distribution must often be built from scratch by using limited data and complicated models—each model with its own specialized methodology and terminology. Importantly, although credit models are often complicated, credit risk is as much about data as it is about quantitative tools and analysis. One of the biggest challenges in practical implementation of any credit risk system is the basic task of developing an effective database of both external and internal data.

Varieties of Credit Risk. The standard approach to measuring credit risk traces back to commercial banks and their portfolios of loans. It is easy to see that for a loan, default risk is dominant: Loans embody credit risk in its quintessential form. Credit risk, however, permeates finance in many forms:

- Single-issuer credit risk, such as for loans and bonds: Default by the issuer means non-repayment of all or part of the principal and promised interest on the loan or bond.

- Multiple-issuer credit risk, such as for securitized mortgage bonds: Default of one or more of the underlying loans creates credit losses.

- Counterparty risk resulting from contracts between parties, often over-the-counter (OTC) derivatives contracts: OTC transactions, such as interest rate swaps, are contracts between two parties, and if one party defaults, it may substantially affect the payoff to the other party. Other contracts, such as letters of credit, insurance, and financial guarantees, also entail counterparty credit risk because there is potential for loss if one party defaults.
- Settlement risk: Associated with delivery and settlement of trades, settlement risk is the possibility that one side fails to settle a trade after being paid.

McNeil, Frey, and Embrechts (2005) nicely summarize the scope of credit risk: "Credit risk is the risk that the value of a portfolio changes due to unexpected changes in the credit quality of issuers or trading partners. This subsumes both losses due to defaults and losses caused by changes in credit quality" (p. 327).

Credit Risk vs. Market Risk. Prior sections focused on market risk, so it is useful to highlight some differences between credit risk and market risk.[110]

▓ *Liquidity and time frame for credit vs. market risk.* The time frame over which P&L is evaluated is often substantially longer for credit risk than for market risk. This longer time frame is primarily a result of the illiquidity of most credit products. Loans are the classic example and have traditionally been held until maturity. Credit events tend to unfold over a longer time horizon than market events—weeks and months rather than minutes and hours.

One result of considering a much longer time period for the P&L distribution is that the mean matters for credit risk but generally does not for market risk. For credit risk, the P&L distribution is often measured over one or more years, and over such a long period, the mean will be of the same order as the volatility and must be accounted for in using any summary measures, whether VaR or other.

▓ *Asymmetry of credit risk.* The distribution of P&L for credit risks will often be asymmetrical, highly skewed with a fat lower tail. **Figure 5.15** shows results for a stylized model for the returns from a simple loan portfolio (discussed in more detail later).

---

[110]Some types of credit can be treated as market risk. A corporate bond is an example where the credit quality of the issuing company will determine the market demand for, and thus the market price of, the bond itself. The line between credit and market risk is sometimes fuzzy, but in many cases (for example, loans that are not publicly traded), it is more fruitful to treat credit risk as separate from market risk. For these cases, the analytical methods used to address credit are different enough that we need to treat credit risk under a separate section.

Figure 5.15. P&L Distribution for a Simple Model of a Loan Portfolio

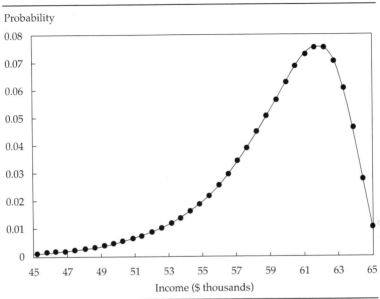

Notes: This is the one-year income (in dollars) from holding a portfolio of 1,000 homogeneous loans of face value $1,000, each with average probability of default of 0.01 and a default correlation across loans of 0.4 percent (roughly representative of BB rated loans). Loss given default is 50 percent; promised interest income is $65. The model is discussed more fully in the text.

It is often said that the asymmetry is the result of the binary nature of credit risks—either a loan or bond pays off as promised, or it does not. If it pays off, there is one possible outcome; if it does not, there is a wide dispersion of possible outcomes—thus the fat lower tail. In other words, a credit portfolio will have many small gains and a few large losses because of infrequent defaults causing a complete loss of principal. In fact, "many small gains, few large losses" will result in lumpy or discrete payouts but not necessarily asymmetry. Some more-fundamental reasons exist for asymmetry in credit risk, most importantly correlation or dependence across defaults.[111] That defaults cluster during times of general economic stress is a simple form of correlation or dependence and a prime candidate for why defaults, and credit risks in general, exhibit asymmetry. Whatever the cause of asymmetry or skewness, it is more prevalent in credit risk than market risk and makes credit risk inherently more difficult to measure.

[111] I use the term "dependence" in addition to "correlation" intentionally. For the multivariate, non-normal distributions that will often arise in credit risk modeling, we have to consider forms of dependence more general than standard linear correlation.

■ *Constructivist (actuarial) vs. market approach to modeling the P&L distribution.* Market risks are, by their very nature, actively traded in the market, which means that the distribution of P&L usually can be derived from observed prices. Credit risks, in contrast, are often not actively traded and market prices are not available. As a result, the P&L from credit-related products must be constructed from a granular model of the fundamental or underlying causes of credit gains and losses, such as cash flows, default, ratings changes, and so on. I call this a "constructivist" (or actuarial) approach to modeling the distribution of P&L.

The contrast between the market-based approach used for market risk and the constructivist approach applied to credit risk is a primary distinguishing characteristic of market risk versus credit risk. Much of the complication surrounding credit risk is a result of the necessity of constructing the distribution from underlying drivers.

■ *Data and legal issues.* Credit risk involves substantial demands for both external and internal data. First, we have the obvious problem that there is no history on the very event of interest: Credit analysis, if it is to be useful, is performed before a particular loan or company defaults, not after. This situation is in stark contrast to market risk, where movements in the price for a particular asset are (relatively) easy to measure. As a result, all sorts of ancillary data about the credit quality and prospects of counterparties and other credit exposures must be used to estimate such things as the probability of default. But much of the ancillary data are difficult to acquire because public data on credit risks are often not available (for example, default history on private loans).

We also face challenges in acquiring and managing what might be termed "internal data," data that are internal to the firm. These data would include the details concerning exactly who a firm's counterparties are and what other credit exposures it has. Such internal data are under the control of the firm, so it is often assumed that they are accessible. Unfortunately, such data are often scattered throughout different units of an organization, in separate legacy systems, collected and stored for reasons unrelated to credit risk analysis, and all too often inaccessible and unusable in the original form. Furthermore, these internal data can be intrinsically complex and difficult to collect.

As an example of the potential complexity of internal data, consider a firm's possible exposure to Lehman prior to that firm's collapse. One unit might hold a Lehman bond, another might hold an OTC interest rate swap with Lehman, and a third might be settling an FX trade through Lehman as prime broker. All of these transactions are at risk when Lehman goes into bankruptcy. Collecting information on the existence of such disparate exposures is not trivial, particularly given their heterogeneity in terms of duration, liquidity, and complexity of underlying assets.

Legal issues are important for credit risk assessment: The legal organization of counterparties, details of contracts (netting, collateral), and priority and venue in the event of bankruptcy are all critical. Such issues generally do not matter for market risk, which usually arises from changes in prices of standardized securities rather than arcane details of legal contracts.

Stylized Credit Risk Model. My overview of credit risk and credit modeling diverges from the approach usually taken in risk management texts. The aim of the present section is to demonstrate the characteristics of credit risk modeling, not to build a realistic credit model. One important goal of this section is to point out that the concept behind credit risk models is simple but also to explain why realistic models are complex and difficult to build.

This section lays out a stylized model to provide a framework for understanding how credit risk models are used.[112] For more standard approaches, Crouhy, Galai, and Mark (2001, ch. 7–12; 2006, ch. 9–12) provide a particularly good review of banking industry practice and models. Marrison (2002, ch. 16–23) has an extensive discussion of industry practice and modeling, with chapter 17 providing a particularly nice overview of the variety of credit structures that a bank faces.

For the stylized model, we consider a portfolio that contains 1,000 identical loans. The time horizon over which we measure the P&L distribution is one year because we want to determine an appropriate level of annual reserves. One year happens to be the same as the loan maturity. The loans are made to a variety of businesses, but all the businesses have the same credit quality so that the chance of default or other adverse event is the same for each loan and the chance of default for a single loan is 1 percent. All the loans are assumed to be independent, so defaults are independent. If a loan does default, we will assume that recovery, from liquidation of the business or assets held as collateral, will be 50 percent of the loan's face value. These characteristics are summarized in **Exhibit 5.4**.

Exhibit 5.4. Characteristics of Loans, Credit Analysis, and Credit Quality

Loans	Credit Quality	Output
• $1,000 initial investment	• All identical credit quality	• Require one-year P&L distribution
• One-year final maturity	• Recovery upon default: 50 percent	
• Promised interest at year-end: 6.5 percent	• Probability of default of an individual loan: 0.01	
	• Individual loans independent	

---

[112]Coleman (forthcoming) expands on this model, provides a taxonomy of models, and discusses specific models by putting them into context using the stylized model of this section.

The initial portfolio value is $1 million (1,000 loans of $1,000 each). The portfolio value in one year depends on the repayment and default experience for the individual loans. If an individual loan is in good standing, the repayment is $1,065 (income $65). If a loan defaults, the recovery is $500 and the loss is $500. These payments are shown schematically in **Figure 5.16**. The actual income (less initial investment) is

$$\text{Actual income} = (\text{Nondefaults} \times \$1,065) + (\text{Defaults} \times \$500) - (1,000 \times \$1,000).$$

We know that the average probability of defaults is 1 percent, so on average, 10 loans will default. Thus, the average actual income will be

$$\text{Average actual income} = (990 \times \$1,065) + (10 \times \$500) - (1,000 \times \$1,000)$$
$$= \$59,350.$$

Beyond the average performance, we need to know how the portfolio is likely to behave in adverse circumstances and how much the bank making the loans should set aside in reserves to cover the contingency that more loans than expected will go into default. We can answer such a question if we know the full income distribution.

Before turning to the "solution" of this model, let me highlight a critical assumption: independence of loans across borrowers. Loans are assumed to be independent; there is no correlation between borrowers (no change in the probability of default because other borrowers do or do not go into default).

Figure 5.16. Initial Investment and Final Repayment for Individual Loans and Overall Portfolio

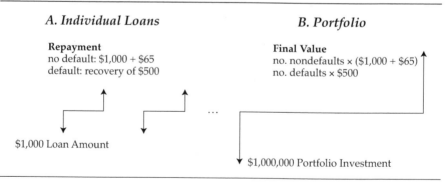

Furthermore, the probability of default does not change with conditions in the economy or other factors—the probability is indeed constant at 0.01 for every borrower.

Under this assumption, the distribution of defaults is actually very simple: a binomial distribution. The outcome for each of the 1,000 loans is a Bernoulli trial, default (probability 0.01) versus not default (probability 0.99). The probability of having k defaults out of 1,000 firms is (by the binomial distribution)

$$P(k \text{ defaults}) = \binom{1,000}{k} 0.01^k \, 0.99^{1,000-k}.$$

Panel A of **Figure 5.17** shows the distribution of defaults, and Panel B shows the distribution of income. Note that the distributions are discrete (the lines have been included only for the visual appeal) but nearly symmetrical, in spite of there being "many small gains, few large losses."

Credit Risk Modeling: Simple Concept, Complex Execution.

If the model just described seems too easy, too simplistic, it is not the model that is too simple but the assumptions or data behind the model, such as the probability of loan default or the independence across loans. Although the model is very simple, it does contain many, even most, characteristics of more realistic credit risk models. The model also helps to highlight why real-world credit risk modeling is so difficult: The difficulty arises not so much from "solving" the credit model once the risk factors are known as from parameterizing and estimating the risk factors underlying the credit process itself.

Four "risk factors" contribute to credit risk, and the model so far highlights three. I will discuss the fourth, correlation or dependence, shortly.[113]

---

[113]Technically, credit risk depends on three factors: default, recovery, and exposure (see, for example, Jorion 2007, pp. 454–455). Loss amount is the product of these factors: Dollar loss = $L = e \times (1 - \delta) \times Y$, where $Y =$ default indicator = 1 if default occurs and = 0 if no default; $\delta =$ percentage recovery (in the current model, 50 percent); $e =$ exposure, the dollar amount at risk if default occurs (in the current model, the loan amount, $1,000). Correlation or dependence between defaults is simply a characteristic of the joint default probability and is subsumed under the "default" factor. Nonetheless, dependence across defaults is such an important element, one that has a huge impact on the shape of the distribution of defaults in a portfolio context, that I include it as a risk factor in its own right. It is particularly important to highlight it alongside "default" because the primary focus when estimating default probability is often on a firm in isolation (the marginal probability) rather than the dependence across firms (the joint probability).

Figure 5.17. Number of Defaults and Income for Portfolio of 1,000 Homogeneous Loans

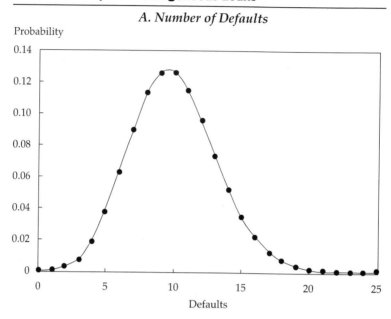

A. Number of Defaults

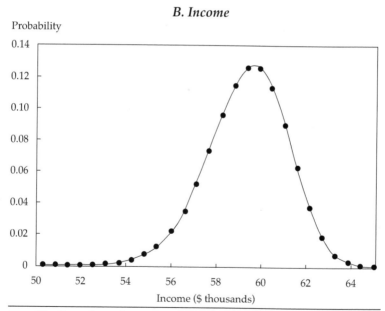

B. Income

Notes: The figure shows the number of defaults (Panel A) and the one-year income (Panel B) for a portfolio of 1,000 homogeneous loans, each with probability of default of 0.01. This is a binomial distribution with 1,000 trials, probability of default 0.01.

- *Default*: Probability that the counterparty defaults and some or all of the value is lost. Termed *probability of default* (PD) or *expected default frequency* (EDF).[114] (In this example, the probability of default is 0.01.)

- *Correlation*: Dependency across firms in terms of default probability. As discussed shortly, correlation has a huge impact on the shape of the distribution of credit losses. (In this example, the correlation is zero.)

- *Exposure*: The amount the firm has exposed to a particular counterparty or at risk to a particular credit, also termed the *exposure at default* (EAD).[115] (In this example, the exposure for each loan is $1,000.)

- *Recovery*: The amount recovered upon default because rarely is the whole amount lost. Also expressed as the *loss given default* (LGD), where Recovery = 1 − LGD. (In this example, recovery is 50 percent or $500 out of $1,000 investment.)

This model underscores why real-world credit risk modeling is so difficult and why it is often more difficult than market risk. The basic problem is data: A good history on defaults and recoveries is rudimentary, knowledge of current status is incomplete, and projections of future default probabilities and other relevant variables are very difficult to make. One must turn to modeling the underlying economic and financial drivers to try to derive realistic estimates. Each of the four factors just discussed must be parameterized and estimated. And estimating these factors is a major analytical, data collection, and data analysis project.

In practical applications, one must spend much time and effort on both making the assumptions reflect reality and building and solving the model. The challenge of marrying assumptions and reality requires that substantial resources be devoted to analytics, data, and programming.

With realistic assumptions for defaults, dependence, recovery, and so on, the stylized model discussed here would be very realistic. The difficulty is that arriving at such realistic assumptions is a complex undertaking. Nonetheless, this stylized model provides a framework for understanding how credit models work as well as a foil for illustrating how and why the concepts are simple whereas realistic implementations are complex.

---

[114]More generally, the probability of default could be extended to include more general transitions between credit states, with the transition from solvent to default being a simple special case.

[115]This term can be confusing because it sounds like "exposure at the time of default" rather than what it is, "exposure upon default," but it is the term commonly used.

Distribution of Defaults and Income. For Figure 5.17, I should note a couple of points regarding the distribution of defaults. First, although in this situation the distribution can be solved analytically, that will generally not be the case. Usually simulation is necessary. Simulation would be easy in this case: Simply draw 1,000 uniform random variables between 0 and 1 and compare each with the probability of default (0.01). If the random variable is above 0.01, the firm does not default; if it is below, the firm does default. Simulation in more complex cases is similar, and although simple conceptually, it is often quite difficult to implement.

The second point is that the distribution of losses and income in Figure 5.17 is symmetrical, which is hardly surprising given the well-known result that the binomial distribution converges to the normal for large n and given that n = 1,000 is large. It does, however, demonstrate that distributions from defaults and credit risk generally are not necessarily asymmetrical and that asymmetry does not arise from "small gains, large losses" as often claimed. This portfolio has many small gains ($65 for each of roughly 990 performing loans) and a few large losses ($500 for each of roughly 10 nonperforming loans), but the distribution is still symmetrical. Credit loss distributions are often asymmetrical, but it is usually because of dependence in defaults across firms. I will return to this issue and consider the asymmetry of the distribution and alternative dependence assumptions shortly.

VaR and Economic Capital. Using the distribution shown in Figure 5.17, Panel B, we can answer questions regarding how much a firm might lose in adverse circumstances. **Table 5.5** shows the cumulative probability, defaults, and income for part of the lower tail (the distribution function rather than the density function displayed in Figure 5.17, Panel B). The average income is $59,350. From Table 5.5, we can see that the 1 percent/99 percent VaR is a loss (compared with the average) of between $4,520 and $5,085. The 0.1 percent/99.9 percent VaR is a loss between $6,215 and $6,780.[116]

Marrison (2002, p. 229) has a succinct description of what the CFO of a bank might require from a credit risk modeling exercise, such as the one we have conducted:

- Provisions: amounts set to cover the expected losses over a period. It would be the expected loss, which in this case is $59,350 (the mean or expected income) − $65,000 (the promised income) or −$5,650.

---

[116] Note that the probability of actually losing money outright from this portfolio is low (if the assumptions about the underlying loans are valid). It might be reasonable to measure income relative to costs, where costs are the original loan plus some cost of funds. If the cost of funds is 5 percent (versus promised interest of 6.5 percent), then average actual income less costs would be $9,350.

Table 5.5. Statistics for Income Distribution for Portfolio of 1,000 Homogeneous Loans

Mean and standard deviation

Item	Amount
Mean	$59,350
Standard deviation	$1,778

Lower tail of distribution

Cumulative Probability	Defaults	Income	Income vs. Average
0.08246	15	$56,525	−$2,825
0.04779	16	55,960	−3,390
0.02633	17	55,395	−3,955
0.01378	18	54,830	−4,520
0.00685	19	54,265	−5,085
0.00321	20	53,700	−5,650
0.00146	21	53,135	−6,215
0.00066	22	52,570	−6,780
0.00026	23	52,005	−7,345

Notes: These data are the one-year income and associated cumulative probability (distribution function rather than the density function displayed in Figure 5.17, Panel B) from holding a portfolio of 1,000 homogeneous loans, each with average probability of default of 0.01. Loss given default is 50 percent; promised interest income is 6.5 percent.

- Reserves: amount set to cover losses for an unusually bad year, maybe set at the 5 percent quantile (5 percent/95 percent VaR) of the distribution.
- Economic capital: loss level for an extraordinarily bad year, maybe set at the 0.1 percent quantile (0.1 percent/99.9 percent VaR) of the distribution, discussed more fully later.

The expected income is $59,350 as calculated earlier. For the reserves, an amount in case defaults are higher than expected, we might want to set them at the 5 percent/95 percent VaR level, between $2,825 and $3,390. For capital, we might set it at $6,500, roughly the 0.1 percent/99.9 percent VaR.

Setting economic capital is a difficult problem. Economic capital is distinguished from regulatory capital because it is set in response to economic circumstances rather than regulatory or accounting rules. Economic capital supports a firm's risk-taking activities, providing the buffer against losses that would otherwise push the firm into bankruptcy. McNeil, Frey, and Embrechts (2005, section 1.4.3) lay out the following process for determining economic capital:

- First, determine a "value distribution," which is the result of quantifying all the risks faced by the firm, including but not limited to market, credit, and operational risk. (For the current simple model, if we assume that the portfolio of 1,000 loans is the total of the firm's business, the P&L distribution shown in Figure 5.17, Panel B, and Table 5.5 is this "value distribution.")

- Second, determine an acceptable probability of default (solvency standard) appropriate for the institution and horizon. A useful basis is company ratings and associated default rates. For example, a firm might target a Moody's Aa rating. Historical analysis of Moody's Aa rated institutions shows a one-year default frequency of 0.03 percent.[117] The firm would want a level of capital high enough so that losses would be worse (implying bankruptcy) only with a probability of 0.03 percent.

- Finally, calculate economic capital as the appropriate quantile (buffer needed to ensure bankruptcy with probability chosen in the second step). For 0.03 percent probability of bankruptcy, it would be the $Z = 0.03$ percent/99.97 percent quantile. (For the current simple loan portfolio example, it would be roughly $7,300.)

Although the conceptual process for calculating economic capital is straightforward, the practical issues are challenging.

Dependence, Correlation, Asymmetry, and Skewness. The stylized model has intentionally been kept simple but is worth extending in one particular direction: correlation or dependence across loans. As noted earlier, asymmetry, or skewness, is an important characteristic of credit risk, and dependence across loans is a major reason for asymmetry.

The model so far produces a symmetrical default distribution and loss distribution—virtually no asymmetry. But it is easy to produce asymmetry by the natural mechanism of dependence across defaults. That is, loans default together. The phenomenon of firms defaulting together is both easy to understand and often observed. The probability of default may go up and down because of common economic factors, with firms more likely to go into default in tough economic times.

We can understand the mechanism that generates asymmetry by considering a two-state world: a low-default regime where the default probability is

---

[117]See, for example, Crouhy, Galai, and Mark (2001, Table 8.3), where they cite Carty and Lieberman (1996); or see Duffie and Singleton (2003, Table 4.2).

0.007353 and a high-default regime where the default probability is 0.025. In each regime, firm defaults are independent, so in each regime, the distribution will be binomial (symmetrical). In these two regimes, the income for our stylized portfolio of 1,000 loans will be as shown in Panel A of **Figure 5.18**.

We now consider the overall situation, which is a mixture of the two regimes. We will assume that at any point in time, there is an 85 percent probability we are in the low-default regime and a 15 percent probability that we are in the high-default regime. At a particular time, we are in one or the other, but beforehand, we do not know which. With this setup, the overall average default probability is 0.01, just as it was originally. But now we have correlation across firm defaults, correlation of 0.004. If one particular firm defaults, it is more likely we are in the high-default regime and thus more likely that other firms will also default—not because of the default of the first firm but simply because the probability of defaults for all firms is likely to be higher.

The overall distribution of income will be a mixture of the two distributions for the individual regimes. This mixture is shown in Panel B of Figure 5.18, and we see that it is, naturally, skewed or asymmetrical. The asymmetry arises because the overall distribution is composed of a large part of the high-income (low-default) distribution and a smaller part of the low-income distribution and the low-income distribution skews the lower tail of the overall distribution.

The mixing of good (low-default) and bad (high-default) worlds naturally produces correlation across defaults and skewed distributions; the correlation and skewness go hand in hand. In either the good or the bad world, defaults will tend to be symmetrical. But at some times, we are in the high-default world and thus will have many defaults, and at other times, we are in the low-default world and will have few defaults. The larger number of defaults during bad times produces both the skewness or fat upper tail of the default distribution (fat lower tail of the income distribution) and the correlation (because defaults tend to happen together).

The default correlation for this example is only 0.004 but produces substantial skewness. Let us compare Figure 5.18, Panel B, with Figure 5.17, where the overall probability of default is also 0.01 but there is no default correlation and little skewness. For Figure 5.17, the 1 percent/99 percent VaR for the losses is between 17 and 18 defaults, or roughly $54,600 ($4,750 below the mean). For Figure 5.18, the 1 percent/99 percent VaR is between 33 and 35 defaults, or roughly $46,000 ($13,350 below the mean). Even the low default correlation of 0.004 produces substantial skewness. There is only a small chance of the bad world (many defaults), but when it occurs, it produces substantially lower income, and it is exactly the low-probability left end of the tail that determines the VaR. It only requires a tiny default correlation to produce substantial skewness or asymmetry.

Figure 5.18. Income Distributions for Low- and High-Default Regimes and Mixture

A. Low- and High-Default Regimes

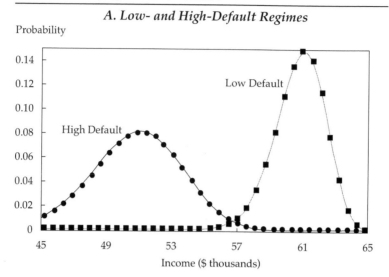

B. Mixture

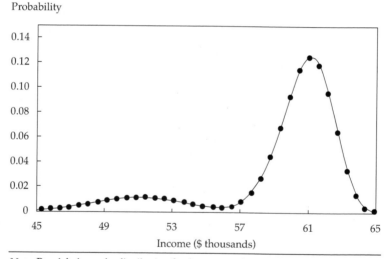

Notes: Panel A shows the distribution for the one-year income from holding a portfolio of 1,000 homogeneous loans, each with average probability of default of 0.025 (high-default regime) and 0.007353 (low-default regime). Loss given default is 50 percent; promised interest is 6.5 percent. Panel B shows the income distribution for a mixture that is 15 percent high default and 85 percent low default.

This model of mixing just a good and a bad state is clearly very simplistic, but it does illustrate two points: first, that correlation can be produced not because firms depend on each other but because all firms are responding to the same underlying factors (in this case, either high or low defaults) and second, that it takes only a very low level of correlation to produce a substantial degree of skewness or asymmetry in the default and loss distribution. (This differs from market price loss distributions, where we usually develop our intuition and where small changes in correlation do not dramatically change the shape of the distribution.)

Let us examine a little more carefully how practical models build in dependence across defaults. Initially, the approach does not look like the mixing just discussed, but in most practical applications, it turns out that it is exactly this kind of mixing that is commonly used.

The most important variable in any credit model is the probability of default, p. A simple model for default, and one that will naturally build in dependence across defaults, is the threshold model and factor structure (used, for example, by credit models such as Moody's KMV). Default is assumed to occur when some random *critical variable* X_i falls below a *critical threshold* d_i:

$$\text{Default when } X_i < d_i. \tag{5.6a}$$

Each loan or firm may have its own critical variable X_i and its own critical threshold d_i. (For the stylized and homogeneous model we have been considering, all loans are set to be identical so that all the d_i will be the same and all the X_i will have the same distribution.)

Credit models of this form, usually based on the Merton (1974) approach, build the relationship between the critical variable and the threshold from realistic economic and financial relationships that are based on historical data and firm analysis.[118] For example, X_i might be the value of the firm (which may go up or down randomly) and d_i the value of the firm's debt. The firm goes into default when the value of the firm falls below the value of the debt, so default occurs when $X_i < d_i$. The important point for now, however, is simply that there is some reasonable story that justifies the relationship between the random variable X_i and the fixed threshold d_i, where default occurs when $X_i < d_i$.

If we assume that X_i is normally distributed with zero mean and unit variance, then the probability of default is

---

[118]See McNeil, Frey, and Embrechts (2005, chapter 8) or Coleman (forthcoming) for more information.

Probability of default: $P(X_i < d_i) = \Phi(d_i)$. (5.6b)

If all the X_i are independent, then the probabilities of default are independent and the model is exactly the stylized model with independent defaults. It is, however, easy to build in dependence across defaults by introducing correlation across the critical variables (X_i) for different loans or firms. Take the extreme example where X_1 and X_2 are perfectly correlated. Then, Firms 1 and 2 will always default together (or not default together). In general, the default correlation will be less than 1.0, and the default correlation is determined by the correlation of the variables X_i. The higher the correlation across the X_i, the higher the correlation in defaults.

Correlation across X_i is commonly introduced by a so-called *common factor structure* that splits the random X_i into one random factor that is common across all firms and one that is specific to the particular firm, i:

$$X_i = \sqrt{\rho}F + \sqrt{1-\rho}\varepsilon_i,$$ (5.7)

where

F = Common random factor, same for all firms

ε_i = Firm-specific independent random factor or idiosyncratic variable

ρ = Correlation in the critical variable F across firms; also is the proportion of variance attributable to common factor

I will now return to a mixing framework. The common factor F represents elements that affect all firms together; a low value of F means bad times and firms more likely to default. These common factors might be economic factors that alter the probability of default, such as economic growth or the level of interest rates, or common industry conditions, such as when airline companies are financially pressured as the relative price of energy rises. The firm-specific variable ε_i represents factors determining default that are specific to the individual firm and are independent across firms.

Whatever the source, correlation across the critical variables X_i produces correlation across defaults. Say we have a default probability as follows:

$$p_i^* = P(X_i < d_i) = \Phi(d_i) = 0.01.$$

Suppose the correlation across the critical variables X_i and X_j is $\rho = 0.05$. We can calculate the default correlation as

Default correlation = 0.004

given

Individual firm defaults = 0.01

Critical variable correlation = 0.05.[119]

The critical variable correlation and the default correlation are both low, but these are typical values for observed credit defaults. McNeil, Frey, and Embrechts (2005, Table 8.8) provide estimates of pairwise correlations from default data for 1981–2000. They find a one-year default probability for BB rated issuers of 0.0097 and a pairwise default correlation of 0.0044; see **Table 5.6**.

Even a low default correlation can give quite substantial asymmetry. We saw this outcome in the simple example of mixing, Figure 5.18. We see the same in more realistic models of correlation and dependence. **Figure 5.19** shows the default and loss distribution, based on the dependence structure of Equations 5.1 and 5.2, for default correlation 0.004.[120] The independent case is the one I explained earlier: no dependence across loans and a binomial distribution for defaults, resulting in a symmetrical distribution for defaults and P&L. The

Table 5.6. Results for a Threshold/Bernoulli Mixture Model

	A	BBB	BB	B	CCC
Average probability of default, $E[p_r(f)]$, implied default correlation	0.00044	0.00227	0.00975	0.05027	0.20776
A		0.00040	0.00076	0.00130	0.00220	0.00304
BBB		0.00076	0.00148	0.00255	0.00435	0.00609
BB		0.00130	0.00255	0.00443	0.00762	0.01080
B		0.00220	0.00435	0.00762	0.01329	0.01912
CCC		0.00304	0.00609	0.01080	0.01912	0.02796

Notes: This table is based on the maximum likelihood parameter estimates for a one-factor Bernoulli mixture model. The underlying data are annual default counts from Standard & Poor's for 1981–2000. The data in this table are slightly adjusted from those shown in McNeil, Frey, and Embrechts: I have estimated a significant digit beyond that published in their table for the average probability of default $E[p_r(f)]$, the mixture mean μ_r, and the scaling parameter σ (0.243 versus 0.24) to more closely reproduce the implied default correlations from McNeil, Frey, and Embrechts, Table 8.8. See discussion in Coleman (forthcoming).

Source: Based on McNeil, Frey, and Embrechts (2005, Table 8.8).

---

[119]See Coleman (forthcoming) or McNeil, Frey, and Embrechts (2005, p. 344)for details of calculating default correlations.

[120]The "dependent" line in Figure 5.19, Panel B, reproduces Figure 5.15, and the "independent" line reproduces Figure 5.17, Panel B. Figure 5.19, Panel A, is close to McNeil, Frey, and Embrechts (2005, Figure 8.1).

Figure 5.19. Number of Defaults and Income for a Portfolio of 1,000 Homogeneous Loans, Alternate Dependence Assumptions

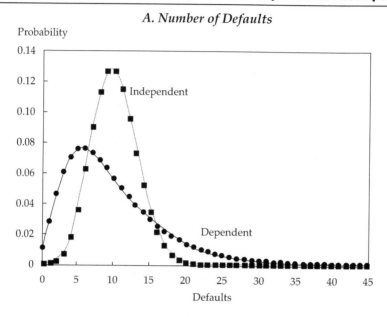

A. Number of Defaults

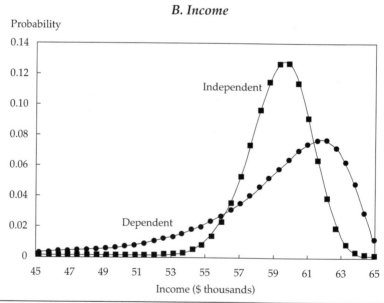

B. Income

Notes: The figure shows the number of defaults (Panel A) and the income (Panel B) from holding a portfolio of 1,000 homogeneous loans, each with average probability of default of 0.01. The default process is the common factor structure as in Equations 5.1 and 5.2. The "Independent" case has threshold correlation = 0%; the "Dependent" case has threshold correlation = 5%, with default correlation = 0.4%.

default correlation 0.004 represents dependence across loans. The dependence is low but still produces substantial skewness and is obvious in Figure 5.19. We can also measure it by calculating the VaR. For the independent case, the 1 percent/99 percent VaR is between 18 and 19 defaults (out of 1,000 loans) and a P&L of roughly $54,600 (between $4,520 and $5,085 below the mean). For the dependent case, the 1 percent/99 percent VaR is dramatically higher: defaults between 34 and 35 and a P&L of roughly $45,500 (between $13,560 and $14,125 below the mean). Once again, we see that an apparently tiny amount of cross-sectional dependence can create large losses in the tail.

The example so far has assumed that all loans are identical, so the default probability is equal across loans, and the distribution (for no correlation) is binomial. Introducing heterogeneity in the loans (while maintaining independence) does not change anything significantly. When independent, the default distribution tends toward symmetry, whereas correlation breaks the symmetry and produces a skewed distribution.

The analysis of dependence and credit risk is challenging. Much of our everyday experience and understanding of correlation and diversification come from the arena of market risk, as applied to correlation across prices and returns. This experience and knowledge do not always carry over well to defaults and credit risk. Default is a rare event. Correlation across defaults will usually be close to zero, but even low correlations can have quite a dramatic impact as demonstrated earlier. Small changes in default correlation can have large impacts on the skewness of the default distribution. The degree of skewness and the sensitivity of the distribution to small changes in the degree of correlation provide yet another example of why credit risk modeling is so difficult: Measuring the degree of dependence in the real world is difficult, but dependence makes such a large difference in the shape of the distribution that it is especially important to measure precisely.

Estimating Default Probability and Correlation. We can use the threshold and common factor framework discussed earlier to estimate average default probabilities and cross-correlations. McNeil, Frey, and Embrechts (2005, section 8.6.4) have done just that using annual default count data from Standard & Poor's for 1981–2000. Table 5.6 is based on their Table 8.8 and shows results for a threshold model with a single common factor. The important point here is the way that the average probability of default and the default correlations vary across ratings.

The probability of default varies from very low (0.0004 for A rated firms or roughly four defaults per year out of a pool of 10,000 firms) to high (0.2078 for CCC rated firms or roughly 2,078 defaults per year out of a pool of 10,000 firms). The correlation across defaults also varies considerably. In all cases, however, the correlation produces substantial skew. **Figure 5.20** shows the default distribution for BBB rated and CCC rated firms, for both zero default correlation and the default correlation shown in Table 5.6. Note from Panel A that even though the default correlation for BBB rated firms is very small, it produces a substantial skew in the default distribution. This outcome reinforces how important dependence across firms is in determining the shape of the default (and thus the income) distribution, particularly when the probability of default and correlation are low. For the BBB rated firms, zero correlation produces a very symmetrical distribution, even though there are very few defaults relative to the size of the portfolio. A small correlation serves to produce a dramatically skewed distribution.

Building and Measuring Default Probability and Correlation.

As discussed earlier, four "risk factors" contribute to credit risk:

Default = *Probability of default* (PD) or *expected default frequency* (EDF).

Correlation = Dependency or correlation in default probability across firms.

Exposure = The amount exposed, also termed the *exposure at default* (EAD).

Recovery = The amount recovered upon default, also expressed as the *loss given default* (LGD), where *Recovery* = 1 = *LGD*.

In its essence, credit modeling is the process of estimating these four risk factors and then using the estimates to generate an income distribution. The stylized model I have been discussing has focused on the first two of these—assuming that exposure and recovery are fixed or known. The latter two are equally important, although I have not focused on them to the same extent.

In reality, estimating each of these risk factors is a very difficult task, and most of the time and effort in credit analysis is focused on estimating one or all of these risk factors. Because we do not usually have observations of default for a firm currently in good standing, we have to estimate these factors from a model. Many practical models use the common factor structure of equations (5.6) and (5.7) as the framework for determining the probability of default and correlation across firms (the first two risk factors).

The critical variable idea embodied in Equation 5.6a,

Default when $X_i < d_i$,

goes back to Merton's (1974) option-theoretic model of default. The idea is to consider default in terms of a firm's assets relative to liabilities at the end of some time period. The critical variable X_i is identified with assets, which are treated as random variables. Default occurs when these random assets are below liabilities (the fixed d_i) at the end of the period. That is, default occurs when the random variable (assets) crosses a threshold (liabilities), or $X_i < d_i$.

Figure 5.20. Default Distributions with and without Correlation Representative of BBB and CCC Firms

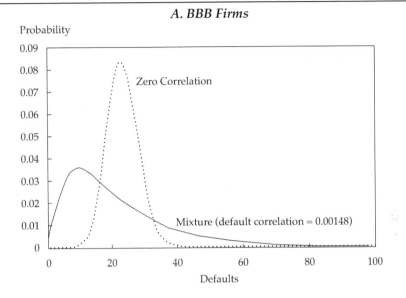

A. BBB Firms

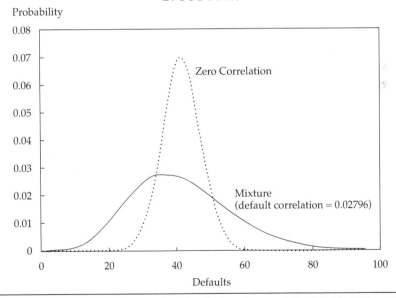

B. CCC Firms

Notes: This figure shows the simulated default distributions for a portfolio of 10,000 BBB rated firms (Panel A) and 200 CCC rated firms (Panel B) using the parameters from Table 5.6. The dashed line is zero correlation; the solid line is for the correlation shown in Table 5.6.

The practical implementation of such an idea requires measuring assets (X_i) and liabilities (d_i) for each firm and then building the relationship between them in terms of how close assets are to liabilities and how likely is default. Both assets and liabilities are difficult to measure, even for publicly traded firms. For private firms, there may be little or no public information on the value of assets or liabilities. Assets and liabilities are heterogeneous, with different firms having often dramatically different capital structures. Consolidating information across a large number of heterogeneous entities into a usable set of data that maps to the simple concepts of "assets" and "liabilities" is a huge task.

The event of default is determined by Equation 5.6a and the probability of default (see Equation 5.6b) by:

Probability of default: $P(X_i < d_i)$.

The "distance" must be calibrated in some way to give a realistic probability of default. Commercially available credit products, such as Moody's KMV, do this by collecting and analyzing a huge proprietary database of public and private company default and loss data.

Default is a rare event and multiple defaults doubly rare, so correlation across defaults is difficult to measure. The common factor structure of Equation 5.7 shifts the problem from measuring defaults directly to that of measuring the correlation across the critical variables (firm assets X_i). The correlation across defaults (joint default of firms i and j) is modeled by considering the correlation across assets (correlation between X_i and X_j) and then inferring joint default by considering the likelihood of both asset levels falling below their critical levels:

Joint default when $X_i < d_i$ and $X_j < d_j$.

Much of traditional credit analysis can be viewed as the estimation of the probability of default, the first of the risk factors. Consider, for example, credit ratings. In one sense, assigning a credit rating to an individual firm is nothing more than an assessment of the probability of default (sometimes with a component of the recovery included).

Poisson as Approximation to Binomial Default Processes.
Default is a binomial process in that default for a portfolio is an example of repeated binary events or Bernoulli trials—default (failure) versus no default (success). For identical loans or firms and no correlation across firms, it is quite easy to write down the binomial distribution and arrive at a graph such as Figure 5.17. In reality, firms are never identical and correlation is critically important,

so the simple binomial distribution cannot be used. The alternative is simulation. Simulation is simple in principle, but the computational expense (time spent in setting up and running the simulation) can be high. In some cases, however, the default process can be approximated by a Poisson process, which can have substantial benefits.

A Poisson random variable is a counting variable that, in contrast to a Bernoulli variable (which is 0 or 1), can take integer values such that $j = (0, 1, 2, \ldots)$. When the event of default is rare, as it usually will be, the Poisson process can provide a useful approximation to the true default process. The value j counts the number of "events" during a period. We can identify no default with $j = 0$ and default with $j \geq 1$. This leaves the possibility that $j = (2, 3, \ldots)$, but when default is rare for any particular firm, the probability of multiple "defaults" for a single firm will be very rare. The benefit of the Poisson framework versus the Bernoulli framework, and it is a substantial benefit, arises when considering a portfolio of multiple firms. For firms that are independent, the sum of the Poissons across the individual firms is itself Poisson, which means that the total number of defaults has a simple mathematical form.[121] Furthermore, correlation or dependence across firms can be introduced in such a way that the distribution, although no longer Poisson, can still be handled analytically or semi-analytically. This allows substantially faster computation and may have considerable advantages in practice.

Actuarial vs. Equivalent Martingale (Risk-Neutral) Pricing.
The focus for credit risk so far in this chapter has been on building the distribution of defaults and losses. The focus has been on doing so from first principles, often using complicated models and limited data, which is appropriate and necessary for products for which there is no traded market. However, there are credit products (and an increasing number of them) for which there is a traded market. For these products, it is often better to use a market-based approach.

In introducing a market-based approach, however, I have to emphasize the subtle distinction between two approaches to the probability of losses and default. So far I have, naturally, used the actual probability of defaults and losses—what we would call the "physical probability" measure. We have not looked at market prices because we have assumed that market prices are not readily available.

---

[121]See McNeil, Frey, and Embrechts (2005, sections 8.4.2 and 10.2.4) and Coleman (forthcoming).

When market prices are available and we use those market prices to infer the distribution of credit losses, however, we need to use something called the "equivalent martingale probability" or the "risk-neutral probability." The distinction between physical and equivalent martingale probability measures is straightforward but can take a little time to get used to. The physical measure is the probability that we actually observe, what we experience in the physical world. All the credit risk distributions I have been discussing so far have been using the physical measure. In contrast, the equivalent martingale or risk-neutral measure arises in pricing market-traded securities. It is an "artificial" probability measure but one that is nonetheless incredibly useful for pricing securities.

The natural question is, why use anything other than the physical, real-world probabilities? The answer is that pricing securities using the physical probability measure is often difficult, whereas pricing with the equivalent martingale measure reduces (for securities with market prices) to the easier exercise of taking an expectation and discounting. For traded assets or securities, when market prices are available, the equivalent martingale or risk-neutral pricing approach is very powerful.

McNeil, Frey, and Embrechts (2005, section 9.3) have an excellent section discussing actuarial pricing (using the physical probability measure) versus risk-neutral pricing. They summarize as follows:

> *Financial and actuarial pricing compared.* The financial-pricing approach is a *relative pricing theory*, which explains prices of credit products in terms of observable prices of other securities. If properly applied, it leads to arbitrage-free prices of credit-risk securities, which are consistent with prices quoted in the market. These features make the financial-pricing approach the method of choice in an environment where credit risk is actively traded and, in particular, for valuing credit instruments when the market for related products is relatively liquid. On the other hand, since financial-pricing models have to be calibrated to prices of traded credit instruments, they are difficult to apply when we lack sufficient market information. Moreover, in such cases prices quoted using an *ad hoc* choice of some risk-neutral measure are more or less "plucked out of thin air."
>
> The actuarial pricing approach is an *absolute pricing approach*, based on the paradigm of *risk bearing*: a credit product such as a loan is taken on the balance sheet if the spread earned on the loan is deemed by the lender to be a sufficient compensation for the risk contribution of the loan to the total risk of the lending portfolio. Moreover, the approach relies mainly on historical default information. Therefore, the actuarial approach is well suited to situations where the market for related credit instruments is relatively illiquid, such that little or no price information is available; loans to medium or small businesses are a prime case in point. On the other hand, the approach does not necessarily lead to prices that are consistent (in the sense of absence of arbitrage) across products or that are compatible with quoted market prices for credit instruments, so it is less suitable for a trading environment. (pp. 412–413)

The authors also point out that as markets develop, more credit products are priced using market prices and the risk-neutral methodology. This raises issues of consistency and uniformity across an institution, with the possibility that the same product may be priced differently by different units of a firm. Managing these issues requires a good understanding of the differences between market-based (risk-neutral) valuation and actuarial valuation.

The financial versus actuarial pricing distinction highlights an important dividing line for credit risk, maybe the most important one in credit risk measurement. When a credit risk is traded, it makes sense to measure risk using the market prices at which it is traded as well as the distribution of prices. One should only use complex, default-based models when instruments are not traded (e.g., for loans, some corporate bonds, counterparty exposure on derivatives).

Market-Based Credit Models. Using the equivalent martingale approach, we can price various market-traded products. Credit default swaps, discussed in Chapter 3 earlier, are the most straightforward example.

Credit Risk Topics Not Covered. There is a wide range of credit risk topics I have not covered. In this section, I will briefly touch on some of these.

Credit risk management is composed of three areas:

- Measurement;
- Setting reserves, provisions, and economic capital; and
- Other management areas—setting limits, portfolio management, and managing people and incentives.

The primary focus of this chapter has been on determining the distribution for defaults, which is only the first component of measuring credit risk. Measurement means determining the P&L distribution. The loss itself depends on default, exposure, and recovery: *Loss = Default × Exposure × (1 − Recovery)*. Defaults have taken center stage because default modeling is the most complex component of credit risk models and because models differ primarily in their modeling of defaults and the process underlying defaults, not their modeling of exposures and recovery.

▓ *Measurement: traditional credit analysis and ratings.* Traditional credit analysis is devoted to analyzing individual firms, loans, and other credit risks with the goal of assessing the likelihood of default and how costly the default would be were it to occur. It usually takes the form of assigning a credit rating to a credit risk. The credit rating may reflect only the likelihood of default or a combination of the probability of default and the severity of loss. In this sense, traditional credit ratings map to the default probabilities of the more formal models discussed in this chapter or a combination of probability and loss given default. In some cases, the mapping is explicit, as in CreditMetrics, where a firm's rating category determines the transition (and default) probability, and in the default probability estimates by rating category from McNeil, Frey, and Embrechts (2005), discussed in their section 6.7.4.

Most rating systems are based on both quantitative and qualitative considerations, but they are usually not based on formal models of the type discussed in this chapter. Traditional credit analysis generally focuses on individual names and not portfolio interactions directly and thus could be termed single-name credit analysis.

In practice, a huge variety of methods and an extensive literature are devoted to single-name credit analysis and ratings systems. There are a number of ratings agencies that rate publicly traded issues, with Standard & Poor's, Moody's, and Fitch being the best known. Private-sector issuers pay ratings agencies to rate a bond issue, and the ratings agencies then make the ratings available to the public. Many investors and regulators rely on these ratings. Almost all public issues in the United States are rated by one or more of the ratings agencies, and many international issues and issuers (including sovereign issuers, such as the U.S. or the Greek government) are also rated.

Many issues and issuers to which a bank is exposed will not have public ratings, so financial institutions often develop their own internal ratings to supplement the publicly available ratings. Crouhy, Galai, and Mark (2001) devote a full chapter (ch. 7) to both public and internal credit rating systems, and Crouhy, Galai, and Mark (2006) split the topic into two chapters, one covering retail credit analysis and the other commercial.

■ *Measurement: exposure and recovery—types of credit structures.* Exposure and recovery are critical to measuring credit losses but have not been covered extensively in this chapter. Exposure refers to the amount that can potentially be lost if default occurs, and recovery refers to the amount (or proportion) of the potential loss that is recovered. They combine to give the loss given default (LGD):

$$\text{Loss given default} = \text{Exposure (\$ amount)} \times \left[1 - \text{Recovery (as a percent)} \right].$$

The current exposure can often be difficult to measure, and what matters is the exposure at the time of default, not simply the current exposure. Because default is in the future and itself uncertain, exposure at default can be doubly difficult to measure. But even measuring the current exposure can be difficult. As mentioned earlier, collecting the data on current exposures can be challenging.

Wide variation exists in the types of exposure. Marrison (2002, ch. 17) discusses various credit structures:

- Credit exposures to large corporations
    - Commercial loans
    - Commercial credit lines
    - Letters of credit and guarantees
    - Leases
    - Credit derivatives
- Credit exposures to retail customers
    - Personal loans
    - Credit cards
    - Car loans
    - Leases and hire-purchase agreements
    - Mortgages
    - Home equity lines of credit
- Credit exposures in trading operations
    - Bonds
    - Asset-backed securities (embodying underlying exposures to corporations or retail customers from such assets as loans, leases, credit cards, mortgages, etc.)
    - Securities lending and repos
    - Margin accounts
    - Credit derivatives
    - Credit exposures for derivatives (that is, for noncredit derivatives, such as interest rate swaps)
    - Trading settlement

For many instruments, exposure will vary over time and with changes in markets. Consider an amortizing corporate bond with five-year final maturity. Because of amortization, the notional value of the bond will go down over time in a predictable manner. For any notional, however, the value of the bond (and thus the exposure or amount at risk of loss) will vary with the level of market risk-free interest rates: Lower interest rates mean lower discounting and higher value. A common way to represent this relationship is by measuring the expected exposure and the maximum likely exposure (MLE). For the bond, whose value depends on interest rates, the expected exposure could be taken as the value implied by the forward curve (or possibly the notional). The MLE could be taken as the exposure at the 95th percentile of the interest rate distribution. The situation for an amortizing bond might be as shown in Panel A of **Figure 5.21**.

Figure 5.21. Expected and Maximum Likely Exposure for Amortizing Bond and Two Interest Rate Swaps

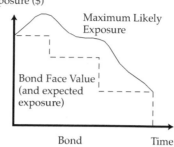

A. Amortizing Bond

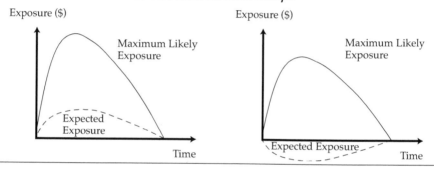

B. Two Interest Rate Swaps

For an interest rate swap and other derivatives, such as options, the credit exposure will be more complicated. The present value for a new at-market swap will be zero, so there is no credit exposure; if the counterparty defaults and walks away, there is no loss in market value. Over time and as interest rates change, however, the market value of the swap may become positive or negative. If negative, then again, there is no credit exposure; if the counterparty walks away, there is no loss in market value. When the market value is positive, however, the credit exposure will equal the market value; if the counterparty disappears, the loss is equal to the market value of the swap.

The exposure for an interest rate swap will start out at zero but then may become positive or remain at zero. The exposure will be random over time, moving between zero and some positive value. It is still possible, however, to calculate the expected and the maximum likely exposures. The expected exposure could simply be taken as the value of the swap traced out along the forward curve. This value might be either positive (shown in the left side of Panel B of Figure 5.21) or negative (the right side of Panel B of Figure 5.21—note that the exposure will actually have discrete jumps on coupon dates, but these are not shown in the figures). The maximum likely exposure could be taken as the 95th percentile of the forward curve distribution, which would be positive for virtually any swap, as shown in both the left and right sides of Panel B of Figure 5.21. Marrison (2002, ch. 17) discusses the concept of maximum likely exposure more extensively and has useful diagrams for many credit structures.

The expected or the maximum likely exposure could be used with the stylized default model discussed earlier to produce a distribution of losses. Indeed, commercial products often do something akin to this. CreditMetrics uses something close to the expected credit exposure. Moody's KMV has the option to use market prices (forward prices) to calculate exposures, which gives roughly the expected exposure.

Using the expected and maximum likely exposure, however, is only an inexact approximation. In reality, the exposure at default will generally be random. Considering an interest rate swap again, the actual exposure may be zero or positive and will change as default-free interest rates change randomly over time. Combining random default processes with random variation in underlying market variables is difficult and not commonly done.[122] This is a major issue to be addressed in future credit risk model development. The problem is particularly important for such instruments as interest rate swaps, where the exposure changes substantially with market variables (specifically, the interest rates on swaps). The issue will be less important for such instruments as short-dated loans, where the exposure is primarily caused by principal at risk.

▩ *Reserves, provisions, and economic capital.* Once the distribution of defaults and losses (the P&L distribution) has been measured, it can be used. The first place it can be used is in the determination of reserves, provisions, and economic capital. This topic was touched on very briefly earlier in this chapter. In fact, the topic deserves a deeper discussion, but it also should be integrated with overall firm risk, not limited to credit risk alone.

▩ *Credit mitigation.* Credit risk management also subsumes a large field that includes credit enhancement, mitigation, and hedging techniques. These range from such traditional techniques as bond insurance and mark to market to such recent innovations as credit default swaps. This book cannot cover these issues, but readers interested in them are referred to Crouhy, Galai, and Mark (2001), who devote chapter 12 to the topic; Crouhy, Galai, and Mark (2006) also cover it in chapter 12.

---

[122]Crouhy, Galai, and Mark (2001) emphasize this more than once—see p. 343 and also p. 411.

6. Uses and Limitations of Quantitative Techniques

Overview

Quantitative techniques work best in the hands of those who understand the techniques but who are also keenly aware of the limits and boundaries of what these techniques can provide. A deep appreciation of the limitations gives the user the confidence to rely on the techniques when appropriate and the good sense to turn elsewhere when necessary. Like most helpful tools, these techniques work well when used properly, and the key is to understand their limitations in order to avoid misusing them. The real risk to an organization is in the unanticipated or unexpected—exactly what quantitative measures capture least well.

Risk Measurement Limitations

Like any set of techniques or tools, risk measurement has definite limitations. This is not a problem; it is just the way the world is. A hammer is a useful tool, but it has limitations. It is good for pounding in a nail but not good for sawing a plank. Appreciating risk measurement limitations helps us understand when and where quantitative techniques are (and are not) useful. Failure to understand the limitations of risk measurement techniques, however, is a problem. Misusing the techniques in the face of limitations leads to mistakes, misunderstandings, and errors.

Models for Measuring Risk Will Not Include All Positions and All Risks.

The models used to measure VaR, volatility, or whatever else will never include all positions and all risks. Positions may be missed for a variety of reasons. Perhaps some legacy computer system does not feed the main risk system, or some new system may not yet be integrated. A new product may not yet have been modeled, or someone may simply neglect to book a trade in a timely manner. A good and robust risk system will have processes and procedures for checking that all positions are captured and reporting those that are not. Nonetheless, there is always some possibility that positions are missed.

Likewise, the risk of positions that are included may not be properly represented. A complex derivative security may not be modeled correctly. Some product may have an unexpected sensitivity that is not captured by the risk system.

Missing positions and missing risks mean that the risk measures reported will not perfectly represent the actual risk. In reality, nobody should be surprised that a reported risk number is not absolutely perfect. It is an estimate, and like any estimate, it will be subject to errors—one possible error being that the positions or risks do not perfectly model the real world. A risk system should be viewed as a tool for summarizing and aggregating a large amount of information in a concise manner. It will not be perfect, and users should recognize that in using the results.

Risk Measures Such as VaR and Volatility Are Backwards Looking. Quantitative techniques can tell us things about how positions and a portfolio would have behaved under past conditions—conditions that are ultimately derived from past experience. This is not a criticism, and contrary to what some commentators say, it is not a weakness of risk measurement techniques. It is simply the way the world is: We can seek to understand the past, but we cannot know the future. Understanding the past is terribly important because understanding current exposures and how they would have behaved in the past is the first step toward managing the future; as George Santayana said, "Those who cannot remember the past are condemned to repeat it."

The mistake here would be to think that these backward-looking tools measure the future. A manager needs to use judgment to interpret backward-looking information and incorporate it into the current decisions that will, together with randomness and luck, produce the future. Recognizing the backward-looking nature of the tools reminds us of the limitations and argues for care in using tools such as VaR and volatility.

VaR Does Not Measure the "Worst Case." Statistical measures such as volatility, VaR, expected shortfall, and others provide summary information about the dispersion of the P&L distribution and will never tell us the "worst case." VaR is often talked about and thought about as a "statistically worst-case loss," but that is a misleading way to think. Whatever VaR level we choose, we can always do worse, and in fact, we are guaranteed to do worse at some point. Expected shortfall is useful relative to VaR exactly because it incorporates information on the losses worse than the VaR level, but expected shortfall does not change the fact that it is simply a summary statistic providing information about the distribution rather than about individual events that have not happened yet.

Litterman's (1996, footnote 1) recommendation for how to think of VaR is good: "Think of [VaR] not as a 'worst case,' but rather as a regularly occurring event with which we should be comfortable" (p. 74). Thinking of VaR as a "worst case" is both intellectually lazy and dangerous. It is intellectually lazy because "worst case" relieves one of the responsibility of thinking of the consequences and responses to yet worse outcomes. It is dangerous because it is certain that results will, at some point, be worse.

VaR, volatility, and other risk measures should be viewed as a set of measuring tools that tell us about the likely level of losses (the "regularly occurring event with which we should be comfortable"). When viewed this way, they push us toward thinking about what to do when something worse occurs, how much worse things could actually get and why, and how to react when things do get worse. Not only do they push us toward thinking about those possibilities, but they also provide quantitative information on how bad "worse" might be.

Quantitative Techniques Are Complex and Require Expertise and Experience to Use Properly. On the one hand, quantitative techniques used in modern risk measurement are indeed complex. On the other hand, "risk management" experts, like other experts, seem to make everything complicated. A balance needs to be struck. General managers and board members have a responsibility to understand the complex businesses they oversee. The financial business overall, not just risk measurement, is complex and is becoming more complex all the time. Managers at financial firms should take their responsibilities seriously and learn enough about the business, including risk measurement, that they can effectively use the available tools. In this day and age, lack of technical expertise cannot be an excuse for failing to use or understand risk measurement information.

"Risk managers," however, have the corresponding responsibility to explain their techniques and results to nonexperts in a simple, concise, transparent manner. Most of the ideas behind risk measurement are simple, even if the details necessary to get the results are complex. Simple ideas, clear presentation, and concise description must be the goals for anyone engaged in measuring risk.

Quantitative Risk Measures Do Not Properly Represent Extreme Events. Quantitative risk measures do not catch extreme events. Experience does not. Imagination can try, but even that fails. Extreme events are extreme and hard to predict, and that is just the way life is. We need to recognize this limitation, but it is hardly a failure of risk techniques. To criticize the field of risk measurement because we cannot represent extreme events very well is just silly, like criticizing the sky because it is blue. Anybody who does not like extreme events should not be in the financial markets. Luck, both good and bad, is part of the world. We can use quantitative tools to try to put some estimates around extreme events, but we have to learn to live with uncertainty, particularly when it comes to extreme events.

Failure to appreciate our limitations, however, is a serious mistake. Overconfidence in numbers and quantitative techniques and in our ability to represent extreme events should be subject to severe criticism because it lulls us into a false sense of security. Understanding the limitations, however, does not mean throwing out the tools, limited as they are, that we have at our disposal for estimating extreme events.

7. Conclusion

Risk management is a core activity of a financial firm. It is the art of using lessons from the past in order to mitigate misfortune and exploit future opportunities. Above all else, it is about making the tactical and strategic decisions to control risks where we can and to exploit opportunities that can be exploited. It is about managing people and processes, about setting incentives and implementing good governance. Risk management is about much more than numbers. "It's not the figures themselves, it's what you do with them that matters," as Lamia Gurdleneck says.[123]

Risk measurement and quantitative tools are critical aids for supporting risk management, but quantitative tools do not "manage" risk any more than an auditor's quarterly report "manages" the firm's profitability. In the end, quantitative tools are as good or as poor as the judgment of the person who uses them. Many criticisms of quantitative measurement techniques result from expecting too much from such tools. Quantitative tools alone are no substitute for judgment, wisdom, and knowledge. A poor manager with good risk reports is still a poor manager.

Managing a firm, indeed life itself, is often subject to luck. Luck is the irreducible chanciness of life. The question is not whether to take risks—that is inevitable and part of the human condition—but rather to appropriately manage luck and keep the odds on one's side. The philosopher Rescher has much good advice, and in closing, it is worth repeating his recommendations:

> The bottom line is that while we cannot *control* luck through superstitious interventions, we can indeed *influence* luck through the less dramatic but infinitely more efficacious principles of prudence. In particular, three resources come to the fore here:
>
> - *Risk management:* Managing the direction of and the extent of exposure to risk, and adjusting our risk-taking behavior in a sensible way over the overcautious-to-heedless spectrum.
> - *Damage control:* Protecting ourselves against the ravages of bad luck by prudential measures, such as insurance, "hedging one's bets," and the like.
> - *Opportunity capitalization:* Avoiding excessive caution by positioning oneself to take advantage of opportunities so as to enlarge the prospect of converting promising possibilities into actual benefits. (2001, p. 187)

---

[123] From *The Undoing of Lamia Gurdleneck* by K.A.C. Manderville, quoted in Kendall and Stuart (1979, frontispiece).

©2011 The Research Foundation of CFA Institute

References

Aczel, Amir D. 2004. *Chance: A Guide to Gambling, Love, the Stock Market, and Just about Everything Else*. New York: Thunder's Mouth Press.

Adler, David. 2009. *Snap Judgment*. Upper Saddle River, NJ: FT Press.

"AIG's Rescue: Size Matters." 2008. *Economist* (18 September): www.economist.com/finance/displaystory.cfm?story_id=12274070.

Appelbaum, Binyamin. 2010. "Cost of Seizing Fannie and Freddie Surges for Taxpayers." *New York Times* (19 June): www.nytimes.com/2010/06/20/business/20foreclose.html?hp.

Basel Committee on Banking Supervision. 2003. "Sound Practices for the Management and Supervision of Operational Risk." BIS (www.bis.org/publ/bcbs96.htm).

Beirlant, Jan, Wim Schoutens, and Johan Segers. 2005. "Mandelbrot's Extremism." *Wilmott Magazine* (March).

Bernstein, Peter L. 2007. *Capital Ideas Evolving*. Hoboken, NJ: John Wiley & Sons.

Carty, L.V., and D. Lieberman. 1996. "Defaulted Bank Loan Recoveries." Global Credit Research Special Report, Moody's Investors Service (www.moodyskmv.com/research/whitepaper/20641.pdf).

Coleman, Thomas S. 1998. "A Practical Guide to Bonds and Swaps" (20 February): http://ssrn.com/abstract=1554029.

———. 2009. "A Primer on Credit Default Swaps (CDS)" (29 December): http://ssrn.com/abstract=1555118.

———. 2011. "Probability, Expected Utility, and the Ellsberg Paradox" (26 February): http://ssrn.com/abstract=1770629.

———. Forthcoming. *Quantitative Risk Management*. New York: John Wiley & Sons.

Coleman, Thomas S., and Laurence B. Siegel. 1999. "Compensating Fund Managers for Risk-Adjusted Performance." *Journal of Alternative Investments*, vol. 2, no. 3 (Winter):9–15.

Cramer, Harald. 1974. *Mathematical Methods of Statistics*. Princeton, NJ: Princeton University Press.

Crouhy, Michel, Dan Galai, and Robert Mark. 2001. *Risk Management*. New York: McGraw-Hill.

———. 2006. *The Essentials of Risk Management*. New York: McGraw-Hill.

Duffie, Darrell, and Kenneth J. Singleton. 2003. *Credit Risk: Pricing, Measurement, and Management*. Princeton, NJ: Princeton University Press.

Eatwell, John, Murray Milgate, and Peter Newman, eds. 1987. *The New Palgrave: A Dictionary of Economics*. New York: Macmillan Press Limited.

Ellsberg, Daniel. 1961. "Risk, Ambiguity, and the Savage Axioms." *Quarterly Journal of Economics*, vol. 75, no. 4 (November):643–669.

Embrechts, Paul, Claudia Klüppelberg, and Thomas Mikosch. 2003. *Modelling Extremal Events for Insurance and Finance*, 4th ed. Berlin: Springer Verlag.

Epstein, Larry G. 1999. "A Definition of Uncertainty Aversion." *Review of Economic Studies*, vol. 66, no. 3 (July):579–608.

Feller, William. 1968. *An Introduction to Probability Theory and Its Applications, Volume 1*, 3rd ed. New York: John Wiley & Sons.

Felsted, Andrea, and Francesco Guerrera. 2008. "Inadequate Cover." *Financial Times* (6 October): www.ft.com/cms/s/0/19e64f6e-93c5-11dd-9a63-0000779fd18c.html #axzz JSPECJ33.

Felsted, Andrea, Francesco Guerrera, Joanna Chung, and Scheherazade Daneshkhu. 2008. "AIG's Complexity Blamed for Fall." *Financial Times* (6 October): http://us.ft.com/ftgateway/superpage.ft?news_id=fto100620081842144671.

Gardner, Martin. 1959. "Mathematical Games." *Scientific American* (October).

Garman, M.B. 1996. "Improving on VaR." *Risk*, vol. 9, no. 5 (May):61–63.

Gigerenzer, Gerd. 2002. *Calculated Risks: How to Know When Numbers Deceive You*. New York: Simon & Schuster.

———. 2007. *Gut Feelings: The Intelligence of the Unconscious*. New York: Penguin Group.

Gladwell, Malcolm. 2005. *Blink: The Power of Thinking without Thinking*. New York: Little, Brown and Company.

Gladwell, Malcolm. 2009. "Cocksure: Banks, Battles, and the Psychology of Overconfidence." *New Yorker* (27 July): www.newyorker.com/reporting/2009/07/27/090727fa_fact_gladwell.

Guerrera, Francesco, and Peter Thal Larsen. 2008. "Gone by the Board?" *Financial Times* (26 June): www.ft.com/cms/s/0/cc02b7d0-4318-11dd-81d0-0000779fd2ac.html #axzz1KXfUc29u.

Hacking, Ian. 1990. *The Taming of Chance.* New York: Cambridge University Press.

———. 2001. *An Introduction to Probability and Inductive Logic.* New York: Cambridge University Press.

———. 2006. *The Emergence of Probability*, 2nd ed. New York: Cambridge University Press.

Hadar, J., and W. Russell. 1969. "Rules for Ordering Uncertain Prospects." *American Economic Review*, vol. 59, no. 2 (March):25–34.

Hanoch, G., and H. Levy. 1969. "The Efficiency Analysis of Choices Involving Risk." *Review of Economic Studies*, vol. 36, no. 3 (July):335–346.

Hoffman, Paul. 1998. *The Man Who Loved Only Numbers: The Story of Paul Erdős and the Search for Mathematical Truth.* New York: Hyperion.

Holm, Erik, and Margaret Popper. 2009. "AIG's Liddy Says Greenberg Responsible for Losses." Bloomberg (2 March).

Jorion, Philippe. 2000. "Risk Management Lessons from Long-Term Capital Management." *European Financial Management*, vol. 6, no. 3 (September):277–300.

———. 2007. *Value at Risk: The New Benchmark for Managing Financial Risk*, 3rd ed. New York: McGraw-Hill.

Kahneman, Daniel, and Amos Tversky. 1973. "On the Psychology of Prediction." *Psychological Review*, vol. 80, no. 4 (July):237–251.

Kahneman, Daniel, Paul Slovic, and Amos Tversky, eds. 1982. *Judgment under Uncertainty: Heuristics and Biases.* New York: Cambridge University Press.

Kaplan, Michael, and Ellen Kaplan. 2006. *Chances Are . . . Adventures in Probability.* New York: Viking Penguin.

Kendall, Maurice, and Alan Stuart. 1979. *The Advanced Theory of Statistics, Volume 2.* 4th ed. New York: Macmillan Publishing Co., Inc.

Keynes, John Maynard. 1921. *A Treatise on Probability.* London: Macmillan.

Kindleberger, Charles P. 1989. *Manias, Panics, and Crashes: A History of Financial Crises,* 2nd ed. Houndmills, Basingstoke, Hampshire, U.K.: Palgrave Macmillan.

Knight, Frank. 1921. *Risk, Uncertainty, and Profit.* Boston: Houghton Mifflin.

Laeven, Luc, and Fabian Valencia. 2008. "Systemic Banking Crises: A New Database." IMF Working Paper, WP/08/224 (www.imf.org/external/pubs/ft/wp/2008/wp08224.pdf).

Lakatos, Imre. 1976. *Proofs and Refutations: The Logic of Mathematical Discovery.* Cambridge, U.K.: Cambridge University Press.

Langer, Ellen. 1975. "The Illusion of Control." *Journal of Personality and Social Psychology,* vol. 32, no. 2 (August):311–328.

Langer, Ellen, and Jane Roth. 1975. "Heads I Win, Tails It's Chance." *Journal of Personality and Social Psychology,* vol. 32, no. 6 (December):951–955.

LeRoy, Stephen F., and Larry D. Singell, Jr. 1987. "Knight on Risk and Uncertainty." *Journal of Political Economy,* vol. 95, no. 2 (April):394–406.

Litterman, R. 1996. "Hot Spots and Hedges." *Journal of Portfolio Management,* Special Issue (December):52–75.

Lleo, Sébastien. 2009. "Risk Management: A Review." *Research Foundation Literature Reviews,* vol. 4, no. 1 (February):1–51.

Lowenstein, Roger. 2000. *When Genius Failed: The Rise and Fall of Long-Term Capital Management.* New York: Random House.

Mackay, Charles. 1932. *Extraordinary Popular Delusions and the Madness of Crowds.* New York: Farrar Straus Giroux.

Markowitz, Harry M. 1959. *Portfolio Selection,* 1st ed. Malden, MA: Blackwell Publishers.

———. 2006. "de Finetti Scoops Markowitz." *Journal of Investment Management,* vol. 4, no. 3:5–18.

Marrison, Christopher. 2002. *The Fundamentals of Risk Measurement.* New York: McGraw-Hill.

Maslin, Janet. 2006. "His Heart Belongs to (Adorable) iPod." *New York Times* (19 October).

Mauboussin, Michael, and Kristen Bartholdson. 2003. "On Streaks: Perception, Probability, and Skill." Credit Suisse First Boston's *Consilient Observer*, vol. 2, no. 8 (22 April).

McNeil, Alexander, Rudiger Frey, and Paul Embrechts. 2005. *Quantitative Risk Management*. Princeton, NJ: Princeton University Press.

Merton, Robert C. 1974. "On the Pricing of Corporate Debt: The Risk Structure of Interest Rates." *Journal of Finance*, vol. 29, no. 2 (May):449–470.

Miletic, Daniella. 2005. "Forex Chief Jailed for 16 Months for Role in NAB Trading Scandal." *Sydney Morning Herald* (16 June).

Mina, Jorge, and Jerry Yi Xiao. 2001. *Return to RiskMetrics: The Evolution of a Standard*. New York: RiskMetrics.

Mirrlees, J. 1974. "Notes on Welfare Economics, Information, and Uncertainty." In *Essays in Equilibrium Behavior under Uncertainty*. Edited by M.S. Balch, Daniel L. McFadden, and S.Y. Wu. Amsterdam: North Holland.

———. 1976. "The Optimal Structure of Incentives and Authority within an Organization." *Bell Journal of Economics*, vol. 7, no. 1 (Spring):105–131.

Mlodinow, Leonard. 2008. *The Drunkard's Walk: How Randomness Rules Our Lives*. New York: Pantheon Books.

New School. "Riskiness." In *Choice under Risk and Uncertainty* (www.newschool.edu/nssr/het/essays/uncert/increase.htm).

Nocera, Joe. 2009. "Risk Mismanagement." *New York Times* (4 January): www.nytimes.com/2009/01/04/magazine/04risk-t.html.

Press, William H., Saul A. Teukolsky, William T. Vetterling, and Brian P. Flannery. 2007. *Numerical Recipes*, 3rd ed. New York: Cambridge University Press.

Reinhart, Carmen M., and Kenneth S. Rogoff. 2009. *This Time Is Different: Eight Centuries of Financial Folly*. Princeton, NJ: Princeton University Press.

Rescher, Nicholas. 2001. *Luck: The Brilliant Randomness of Everyday Life*. Pittsburgh: University of Pittsburgh Press.

Rosenhouse, Jason. 2009. *The Monty Hall Problem: The Remarkable Story of Math's Most Contentious Brainteaser*. New York: Oxford University Press.

Ross, Stephen. 1973. "The Economic Theory of Agency: The Principal's Problem." *American Economic Review*, vol. 63, no. 2 (May):134–139.

Rothschild, M., and J.E. Stiglitz. 1970. "Increasing Risk I: A Definition." *Journal of Economic Theory*, vol. 2, no. 3 (September):225–243.

———. 1971. "Increasing Risk II: Its Economic Consequences." *Journal of Economic Theory*, vol. 3, no. 1 (March):66–84.

Schmeidler, David. 1989. "Subjective Probability and Expected Utility without Additivity." *Econometrica*, vol. 57, no. 3 (May):571–587.

Selvin, S. 1975a. "A Problem in Probability." *American Statistician*, vol. 29, no. 1 (February):67.

———. 1975b. "On the Monty Hall Problem." *American Statistician*, vol. 29, no. 3 (August):134.

Stiglitz, J.E. 1974. "Incentives and Risk Sharing in Sharecropping." *Review of Economic Studies*, vol. 41, no. 2 (April):219–255.

———. 1975. "Incentives, Risk, and Information: Notes Towards a Theory of Hierarchy." *Bell Journal of Economics*, vol. 6, no. 2 (Autumn):552–579.

Taleb, Nassim. 2004. *Fooled by Randomness*, 2nd ed. New York: Random House.

———. 2007. *The Black Swan: The Impact of the Highly Improbable*. New York: Random House.

Tremper, Bruce. 2008. *Staying Alive in Avalanche Terrain*, 2nd ed. Seattle: Mountaineers Books.

Tversky, Amos, and Daniel Kahneman. 1974. "Judgment under Uncertainty: Heuristics and Biases." *Science*, vol. 185 (September):1124–1131.

———. 1983. "Extensional versus Intuitive Reasoning: The Conjunction Fallacy in Probability Judgment." *Psychological Review*, vol. 90, no. 4 (October):293–315.

Valencia, Matthew. 2010. "The Gods Strike Back." *Economist* (11 February): www.economist.com/node/15474137.

vos Savant, Marilyn. 1990a. "Ask Marilyn." *Parade* (9 September).

———. 1990b. "Ask Marilyn." *Parade* (2 December).

———. 1996. *The Power of Logical Thinking*. New York: St. Martin's Press.

Wilmer Cutler Pickering Hale and Dorr. 2008. "Rogue Traders: Lies, Losses, and Lessons Learned." WilmerHale Securities Briefing Series (March).

RESEARCH FOUNDATION
CONTRIBUTION FORM

☑ **Yes,** I want the Research Foundation to continue to fund innovative research that advances the investment management profession. Please accept my tax-deductible contribution at the following level:

Contributing Research Fellow . . . .$25,000 to $49,999
Research Fellow . . . .$10,000 to $24,999
Contributing Donor . . . .$1,000 to $9,999
Donor . . . . Up to $999

I would like to donate $_____ .

☐ My check is enclosed (payable to the Research Foundation of CFA Institute).
☐ I would like to donate appreciated securities (send me information).
☐ Please charge my donation to my credit card.
　☑ VISA ☑ MC ☑ Amex ☑ Diners ☑ Corporate ☑ Personal

| | | | | | | | | | | | | | | | | |

Card Number

____/____
Expiration Date

☐ Corporate Card
☐ Personal Card

Name on card PLEASE PRINT

Signature

☐ This is a pledge. Please bill me for my donation of $_____ .

☐ I would like recognition of my donation to be:
　☑ Individual donation ☑ Corporate donation ☑ Different individual

PLEASE PRINT NAME OR COMPANY NAME AS YOU WOULD LIKE IT TO APPEAR

PLEASE PRINT ☐ Mr. ☐ Mrs. ☐ Ms.　MEMBER NUMBER_____

Last Name (Family Name)　　　　　First　　　　Middle Initial

Title

Address

City　　　　　　State/Province　Country ZIP/Postal Code

11CO

Please mail this completed form with your contribution to:
The Research Foundation of CFA Institute • P.O. Box 3638
Charlottesville, VA 22903-0638 USA

For more on the Research Foundation of CFA Institute, please visit www.cfainstitute.org/about/foundation/.

Named Endowments

The Research Foundation of CFA Institute acknowledges with sincere gratitude the generous contributions of the Named Endowment participants listed below.

Gifts of at least US$100,000 qualify donors for membership in the Named Endowment category, which recognizes in perpetuity the commitment toward unbiased, practitioner-oriented, relevant research that these firms and individuals have expressed through their generous support of the Research Foundation of CFA Institute.

Ameritech
Anonymous
Robert D. Arnott
Theodore R. Aronson, CFA
Asahi Mutual Life
Batterymarch Financial Management
Boston Company
Boston Partners Asset Management, L.P.
Gary P. Brinson, CFA
Brinson Partners, Inc.
Capital Group International, Inc.
Concord Capital Management
Dai-Ichi Life Company
Daiwa Securities
Mr. and Mrs. Jeffrey J. Diermeier
Gifford Fong Associates
John A. Gunn, CFA
Jon L. Hagler Foundation
Investment Counsel Association
    of America, Inc.
Jacobs Levy Equity Management
Long-Term Credit Bank of Japan, Ltd.
Lynch, Jones & Ryan

Meiji Mutual Life Insurance Company
Miller Anderson & Sherrerd, LLP
John B. Neff, CFA
Nikko Securities Co., Ltd
Nippon Life Insurance Company of Japan
Nomura Securities Co., Ltd.
Payden & Rygel
Provident National Bank
Frank K. Reilly, CFA
Salomon Brothers
Sassoon Holdings Pte Ltd.
Scudder Stevens & Clark
Security Analysts Association of Japan
Shaw Data Securities, Inc.
Sit Investment Associates, Inc.
Standish, Ayer & Wood, Inc.
State Farm Insurance Companies
Sumitomo Life America, Inc.
T. Rowe Price Associates, Inc.
Templeton Investment Counsel Inc.
Travelers Insurance Co.
USF&G Companies
Yamaichi Securities Co., Ltd.

Senior Research Fellows

Financial Services Analyst Association

For more on upcoming Research Foundation
publications and webcasts, please visit
www.cfainstitute.org/about/foundation/.

Research Foundation monographs
are online at www.cfapubs.org.

Made in the USA
Middletown, DE
12 January 2016